THE MURDERS OF MOISÉS VILLE

ALSO BY JAVIER SINAY

Available in Spanish

Camino al este (Tusquets)
Cuba Stone, with Jeremías Gamboa and Joselo (Tusquets)
Sangre joven (Tusquets)

THE
MURDERS
OF
MOISÉS
VILLE

*The Rise and Fall of the
Jerusalem of South America*

Javier Sinay

Translated from the Spanish by Robert Croll

RESTLESS BOOKS
Brooklyn, New York

First Restless Books hardcover edition February 2022

Hardcover ISBN: 9781632062987

Work published within the framework of "Sur" Translation Support Program of the
Ministry of Foreign Affairs and Worship of the Argentine Republic

Obra editada en el marco del Programa "Sur" de Apoyo a las Traducciones del Ministerio
de Relaciones Exteriores y Culto de la República Argentina

This work is published with support from David Bruce Smith,
Grateful American Foundation.

This project is supported in part by an award from the National Endowment for the Arts.

NATIONAL ENDOWMENT for the ARTS
arts.gov

Programa Sur

Library of Congress Control Number: 2021948327

Cover design by Emily Comfort
Text design by Sarah Schneider

Printed in the United States of America

1 3 5 7 9 10 8 6 4 2

Restless Books, Inc.
232 3rd Street, Suite A101
Brooklyn, NY 11215

www.restlessbooks.org
publisher@restlessbooks.org

Contents

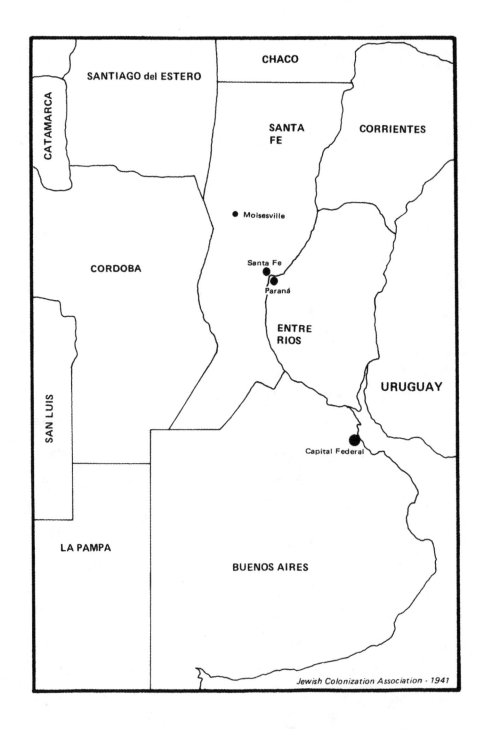

Source: Jaime Barylko et al., *Los judíos en la Argentina*, Betenu, Buenos Aires, 1986.

To Manuel, this story, the ancestors' story, my story, your story.

"In the sordid, snow-covered city of Tulchin, a city of glorious rabbis and hoary synagogues, the news of America filled the Jews' hearts with dreams."

ALBERTO GERCHUNOFF, *The Jewish Gauchos of the Pampas*
(translated by Edna Aizenberg)

"I've doomed myself, old father, I've killed a man."

The old man lifted his head, looked at Moreira through a veil of tears and simply asked him.

"In a fair fight?"

EDUARDO GUTIÉRREZ, *Juan Moreira*
(translated by Daniel Bernardo)

Preface

On the night of June 9, 2009, an email arrived in my inbox. It was from my father, Horacio, and had the subject line "Your great-grandfather":

> Hola Javi,
> Go to this address: www.generacionesmv.com/Generaciones/Victimas.htm. The author, Mijl Hacohen Sinay, is your great-grandfather. I just found it and, apart from everything it means for us emotionally and historically, there's a touch of a crime report about it.

With some curiosity I clicked through and read the title of an article: "The First Fatal Victims in Moisés Ville," which was completed farther down with: "An account of the first murders suffered by the colony." The site proclaimed itself as "The Generations of Moisés Ville, a website dedicated to the first Jewish agricultural colony in Argentina." I skimmed through the text and confirmed that the touch of crime my father had referenced was obvious.

It contained the account of a killing: in the year 1889, a group of Jewish immigrants was starving, begging for scraps from anyone who would spare them a look. A gaucho wanted to take a wretched princess of a girl from their ranks in exchange for a simple dowry; the whole thing ended in bloodshed. This was a real case that had taken place in Argentina. After that, another crime was narrated, then another, and another, until more than a score had been detailed. The text was powerful and gruesome, historical and eye-opening, forgotten and yet valuable. A very dark piece of Argentine life and the saga of immigration had been preserved there.

For my own part, I had heard, as far back as I could remember, that the colonization of the Jewish gauchos had been a pastoral adventure. I had never considered that it might have been tinged with blood or that this immigration could have met with such resistance.

To tell the truth, I also lacked any knowledge of who my great-grandfather, the author of the article, had been. The family's memory didn't stray that far back around the Sunday table, which my grandmother Mañe loaded down with delicious plates of gefilte fish with carrots and salads in many colors and flavors. "Your grandfather's father ran a newspaper," I had once heard, between one dish and the next, but I let the comment pass. And now my grandfather Moishe—the son of that great-grandfather, Mijl Hacohen Sinay—is dead. He passed away in the fall of 1999 without ever telling me a word about his father. I still wonder why. But his wife, my grandmother Mañe, is still with us. She was Mijl's daughter-in-law and remembers him well.

And what was that about "Hacohen"? A first name or last? "It means 'the kohen,'" my grandmother told me, in the colorful melody of her Santiago Yiddish—for, although she was born in 1922 in the town of Lanivtsi, within the region of Volhynia (then part of Poland, today in Ukraine), she was raised in La Banda, quite close to the provincial capital of Santiago del Estero, Argentina. Of religion she knows what she absorbed in her Polish home in Santiago del Estero, which is to say, what any girl from a shtetl, or Jewish village, would know, and that, to be sure, is far more than is within my grasp. "The Kohanim have a special status: they're the direct male descendants of Aaron, brother of Moses, and were the priests of the Temple in Jerusalem. The tribe passes from father to son. You too are a kohen," she said when I asked her that day.

Searching online, I easily find a monograph on the journalists who arrived in Argentina in the period of 1850–1950, which includes a few lines about my great-grandfather: "Mijl Hacohen Sinay was born in 1877. In 1894, the Sinay family immigrated to Argentina and settled in

Moisés Ville, in Santa Fe province. There, Mijl became a teacher at the first school in the colony. In 1898, his family moved to Buenos Aires, where, at twenty-one, he founded the first Yiddish-language newspaper in Argentina, *Der Viderkol*. He went on to found other publications as well and reported for many more, both local and international. He died in Buenos Aires on August 8, 1958." A note indicates that the text is quoted from the book *La letra ídish en tierra argentina: Bio-bibliografía de sus autores literarios*, by Ana Weinstein and Eliahu Toker.

It's no common thing to discover, four generations back, a figure who seems so close. The matter digs into me like a thorn, keeps me up at night: if I found this much with so little, it's because more is out there.

However, the internet does not hold the answers; the trails end quickly. But the most serious issue is not to do with the lack of results, but my ignorance: I don't know what title I'm searching for or where more information about the crimes of Moisés Ville might be found.

So, I turn to the only person I'm sure can help me: the writer Eliahu Toker, author of that short biographical note, and ask him about my great-grandfather, Moisés Ville, and the periodical that Mijl founded. I suspect that this newspaper, *Der Viderkol* (The echo), which was produced in 1898—during the same period in which the murders were committed—might well have recorded them. As I draft my message to Toker, I'm scarcely aware of his standing as a nobleman of the local Jewish population, a champion of Yiddish culture, and also a poet, writer, and researcher.

"The place where I once saw a copy of *Der Viderkol* was the IWO, I think before the attack it suffered in 1994," he responds, barely three days after the email from my father that set everything in motion. Those first hours, fed solely by the fuel of excitement, had already led me to a reference to the IWO, the Institute for Jewish Research or, in Yiddish, Idisher Visnshaftlejer Institut, an organization dedicated to the research, dissemination, and conservation of Jewish culture. Although it no longer operates out of the building that houses the AMIA (the Argentine Israelite Mutual Association, the largest community center in the country), it was there on July 18, 1994, when the building was destroyed by a terrorist attack. Toker goes on in his email: "I don't know if they still have that copy or any other. It appears in facsimile form in a few books, including one that I have, but I suggest you begin your investigation at the IWO. Your great-grandfather was an interesting character, and it would be good to do something with his biography, maybe conducting research within your own family. Can you read Yiddish? There's a book by Pinie Katz about Jewish journalism in Argentina that must have some material about your great-grandfather and his newspaper. That's all that occurs to me at the moment."

But no, I can't read Yiddish.

And *Der Viderkol*, my great-grandfather's newspaper, which might well lead me to the murders, will not be easy to track down. For several nights, one question has been keeping me awake: how can I investigate a crime that took place in the twilight of the nineteenth century, out in the barren plains of Santa Fe? Used to walking the courtroom hallways and seeking out witnesses, to speaking with investigators and looking at a crime scene through the eyes of the victim or the killer, in short, accustomed to a justice system that answers through a press office and to the media-hyped crime of the twenty-first century, where the protagonists love the cameras or seek to profit through them, I discover that in this text left behind by my great-grandfather there is nothing of the kind. Here, the victims' names run one after the other: Lander, Iegelnitzer, Seivick, Fainman, Kantor, Gerchunoff, Horovitz, Wainer, Bersanker, Kristal, Finkelstein, Schmucler, Waisman, Aliksenitzer, Reitich, Tzifin . . . But the criminals' names don't even appear. As if they didn't matter. They are always just gauchos; or *gauches*, in the original Yiddish text.

In a comment on brutality as a literary virtue, Borges references the nineteenth-century writer Eduardo Gutiérrez and "the monotonous scenes of atrocities that he dispatches with resignation." It isn't a fair comparison—it does credit neither to one nor the other—but that Borgesian footnote echoes in my head as I face this text by Sinay the older, whose words usher us from one pool of blood to another. That is also the sense of the brief summary in Spanish that accompanies the original lines, published in Yiddish so long ago, by way of introduction:

It was not without victims that Jewish colonization in the Argentine Republic began. More than twenty young lives were cut short in this area alone. Not long after their arrival, the Jewish pioneers in the territory of Santa Fe paid their first blood tribute to the customs of the gaucho. The bloody and barbarous events narrated in this article play out with an abundance of detail, one by one, following the crime report. The author does not categorize the events but presents and documents them using the available literary testimonies, turning them into more interesting reading, to understand the gauchos' methods in that period.

I should now add that the first of these killings occurred in 1889 and the last in 1906. The balance stands at twenty-two victims in seventeen years. It isn't particularly strange: in the countryside of Santa Fe, homicide was routine, and outlaws didn't hesitate to slit their victims' throats before or after robbing them of their belongings.

In many cases the victims numbered among the colonists. They, unlike the rugged gauchos, were generally mundane, hardworking, bound to the slow cycles of agriculture. Moisés Ville remained the only colony of Russian Jews in Santa Fe province for more than twenty years, until that of Montefiore was founded in 1912. In other settlements the colonists were Catholics and Protestants of Italian, French, German, and Swiss origin, the same nationalities that had populated the first and largest of all the colonies, that of Esperanza, since 1856.

Nevertheless, it was nothing new to anyone that immigrants could generate resentment among the locals after 1872, the year when some fifty gauchos attacked the town of Tandil under cries of "Long live the Argentine Confederation! Long live the faith! Death to gringos and masons!" Thirty-six foreign immigrants were massacred. The event was instigated by Tata Dios, a mysterious witch doctor who died not long after, in prison. That same year, José Hernández published *The Gaucho Martín Fierro*, in which that most famous of all gauchos sang: "I don't know why the Government sends us / out here to the frontier, / these gringos that don't even know / how to handle a horse." In the background, political struggle fueled the words: Hernández rejected the liberal ideas of Domingo Faustino Sarmiento, the nation's president at the time, who viewed these immigrants as civilizing agents.

In an article written two decades later, Gabriel Carrasco—a politician, lawyer, and journalist from Rosario—reported an average of seventy-one murders per year in the province during the period of 1874–1892. Some inhabitants of Moisés Ville must be counted among those victims as well: the three Iegelnitzer brothers, killed out of vengeance; Wainer and Bersanker, murdered and robbed, like many others, out on the lonely road; Kantor, finished off mysteriously inside his own locked room; Gerchunoff, stabbed by an impulsive drunkard. And statistics from a later period must include the homicides of still others from Moisés Ville: Horovitz, who went out looking for his horse on the vast plain and never returned; the Waisman family, massacred in their own home for a couple of pesos; the beautiful young Aliksenitzer, assaulted by a policeman; Reitich, Tzifin . . .

Fifty years later, my great-grandfather gathered all of those killings together once more, yet this time not with the coldness of figures but the warmth of narrative. In 1966, the researcher José Liebermann wrote in his book *Los judíos en la Argentina*:

> One devout author—Miguel Hacohen Sinay—wrote the history of the colonists murdered in Santa Fe, paying a well deserved homage to all the pioneers of our rural epic whom we honor here once more. May these words be the 'Kaddish' for their memory, with a fervent vote for the eternal remembrance of their names even if unmerciful time has erased them from fallen headstones in the lonely cemeteries of the colonies.

In the early days of the 1900s, the French criminologist Edmond Locard, head of the police laboratory in Lyon, formulated his famous exchange principle: whenever an object makes contact with another, it transfers part of its material onto it. That is, a murderer leaves something of himself on the victim and takes something of theirs with him, and it is impossible for him to act, especially amid the tension of a crime, without leaving any traces. Investigators confirmed the exchange principle using fingerprints, footprints, and trace evidence. Applied within these pages, Locard's principle is cultural: the colonists and gauchos exchange something in their conflicts, but also in their agreements. The encounter between two such uneven worlds knows nothing of bargaining or terms and conditions.

But time is part of the problem as well. The long century that has passed since the crimes took the memories with it. The nineteenth-century dénouement is far away, and delving into its wilderness will require ingenuity and skill. I repeat: how can I investigate so distant a crime? And a still more complex question: why investigate it? If, becoming immersed in the abyss of time, one can extract something more than one or two names and the memory of a bloody knife, it must be owed to the notion that one is now heir to all of it.

The first people who missed their chance to record everything—and hand down a few useful clues to us—were the same Jews who arrived in Argentina as part of the migratory boom and shaped a community that would become one of the most fruitful of its kind in the world (comparable, in the interwar period, to those in Odessa, Moscow, and New York). That first group established the basis for the creation of the new Judeo-Argentine element, but it all happened too quickly for anyone to realize it. Not even them. Many (all?) believed that the community was only passing through South America and would be expelled from there sooner or later as well, or, given a favorable wind, would emigrate to Israel following the precepts of the Zionist movement, as cemented by Theodor Herzl at the Basel Congress in 1897—eight years after the first Moisés Ville killing and one before the publication of my great-grandfather's newspaper. And if the community would have to break camp again someday, there didn't seem to be much use in sitting down to record history.

In a very short time, Argentina had emerged as an attractive option for Jewish emigrants from Russia thanks to the agricultural colonization being promoted by the local government and the German philanthropist Maurice de Hirsch, founder of the Jewish Colonization Association. In fact, Theodor Herzl himself had to fight against the expectations generated by this exotic destination. Proposing that Zionism's efforts should concentrate on the foundation of a political state in the Land of Israel, in 1896 Herzl wrote *The Jewish State*, a book in which one chapter is entitled "Palestine or Argentina?"

New Jewish print media have been appearing here one after the other ever since my great-grandfather's newspaper, Der Viderkol, first hit the streets in 1898. Within that same year two more appeared, published weekly, and a decade later there was a daily paper in circulation. In 1914, the largest of them all, *Di Ydische Zaitung* (whose own front page used that spelling to transliterate its name) was founded, and 1918 saw the birth of its counterpart on the left, *Di Prese*. Today, much of the account of the homicides can be found scattered among all of those pages.

On the other hand, in his email Eliahu Toker had turned my attention to a simple and decisive question: "Can you read Yiddish?" The popular Jewish language had long since fallen out of everyday use by the time I set myself to investigating the crimes of Moisés Ville. Which posed another problem: all of the colonists spoke Yiddish, and even the commentators on their adventures and misfortunes wrote in Yiddish. Without looking any further, the original version of "The First Fatal Victims in Moisés Ville" (according to the title on the website my father directed me to) was published in 1947 in Yiddish: its actual title is "Di ershte idishe korbones in Moisés Ville" ("The First Jewish Victims in Moisés Ville"). It appeared in the fourth issue of the series *Argentiner IWO Shriftn* (or Annals of the Argentine Jewish Scientific Institute), a collection of historical, sociological, and literary studies. The article isn't brief: it stretches on for twenty-seven pages. Taken in terms of its singularity, the article is more like a small book. For that matter, in the 1980s a Judeo-Argentine historical studies association republished it in the format of a sixty-page pamphlet.

At this moment I have the original *Argentiner IWO Shriftn* book on my desk: its cover is a dull sky blue and it is two hundred pages long. The Yiddish letters look, to my novice eyes, like ants in a line; the language is now, and always will be, a barrier in reuniting with my great-grandfather, with his textual legacy. The IWO began publishing these yearbooks in 1941, always in Yiddish, and they continued with few interruptions until the 1980s and even into our own time: as I write these lines, I wonder at the contents of the yearbook's sixteenth issue, soon to be published online.

And, like the IWO yearbooks, almost all the documentary sources I might wish to turn to in order to follow the trail of the crimes of Moisés Ville have been written in Yiddish.

But no. I repeat: I can't read Yiddish.

And I know very little about the language. I've heard only the sayings with which my grandmother seasons her gefilte fish and borscht, that soup derived from a Russian recipe.

It was against this backdrop that, sometime after receiving the first message from my father, I set course for Moisés Ville.

The Journey

We make our way through the corners of the grand old building that houses the Buenos Aires Jewish Museum, following the guide—an elegant woman with a friendly smile—and looking at passing displays showing old prayer books decorated in mother-of-pearl and gold leaf, a letter from Albert Einstein to the Argentine Jewish community, and even a table set with plastic food and electric candles in imitation of the Shabbat ceremony.

"For Jewish people, Shabbat is the most important festival. Why? Because it was given to us in the Ten Commandments," the guide says, watching the group. She wants to make sure that each of us understands properly. I imagine she must work, at other times, as a teacher at Hebrew school. "We have to observe and keep Shabbat; that's why we light two candles. And we cook traditional foods like fish or roast chicken with potatoes and peas, for example."

It's all there behind a glass display, along with place settings, cups, chairs, a tablecloth, and table, ready for a family of mannequins to sit down for the meal.

The museum is quite large, and we continue down another corridor where we can see a few Torot. "Torot" is the plural form of "Torah," the five books of Mosaic Law laid down upon long parchment scrolls. The three Torot here are all of Moroccan origin and quite old, from the seventeenth, eighteen, and nineteenth centuries, and the woman from the museum looks at them with reverence, admiration.

"The Torah is ornately decorated: it is our most important symbol," she explains, pointing out the details covering the scrolls, and then, through an inner door, we enter the synagogue, the first grand temple of the City of Buenos Aires, which stands at 785 Calle Libertad.

Inaugurated in 1897 and restored in 1932, the synagogue is constructed in the Byzantine style, with imposing vaults ascending overhead.

"I'll request that you please cover your heads before entering this area," says the guide. She hands me a kippah, and I put it on as we walk through the central nave; I hear her explaining that there are no human representations here, as it's forbidden in Jewish tradition, though there are menorahs and Stars of David like those visible in the stained-glass windows through which a faint, bluish, gentle light filters in.

Her voice cuts through the silence of a temple that can accommodate as many as a thousand congregants. For the moment, there are only six of us. And four are not even Jewish.

"Before we started the tour, you told me that you don't have saints either," the guide remarks to the four foreigner visitors, two women and two men who are Evangelicals, of the kind who haven't entirely embraced the liturgy of Christianity nor entirely abandoned that of Judaism. "Do you follow Christ? Also no? And what's the name of your church?"

"Cristo Viene," says one of the men.

"Ah, Cristo Viene . . ." she smiles, cordial. The name of the small church sounds facetious inside this imposing temple. The woman presses further: "Is it a new movement?"

"We've been around in Bolivia for some time."

"Very good. And you?"

Now it's my turn.

"What brings you here?" she asks, with a certain delight. I feel like hiding, uncomfortable, but there's nowhere to go. "I'm doing some research," I say.

The less said, the better. I try to think of some excuse. I need to invent some story to forestall her. But she beats me to the punch.

"What kind of research?"

"About . . . about a series of crimes. That took place. In the Moisés Ville colony."

"Ah . . ." Her smile remains perfectly intact. Yet I discern, beneath it, a certain unease.

Then she invites us to exit the temple and reenter the museum, where she goes on, as if nothing happened:

"The plot of land beneath this temple was acquired thanks to a donation from Baron Maurice de Hirsch. He was born at the beginning of the nineteenth century, in the house of the banker to the Bavarian king, and went on to marry the daughter of another banker. His mother came from an Orthodox family, and he inherited her affection for the children of Israel. The Baron had a son named Lucien who died tragically young, and so he decided that his fortunes would go toward the plight of the Jewish people."

The story, which sounds like a fairytale for the displaced, will sometime later reveal itself as a more complex matter, one involving important sociological elements and novel economic concepts. But it's still too soon for me to understand all that when the guide positions us before a model ship: it is the *Weser*, the iconic steamship that transported the founders of the town of Moisés Ville—including several of those who would fall victim in the crimes of its earliest days.

"It was on the *Weser* that Jews escaping from the pogroms arrived. The ship reached Argentina in the year 1889 with 129 families, who sadly faced an incredibly difficult journey, and terrible hardships were in store for them here as well. And here's a little gem, a typewriter with Hebrew keys . . ."

She continues, but I detach myself from the group. I let them move ahead and remain there, facing the ship. The proportions, the details, even the colors have been respected and reproduced by the skilled hand of an artisan who, having no original plan to rely on, worked against the clock on the basis of a few old daguerreotypes printed on 18-by-24-centimeter glass plates. He delivered his handiwork in August of 2009, shortly before the one hundred twentieth anniversary of the real steamship *Weser*'s arrival in Argentina. At its 1:70 scale, the replica is perfect.

. . .

A prow in black, white, and red (like the flag of the Kaiserreich, the German Empire that would arise in central Europe beginning in 1871) cut through the waves of the Atlantic Ocean with ferocity and skill over the course of July 1889, under optimal conditions for navigation: the prow of the steamship *Weser*. The ship, which connected the European coasts to the shores of America several times per year, had put to sea for the first time on June 1, 1867, making a journey from Bremen to New York. Weighing 2,870 tons and measuring 99.05 meters long by 12.19 wide, the ship traveled at a speed of 11 knots, with two masts for sails and a single smokestack. It carried 60 passengers in first class, 120 in second, 700 in the hold, and a crew comprising a hundred-odd sailors. In July of 1889, the *Weser* embarked with a large company of passengers from Russia. It had set sail once again from Bremen, the largest port in Germany, this time plotting a course far off to the south, to a point that had quickly become a common destination for European immigrants: Buenos Aires.

Among these Russians traveled David Lander: a large man, but not enormous; heavy, but well-built; poor, but educated. A common man among the hundreds, unremarkable save for one detail: he was one of the few—the only one?—to be traveling on his own. Surrounded by so many families, he brought only two trunks. Hundreds of other Jewish immigrants of Russian origin—824 individuals among 136 families—boarded the steamship along with him on that day, July 1, 1889. But perhaps the statistics of today reflect only an expression of desire: it has never been entirely certain how many families there really were. Some historians believe there were 120; others claim 88, or 104, or 129, or 130. This confusion is owed to the fact that the *Weser* was carrying other passengers as well. But, for the purposes of this story, the Jews are the people of interest.

The name Argentina had rung out joyfully through the eastern shtetls the year before, when a contingent of persecuted Jews departed Russia in search of aid. In the czarist empire, a series of rules implemented in 1882 in retaliation for the assassination of Czar Alexander II—unjustly attributed to the Jews—prohibited them from settling in the countryside or in border regions and also barred their access to liberal professions and public education. Jews had become the scapegoats for a decadent empire. But it didn't end there: they were sentenced, furthermore, to live in the Pale of Settlement, a strip running north to south across the western territory of Russia. There, as though inside a vast outdoor ghetto encompassing cities and villages on the steppes that today form part of Ukraine, Lithuania, Poland, Belarus, and Russia, some five million individuals crowded in.

And so, when the suffocating atmosphere in Russia became too much to bear, a few delegates originating from Podolia (in Western Ukraine) and Bessarabia (a region comprising parts of Romania, Moldova, and Ukraine) gathered in the city of Katowice in order to find a way out—a destination. The only solution they could find was emigration. But where would they go? To the Land of Israel? Africa? The United States? The first destination was the most popular: in the dark alleyways of the czarist empire there had been a rebirth of Zionism, a distinctively European nationalist movement that saw its goal as the return to the Holy Land and cultivation of the soil—an activity forbidden to these people wasting away in Eastern Europe. And support from the Baron Edmond James de Rothschild, a powerful English banker and Jewish philanthropist, was emboldening the movement. Some, however, believed that only the elderly should go to the Promised Land, to die there in holiness. Africa had the draw of the mines, which seduced the more adventurous spirits. And the United States seemed to be the simplest option: in the first few years of the 1880s, more than two hundred thousand people had set out toward that destination. But by 1889, the country had already begun shutting its doors to new immigrants.

The delegates were therefore inclined to make for the Land of Israel, and three envoys set out for Paris to seek Baron de Rothschild's help.

But they secured nothing. On the other hand, someone did bring them to see the Chief Rabbi of Paris, Zadoc Kahn by name, who connected them to the Alliance Israélite Universelle, a group of Parisian philanthropists who favored that spirit of *"Kol Yisrael arevim ze la ze"*: "All of Israel are responsible for one another."

"Argentina?" The delegates were astonished to hear, from the gentlemen's lips, the name of a country so foreign to them that they hadn't even considered it. They were unaware that this nation, set to become the world's breadbasket, was captivated by a mission to draw in the masses being expelled by the powers of Europe. A liberal model had been imposed: Europeans, rather than criollo people (who were viewed as rebellious or lazy), should populate the lands of Argentina and set the extraordinary machinery of the agro-export model into motion. And this would be done by means of agricultural colonies: the land would be divided into lots, populated with colonists, and then sold to them in installments paid over the course of several years, no matter which God they might like to pray to.

And so, at the Bureau officiel d'informations de la République Argentine in Paris, a representative made contact with the delegation from Russia, offering them land in Buenos Aires that belonged to a senator, Rafael Hernández, whose brother was the author of *Martín Fierro*. The future colonists' contract could be paid off over the course of twenty-two years, and if they made it to Bremen, they would be admitted aboard a steamship financed by the Argentine government for the voyage south.

They accepted, of course.

But the journey would prove that the shadow these emigrants had borne upon them in Russia in fact extended throughout the whole length of Europe. After crossing the border, they drifted like ghosts for several weeks through the cities and roadways of the Old World as though condemned in advance, as though warned of what lay in store. For them, reaching Bremen would mean enduring prison (after they were arrested in Kraków for using counterfeit tickets, having fallen victim to a scam) and a forced delay in Berlin (where their itinerary drew suspicions from the inspectors). And when that city's chief rabbi warned that they'd be sold as slaves the moment they set foot on Argentine soil, a new group of delegates made for Paris to inquire, once more, about their destination.

· · ·

In the end, the emigrants wanted to believe the words of the Parisian philanthropists, who assured them that Argentina was a free republic. And so it was that the ship, which they might have found revolting after thirty-five days on the high seas, passed on into history. Just as the *Mayflower* bore those first English colonists to the shores of North America, within its four levels (and more besides, for the vessel was over capacity and some dared to travel out on deck), the steamship *Weser* carried the first Jewish colonists to Argentina.

The arrival of the group from Kamenetz-Podolsk—known thereafter as "Podoliers," since they came from the region of Podolia—was in line with all the suffering they had already experienced and still had yet to endure. The ship dropped anchor in the port of Buenos Aires on August 14, 1889, but the quiet David Lander and his fellow immigrants were unable to disembark until three days later, the same August 17 when the newspaper *La Prensa* announced that "Yesterday, due to an error on the part of the immigrant landings inspector, 104 Jewish families, contracted in Europe by Sr. Franck upon request of Sr. D. Rafael Hernández and bound for the 'Nueva Plata' colony, were left on board the *Weser*."

The Russian Jews stood out, even in a port that each day received travelers from all corners. The fortune that awaited them in Argentina was quite different from the one they had yearned for: the first disappointment on dry land came when the group received news that the property of Rafael Hernández—the landowner who'd extended his offer to them in Europe—was already occupied by other colonists. At the Banco de la Colonización, the contracts they'd signed before their departure were recognized as authentic, but not valid. The Podoliers had fallen victim to yet another scam (or an innocent accident, as the authorities insistently explained), but they were already on American soil, ready to find their homeland, and for five days they stayed at the Hotel de Inmigrantes, unsure what to do. One night they experienced the great unrest of La Plata River when a storm deluged the city, and they watched the hours crawl by inside the vast and overcrowded rooms through which seven thousand disoriented people circulated each day.

It was only after members of the very chivalrous Israelite Congregation of the Argentinian Republic put them in contact with one of their associates that the Russians discovered a new path lay before them. This new character, Pedro Palacios, owned land in the province of Santa Fe and was offering them a small piece of his hundred thousand hectares where everything was yet to be done. A committee of Podoliers signed their first contract with him on August 28, 1889. The bill of sale specified that each twenty-five-hectare lot would be paid off in three annuities, with a yearly interest of 8 percent. The colonists could purchase up to fifty hectares in addition to their means of subsistence and the tools they would need for the first harvest.

Although this was yet one more scam (as the value per hectare in that region was ten times less than what was being asked of them), they accepted, caught unawares. They set off, not imagining that the worst still lay ahead.

And I, having seen the replica of the steamship *Weser* in miniature as if it were an illustration in a children's story, search the map for the exact site where they arrived, in the province of Santa Fe, called Moisés Ville. Now the train moves lazily along and, heading out of the large Retiro Station, in Buenos Aires, the railway sheds glide past. It's a familiar landscape: all trains have the same way of departing. But now the destination is distant, exotic, hazy at times. And quite different from the city rising up behind the scenography of tin and zinc that surrounds the tracks. I look out at the cargo compartments, piled up like game pieces in every color; the skyscrapers, arrogant from this distance; the graffiti, cryptic, on banks of concrete; the wires that cleave the air in secret connections between sky and earth; the cardboard shelters along the edge of the tracks, too close to the locomotive's path, too fragile and fleeting.

I'm traveling in a threadbare cabin from the seventies where the cheap abstraction of two geometric paintings does nothing to decorate or enrich the ambience. "Dear Passenger," a notice advises, "During your daytime journey, the lower bed in this cabin may be converted into a comfortable seat with a backrest. If you should wish to use it, please ask your attendant, who will gladly carry out the operation." When I attempt the operation in reverse—without calling for anyone—the seatback, upholstered in fake leather, drops down with a thunderous crash and transforms into a bed. And then the attendant appears, verifies that all is in order, and leaves me with a towel and a set of white sheets.

"The lunch menu is ham and Russian salad for the starter, flank steak à la pizza and mashed potatoes for the entree, and bread pudding for dessert. Shall I put you down on the list?" he asks.

I don't know how to respond, yet some hours later I'll find myself in the dining car, unenthusiastically trying the menu, watching cultivated fields pass by through the window. Retiro Station will have been left definitively behind, and by then even the suburban strip will be a grimy memory.

When time and space enter this exclusion zone, the rhythms of life cease to exist, and it is indeed then that the real journey has begun, and I feel I am finally experiencing the famous vastness of the Pampas first-hand. The iron worm moves across the country, heading toward what is today a small town situated in the center of Santa Fe Province, more than 600 kilometers from Buenos Aires, although the station where I'll get off is not that of Moisés Ville (which has been overgrown with weeds for many years) but Rafaela, the most prosperous city in the region. Then I will complete the remaining distance of just under one hundred kilometers via National Route 34 and Local 13. But that is all still a long way off when several children glide past the little windows of our convoy: in the small towns, they salute the train's passage with white handkerchiefs; in the shanties, they amuse themselves by throwing rocks.

Meanwhile, I read about Moisés Ville's turbulent history as recorded by José Mendelson in the book *50 años de colonización judía en la Argentina*, a subject also evoked by the colonist Noé Cociovich in his *Génesis de Moisés Ville*. And I surmise that Moisés Ville today is a tranquil, quiet town. A corner of the Pampas where it seems like a lie that so many things should have once taken place there.

When they reached the landowner Palacios's colony, the Russian Jews were left all alone on the wicked plain. No one had come to receive them. And so they waited. And waited. And waited longer still.

After a month in the countryside, all remained as before except for those people, who were dragging themselves about like specters among the empty sheds of a railway station that would not be inaugurated with the name "Palacios" until February 20, 1890, six months later.

The immigrants had begun their passage to these lands on Friday, September 6, 1889, when a boat transported them up the Paraná River as far as the city of Santa Fe, and from there they had continued by train to this brand-new station, authorized for their use by special exception. They got out, clattering with all their gear, trunks, and tools: the group numbered several hundred people, ready to leave the long journey behind them and take some local hand in a firm handshake. But there was no one there. When the train they'd been traveling on departed, and they confirmed that no landowner was there to greet them, they preferred to believe that the rancher Palacios would arrive in short order or send out an administrator at the very least. But all he sent them—and a few days later at that—were a few sacks of cornmeal, which came infested with worms, and some beef, which was butchered by Rabbi Aharon Halevi Goldman, the spiritual leader of the group.

They soon realized that it hadn't been in Europe where they would experience their true misfortune, but in the hostile landscape of Santa Fe. Here, there were neither houses nor tents, and for weeks they slept inside the sheds of the station, which would become their refuge, as well as a few broken-down train cars. Beyond extended a terrain sewn with cordgrass, tacurú ants, iguanas, armadillos, chañar trees, and white carob; nothing like the cleared plains they had imagined.

Their first few months in Santa Fe slipped by quickly, and the calendar soon showed November 1889. The next year was not far off, and reserves were running low. It was at this point that they began, each morning, to make wayward excursions, searching for any scrap of food. Sometimes David Lander, the solitary man, was part of the company that went off to visit the sawmill and the railroad works in the neighboring town of Sunchales, the only place in the area with any vestige of progress to be seen. They'd arrive on foot after walking some thirty kilometers, wearing tattered coats over filthy clothing. Some went barefoot; others clad their feet using sacks already riddled with holes. They knew that a train arrived from Tucumán each morning to provide food for the workers. They'd ask for something to eat in their modicum of Spanish, the words badly stammered. They wanted *"galletn."* They begged, "Please, give me bread," "I'm hungry," "Give me sugar," and held out their hands; the hunger was gradually killing them. They walked close to the tracks in order to be right there when the train went by and would run alongside until the windows opened and the food dropped out, and it was not unusual for children to fight feebly over a crust of bread or scraps from a piece of fruit. Anything to stay alive.

The ones who stayed back in the railway sheds—the elderly, a few frail women, the smallest children—placed their hopes on the others. If those did not eat, neither would they. Under such circumstances, dozens of would-be colonists chose to leave the group behind, abandon the dream of agriculture, and return to business, and they made their way back to Santa Fe or Buenos Aires. Only the most determined remained: barely more than half.

But whether they stayed or left, all remembered those back in Russia who had preached progress and spoken of an end to oppression. They never suspected that the cost could reach that of a biblical calamity. They had been warned about sacrifice, about estrangement and privation, but not about the end of meaning. And in those railway sheds it came to pass that the children were the first to fall. In the beginning one died, in fever, trembling from unending chills. Then another. And another. Within a few weeks, more than sixty perished. It was an epidemic of typhus.

David Lander helped to erect the earliest traces of this failed colony: two cemeteries, one standing some distance away from the Palacios sheds and another in the nearby town of Monigotes, where more Jewish children had contracted this plague. A small farmer from the area contributed a few kerosene drums, and the railway workers gave boxes left over from nuts and bolts. The parents nestled their children inside these vessels and lowered them into the ground. Lander witnessed the pathetic scene. Perhaps he cried. After a little time, the soil held shrouded in its depths the future colonists.

. . .

But for those who remained standing, life went on. One day, they saw a horseman from afar, silhouetted among the treetops. He wasn't the first to pass through. A few criollo people worked on the ranches, driving cattle; others had never been able to adapt to the onslaught of the modern economy in the fields of Sante Fe. Barbed wire fencing and gates had turned the territories into prisons, and these men already sensed that they were nearing extinction. In 1889, the gaucho was a corralled species. And if he kept his facon knife well sharpened, it was because he didn't want to go out alone.

The figure of the horseman grew larger until he was right in their midst. Most of the gringos were to be found scavenging around the vicinity in search of a bite to eat, and the rider walked his horse among the ones who had stayed in the railway sheds, not making up his mind to dismount.

It was an encounter between two universes that shared not a single star. The criollo acknowledged the women, children, and elderly from the saddle with a surly gesture. His swagger contrasted with the deplorable appearance of the others. A narrow-brimmed hat and headscarf to shield against the noonday sun framed his dark face. A vest, a shirt, chiripa trousers, and a sash completed his ensemble. The Russians, by contrast, had nothing more to wear than makeshift garments fashioned from the large sacks of meal they received every once in a while from the landowner Palacios.

The horseman touched the ground with his riding boots and barged through, and he seemed on the point of addressing them yet held his silence. He paused only in front of one girl. Even all the poverty in the world had not managed to quell the beauty of this young woman who, weak as she was, had been unable to go out in search of bread. The paleness of her face and the cloudy gleam of her eyes fascinated him—no farmhand's wife was anything next to this feeble angel. The gaucho touched her face and spoke gently to her in plain sight of everyone. One of the Jewish men wanted to ask him something but couldn't find the right words in his meager Spanish vocabulary, and so the criollo hastened to respond with what he believed was appropriate. The gringo, uncomprehending, repeated, "Sí, señor, sí!" which may well have been the better part of what he was able to say in that unrevealed tongue. The marvel of this communication disrupted the apparent calm of the needy people, who rallied in an instant and launched themselves toward the gaucho, touching him and holding out their hands, a hundred hands, a thousand hands: "Give me bread!" "*Deme galletn!*"

Somehow the criollo broke free, turned tail, and fled. The Russians thought they must have scared him away, but none noticed that, as he rode off, he was smiling.

They went back to lying in their moldy corners, yearning for nothing, awaiting the return of their own who'd bring back something to eat, until they saw something they couldn't quite believe: the gaucho had returned, and was bringing food for everyone. But he hadn't come alone. Beside him galloped another man, who assisted him in carrying two bottles of caña spirits and a large sack of biscuits, which the immigrants leapt upon, digging their hands down to the very bottom.

As the tumult grew, the gaucho pointed to the girl he'd met on the first visit, exhibiting her to his cohort, who seemed to approve, enchanted by a kind of beauty unknown on these plains. Then the first man took her by the arm to lift her up onto his saddle, but she resisted. He kept trying, grappling with her. And he nearly had her over his back when her cries summoned the attention of the starving people, who dropped what they were doing and ran toward her. An uproar broke out in an instant: bodies shoving, curses hurled in Yiddish, in Spanish, in Guaraní, and a dagger in a skillful hand.

Thus sprouted the seed of the misfortune these beggars still had yet to know.

A dust cloud shrouded the gaucho and gringos in their combat. Like a panther, the criollo made a swift turn and broke away from the aching hands that held him, but the girl slipped free, and her sorrowful eyes disappeared behind the fury of the others, who didn't know that the gaucho was like the wind with his knife—in an instant, he'd buried it in the chest of the closest man, who suddenly tasted steel and was already whimpering, stunned by the sight of his own blood. It was David Lander, the solitary man, the quiet one, who now cried out in terror, stumbling back until he fell to his knees, and still able to hear, far off in the distance, the gaucho, running with long strides, though he did not manage to escape.

For fate did not look kindly on the horseman either. The small crowd fell upon him, and, although he clung to his blade, slashing open more gutters of blood, someone managed to wrest it from him and then the others (even the women) took him down by blows. The beating continued until his dirty cries subsided into hoarse moans.

And then they bound him by the hands and feet. With the gaucho now subdued, they buried their shoes in his sides, kicking, stamping down upon him until they heard the *crack, crack!* of ribs and saw how his blood fertilized the Argentine soil.

David Lander's Kaddish, the prayer meant for sending off the dead, was recited the following morning. He hadn't made it past fifty.

Some days later the inspectors arrived: a party of officers dispatched by the Santa Fe government from the town of San Cristóbal, which stood close to the Palacios lands and was the seat of the department of the same name. At long last, representatives of the state had taken notice of the destitute Jews living in the railway sheds. However, they were not interested in their pleas. Neither "Give me bread" nor *"Deme galletn!"* There came the man in charge of writing the report, with his decorated quill and his testifying ink. A man prepared to recount everything, yet who, however, had nothing to write: when the chief tried to question the Jews, none would respond. They either didn't understand or didn't want to understand.

It was a crime without witnesses, even though it had occurred in front of all of them.

Only the other gaucho, who'd managed to flee in time and alert the police, was able to relate the events. He told the chief of the guard that his friend had been murdered by a gang of savage and traitorous gringos, who had failed to recognize their agreement and sworn oath. What happened was that his friend had taken a fancy to a girl, and, since she'd liked him as well, he had asked those present if he could take her as his wife. "Sí, señor, sí," the Russians had answered. Then they had begged him for bread and biscuits, so his friend had gone to the shop to buy food and two bottles of spirits to raise a toast with everyone. And these filthy Russians had taken advantage of him, eating and drinking without fulfilling their side of the bargain. Then, as if that wasn't enough, they had attacked him. His friend, may he rest in peace, had no recourse but to unsheathe his blade.

After many attempts to draw even a minimal testimony from the Russians, the chief from the party of officers realized he wouldn't get anywhere. And so, downhearted, he gave his scribe the order to pack up his things and leave.

And then I arrive.

The train stops at Rafaela station—where I get out—and then heads on its way toward Tucumán. I leave my cabin behind after fourteen hours to sleep in a fleabag motel before continuing aboard a bus the next day for just under a hundred kilometers. Moisés Ville is the last stop on a route through tiny towns with neat outlines and colonial pasts: Lehmann, Ataliva, Humberto Primo, Virginia. As was the case for many of them, life in Moisés Ville transformed to such an extent that the majority of colonists left: many Jewish people emigrated to the big cities or departed for Israel to live out the same colonizing ideal that their parents and grandparents had known here, and criollo people took their place.

It's early morning when I get off the bus. I walk with my suitcase over one shoulder and discover that I'm following Calle Barón Hirsch, where grass grows up between the paving stones and the bricks of old houses, and dew lies damp over everything. I cross an empty square, pass in front of a clothing shop displaying the latest fashion from fifty years ago, and pause to buy a drink at the kiosk in a service station. I avoid the schoolchildren in white uniforms on their way to class and, after going a few blocks, scarcely traveled, reach a house on Calle San Martín. This is the address I have written down in my notebook: this is the place I've been headed, half a block from the main square and just a few steps from a synagogue where no one now prays, one of three temples to be found in this town. I open a little latticed gate and reach the entrance. I catch myself waiting for the sound of dogs barking, though it never comes. I ring the bell.

Señora Sofía, my host, opens the door a moment later; I sense that she has been waiting for me with some anxiety. She's a slight woman, retired, with curly hair, who lives alone and waits up every night for a call from her daughter, a scientific researcher living in Buenos Aires. For several days she will lodge me in the room where that same daughter grew up; beyond it reign family portraits. The service is half-board: breakfast each morning, prepared by Señora Sofía herself, is abundant and delicious. Otherwise, there haven't been any lodgings in Moisés Ville for a long time apart from the Mordechai Goldman Complex, a collection of bungalows managed by a descendant of the first rabbi, which opens its doors to tourist groups.

"Aren't you going to take siesta after such a long journey?" It's the first thing Señora Sofía asks me, the moment I've put down my luggage.

But all I want to do is to comb through the history that has led me here. (Sometime later, yes, the stillness of this town will start to get the better of me.) Back outside, then, I walk without much of a set course, as though wanting to recognize this stretch of twenty-five blocks that constitutes the town. I pause at the intersection of Calle Barón Hirsch and Calle San Martín—a typical Moisés Ville crossroads—and take note of the old community buildings (a library, a theater, a bank, a school), which follow one after the other and speak to the significance of this town, the vigor of its early days.

The fields are the primary source of work for the old colonists' heirs—today, simple men, now grown older—but there isn't enough for everyone. The others live off commerce. In either case, at siesta time all sorts gather inside a little bar with high ceilings, in a corner of the plaza, and play cards while the manager—a young but unhurried man—serves up drinks, and news from a nation in constant unrest files past on the TV, distant and strange. A grandfather and his grandson, dressed in meticulous gaucho garb from beret to boots, play dominoes while I drink my first coffee at a table where, before I arrived, a little dog lay sleeping, curled up on one of the chairs. The grandson celebrates when he beats his grandfather in the game and orders some cocoa. And as he heads up to the counter to collect it, he walks past another table occupied by an old man. He spies on the man's cards and asks him:

"Are you playing for cash, León?"

Not even David Lander's bones remain at this moment when I insert myself into the life of Moisés Ville. More than one hundred twenty years later, the dust has turned to dust. And when I tell a few of the neighbors why I have come—and what it is I want to know—they wrinkle their noses at the nasty smell of the word "crime."

2

An Argentine Jerusalem

Alone opposite the plaza appears a light, peeking out from a bar called Leshanto. The town of Moisés Ville lies in half shadow on a winter's night made colder still by the crisp country air. It is my first night here, and my arrival some hours ago seems like a distant episode now. Inside the bar—one of only two or three places where you can sit down for a bite to eat—the men seem to be hunkering down among themselves. Some share coffee, others play dominoes, the rest watch a soccer game. The fluorescent tube light illuminates their weary faces and ricochets off old alcohol bottles stacked along the counter. The electric buzz of the soccer commentary drowns out their muttering, and the man tending bar hands me a dark fizzy drink that contrasts with the bright green of the plastic tablecloth. The rest of the town is sleeping.

A man wearing thick glasses and bundled in a short woolen jacket tells me that, back when he was a boy, he used to come to this very bar to buy little cones of toasted sunflower seeds topped off with two peanuts. Shie Godl Kleiman and his father, old man Idl, two characters who are no longer around but left their mark, used to wrap the cones in newspaper (using pages from the most widely read Jewish papers in Argentina, *Di Ydische Zaitung* and *Di Prese*) and would serve them up, one after the other, as the sun was setting. I haven't been here more than twenty-four hours and have already heard several anecdotes of the kind.

I've also heard "Moisés Ville," one of the songs by Jevel Katz, a singer who came to Argentina from Vilnius in 1930 at the age of twenty-eight. His unquestionable artistic talent led him to become the favorite of his fellow countrymen. Between klezmer, tango, cabaret, ranchera, foxtrot, and rikudim tunes, he had written and performed some five hundred songs by the time of his death, in 1940, after a tonsil operation. "The happiest of the Argentine Jews, the most popular and beloved artist of Buenos Aires, Jevel Katz, is dead," ran the story in *Di Ydische Zaitung* at the time, and the procession accompanying his cortege to the cemetery was enormous. Five years earlier, a similar thing had occurred with the burial of tango legend Carlos Gardel; perhaps for that reason, Katz is known as "the Jewish Gardel."

In the song "Moisés Ville," a clarinet plays long and sorrowful notes, but the lyrics are happy. Jevel Katz saw a town that many of his own kind in Europe had dreamed of, a town where everyone was Jewish: the pharmacist, the lifeguard, the chief of police, the judge, and even—so he sings—the gaucho, a man in espadrilles who whistles a local song, but . . . "You may be sure sir, that criollo is a Jew," the song declares in Yiddish. In the chorus, Katz aggrandizes the town's epic, singing: "You are a Jewish state, a pride in Argentina, Moisés Ville!"

Even so, all I can confirm is that nothing seems much like that today, and the original epopee is now a myth that fills even those who don't know it very well with pride. Here, a wall along one street has been painted by students to show a calm blue sea, a starry night crowned with crescent moon, and a ship with "WESER 1889" written across the prow that carries three smiling immigrants: father, mother, and daughter. A short walk away, a bronze bust of Baron de Hirsch emerges, showing eyelashes painted on in white marker, the work of some prankster. All of this is part of the myth as well.

For my part, I'll have to get used to referring to the town with that very Argentine pronunciation employed by everyone around here when they say "Moisesvishe."

"What would you like the colony to be called?" asked the man, painstakingly elegant, whose very presence there in the fields seemed impossible.

Thus far, the Podoliers' life in the Pampas had been neither easy nor pleasant, but the immigrants who still remained after two months had decided that the colony they'd come there to found should have a captivating name, one with biblical echoes, one that no one could forget.

"What would you like the colony to be called?" the landowner Pedro Palacios asked again, having finally come from Buenos Aires to visit them. All of the Russians had gathered to welcome him with bread and salt, in the traditional way, on a hot day in late November or early December 1889. They had washed and dressed in their tattered garments with propriety, as though the penuries of their journey and scrounging had been left behind.

Rabbi Aharon Halevi Goldman, the spiritual and community leader, took a step forward. At thirty-six, his long beard and frown made him appear older. Like many of his fellows, Goldman had been born in Russian Podolia and ordained while still a boy. He had never wished to make economic gains off of religion; rather, he preferred to earn his living as a *shochet* (or ritual slaughterer). The rabbi had found little joy along this odyssey and his five children now looked as hungry as all the rest, but, in spite of everything, he was poised to pronounce some magnificent words. At his side waited David Horovitz. The latter, originally from Minsk (today the capital of Belarus, then a frostbitten city in the far western reaches of the czarist empire), was a man of long, dark features who had arrived a few years before on his own account, along with two brothers: Abraham Itzjak and Noaj. The three had taken up in Buenos Aires, and he, having earned Palacios's trust through his talents as a translator, had been sent to the colony as a temporary administrator.

Then the rabbi spoke the name in Hebrew: "Kiriath Moshe." And he explained that, just as Moses had brought the Jews out of slavery in Egypt and led them to a free country, the contingent gathered there had left behind the tyranny of Russia to make their way to Argentina. David Horovitz translated the name, with an elegant, Gallicized turn of phrase, as "Moisés Ville," Moses Town. Palacios, the landowner, smiled. And he launched into an optimistic speech filled with promises, which the colonists met with applause. After so many travails, they longed to hear sweet words.

There were strong handshakes and words of goodwill that day, and then, with the setting of the sun, the Russians took shelter inside the canvas tents they now inhabited—except the rabbi, the only one who had been given lapacho wood to build his house. Some few weeks before, perhaps near the end of October 1889, they had left the railway sheds of the Palacios station and settled in another area, eighteen kilometers away, on the land where the town of Moisés Ville now stands. Yet, despite this day of celebration, the landowner and Russians could never stop eyeing each other with suspicion. A month before, on October 29, the newspaper *La Nación* had drawn attention to the "wretched" people in the Palacios colony and demanded punishment for the man responsible for their destitution in a short article entitled "Immigration," which reproduced a letter signed by Estanislao S. Zeballos, the minister of foreign relations under President Miguel Ángel Juárez Celman.

In no way could those hungry pioneers have been able to reach the pages of a powerful newspaper like *La Nación* through their own means. But they had an unexpected protector: a Romanian doctor who lived in Berlin and was traveling through Argentina. His name was Wilhelm Loewenthal, and he'd been moved by the pleas of those children in rags begging for food. The doctor recognized the harsh accent of their miserable words: they wept in the same language he had heard in Romania and again in certain alleyways of Berlin. They wept in Yiddish.

The writer Pedro S. Lamas, who was in charge of the office of information at the Argentine consulate in Paris, had entrusted Loewenthal with an investigation into the colonies, and the doctor was making his way back to the city of Buenos Aires when he stopped in Palacios. Not long before, at the same time that the pioneers were embarking on their Atlantic journey, the philanthropists from the Alliance Israélite Universelle in Paris had also asked this emissary, knowing about his mission, to look after them. And so Loewenthal wasn't just any bourgeois but a bourgeois who was Jewish, had contacts, and was *elegantly* European; that is, he belonged to the bourgeois class that the travelers from the *Weser* needed to get to know.

In the report that he presented to the Argentine government for his scientific mission, Loewenthal made reference to this *"affaire des immigrants russes.*" But that wasn't all: before boarding the ship back to Europe, the scientist tracked down Pedro Palacios himself to inquire about them and, once back in Berlin, shut himself away in his office to write about the unhinged and brilliant idea that had obsessed him on the high seas. Loewenthal sought to develop a vast project that could transform the destitution he had seen and turn the Argentine Republic into the potential destination for a mass Jewish colonization.

He nourished his dream of one million francs to mobilize the idea; a transoceanic flow of five to ten thousand immigrants per year; and small farms of fifty to one hundred hectares where each family could settle and, from the harvest, make enough money to buy the land in installments. Of course, Loewenthal was not naive: he knew quite well that a rich banker had also been taking an interest in the fortunes of his oppressed brethren. Like that of the Rothschilds, the fame of Baron Moritz von Hirsch auf Gereuth (or "Maurice," in the French fashion of the era) was well known throughout Europe. Hirsch had established his fortune on currency trade, finances, copper, and railroads, having multiplied the thousands of francs and marks bequeathed to him by his father and grandfather several times over. Baron de Hirsch, as he was known—or simply Baron Hirsch—had come to have it all, but he lost what he loved the most: his first daughter had died shortly after birth, and his second child, Lucien Jacob Moritz, passed away from pneumonia before he turned thirty. The man then fell into a deep depression, which he could only break free of with one decision: having no descendants, he would bequeath his inheritance to the Jewish people.

And so, bit by bit, he entered into a philanthropic frenzy.

To raise the standard of living for the Jewish masses he was initially prepared to invest fifty million francs in the Russian territory, but the czar objected: he didn't wish to receive any aid for those pariahs and instead meant to control the donated money at his own discretion. The Baron thus resigned himself to organizing their emigration and facing the challenge of transporting five million individuals to other countries. But, unlike Rothschild—or perhaps so as not to get mixed up in his affairs—he wasn't inclined to fund the emigrants heading for the Land of Israel. He feared that the Russian empire would advance on the Ottomans and take Jerusalem, and it made no sense to remove the Israelites from one region of the czarist empire only to bring them to another.

Argentina—that wedge of America—would, then, be their new destination.

With his impressive introduction, the Romanian doctor Wilhelm Loewenthal earned the favor of the philanthropist. And one year later he returned to Buenos Aires to cement the project. He stationed himself at 359 Calle Perú, behind a door that for several months blazoned the inscription "BARON HIRSCH COLONIZING COMPANY": from that dark office with its creaking floors, in the heat of bustling Buenos Aires, half a block from the very historic Manzana de las Luces, Loewenthal began to organize the rescue of the Hebrew masses from Russia.

On August 24, 1891, a year after he'd begun thinking about the project, Baron de Hirsch founded the Jewish Colonization Association (JCA), registered in London as a "charity society" and supported by an endowment of two million pounds sterling (equivalent to about one hundred twenty million in today's pounds, a sum the Baron would quadruple not long afterward). In total—with the contributions it would receive from its creator himself—the organization came to exceed all of the public Jewish funds in Europe and America combined: in its day, it was the largest philanthropic institution in the world. Even so, Maurice von Hirsch, in the happiest days of the bourgeoisie, never ceased to be a capitalist who conceived of his philanthropy as a business. The capital invested had to grow steadily to feed back into the work, and the colonists had to become productive, capable of paying for their lands in timely installments in order to keep the machinery running smoothly.

Only at the end of the same year—on December 28, 1891—was Loewenthal able to sign a contract with the ranch owner Palacios to buy the 10,163 hectares of his land being cultivated by the pioneers in Moisés Ville. That was the first step. Later, over the course of the twentieth century, the JCA would found some fifteen colonies in Argentina: it was from these that the legend of the Jewish gauchos and the mystique of the agricultural cooperatives arose. But Moisés Ville was always the main seat, the most expansive (at 118,262 hectares, nearly four times the locality's area today) and most populous (more optimistic estimates say that it accommodated as many as 6,000 inhabitants at its peak, although the largest census figure, that of 1914, counted 3,837—perhaps 1,000 more than today). As a result, it was known for many years as "the Jerusalem of South America."

Not for nothing, then, is Baron de Hirsch's name scattered throughout the length and breadth of the town today. The hospital, a street, a small plaza, one of the two libraries, and the largest synagogue are all named in his honor.

Other buildings stand out alongside them: the lavish four-hundred-seat theater of the Kadima ("forward" in Hebrew) Cultural Association and Library; the Rabbi Aarón Halevi Goldman Museum of Communal History and Jewish Colonization, the Arbeter and Brener synagogues, the Iahaduth Hebrew School/Iosef Draznin Seminary, and the Hebrew Teachers' Boarding School. All of these proud façades show that Moisés Ville progressed after its pioneers' sacrifice, that from amid those weeds a cultural clearing was able to emerge, that the dream finally became reality. But time went running on. And today, some of the buildings look asleep, as though this "Moisesvishe" were only a dull reflection of that Moisés Ville of myth.

In fact, it is inside the Baron Hirsch Synagogue, a block from the main square in town, where for the first time in my life I take part in a Kabbalat Shabbat ceremony to welcome the Sabbath. The first star is glimmering in the sky and the fellow believers crowd together in the doorway just as they do every Friday, greeting each other yet again—even though they pass each other along the few blocks in town all the time—with a certain anxiousness to begin the ceremony. There aren't many of them. And the reason there aren't many is partly because there aren't so many Jews left in Moisés Ville, but also because their stances toward religion tend to be mixed. There are still some Jewish atheists, heirs to the old progressives.

Inside the temple, one voice intones the prayers and several others follow. The speaker is not a rabbi—it's been a few decades since one has lived here—but rather a devout resident who, like all the other neighbors, has come in his best clothing, his "Shabbat clothes."

"Since there was no officiant and all the rabbis had died, I stepped up," he will tell me later, after the ceremony has ended.

The man's name is Luis Liebenbuk, and he is the great-grandson of a colonist brought here by the JCA from Lithuania in 1906. A typical country man, he grew up on his grandfather's plot, in a rural area of German immigrants known around here as "Berlin." And although he doesn't like to call himself religious, he does consider himself an heir to his ancestors' traditions, being educated at the local Hebrew School, and a decent *ba'al tefillah*, or master of prayer.

The temple today has nothing in common with the humble synagogue that once was. After a renovation between 1926 and 1927 it took on a magnificent appearance, with three bronze menorahs; the Aron HaKodesh, an ark where holy books are kept, which holds the little treasure of ten Torah rolls—as was the custom in the great temples of Russia—including one brought from Kamenetz-Podolsk by Rabbi Goldman himself; and three ritual objects donated by Baroness Clara Bischoffsheim, wife of Baron de Hirsch. The meetings here to discuss the Bible, the Talmud, theology, and messianism were once weekly and well attended: the habits of Europe lingered for several decades.

Now, as my attention strays from reading the prayer book that someone has placed before me, I notice the whispering of young voices: tonight, the synagogue is packed with a contingent of students visiting from Tucumán. As pupils at a Jewish high school, they can follow the prayers, and if they get distracted—exchanging brief glances—are able to return to the text with the ease of initiates, which I most assuredly do not share. I, by contrast, struggle to follow the words and, after a while, very gradually, let myself be swept away in the mantra of supplications that drag me out to sea in their strange waters.

Be that as it may, it is a fact that those unaffiliated with Judaism (that is, the descendants of Christian Europeans and criollo people), who were formerly a minority of the population, now make up 90 percent of the population today. One hundred twenty years after the generous hand

of Baron de Hirsch opened over the first colonists, the Israelite Mutual
Community of Moisés Ville comprises just 117 families.

"But the Jewish people are greatly respected and still remain the spirit
of the town, even though it's no longer like that Jevel Katz song where
he said even the police chief was Jewish. It's nothing like that now, but
there'll never be an initiative that doesn't involve the participation of
some Jewish person either," says Abraham Kanzepolsky, better known
around here as "Ingue," which means "boy" in Yiddish . . . though he's
more than eighty years old.

Ingue is a fine conversationalist, a frank man who doesn't shy away
from unofficial versions of history, and a generous host who gladly
accepts conversations with outsiders in search of answers. Of course, I'm
not the one who recognizes him when the doors of Leshanto bar open
and he appears, but he me. Ingue wears a beret on his head and moves
slowly, with care, as he approaches my table and introduces himself with
a smile. He removes his hat; his silver hair is divided in a neat part.

What Ingue points out can be seen on every corner: Moisés Ville is
a place where the old Judaism is still alive and displays itself with pride.
It's more than that: contrary to what I would have expected, Yiddish can
still be heard here as well. There are little sayings, words that slip into
speech, and nicknames like Kanzepolsky's. What's more, children in the
community are taught Hebrew. And Jews are treated with respect, with
such respect that this name is barely ever mentioned: the Jewish people
call each other "paisanos" and are referred to by the others as "Hebrews,"
in an ancient and polite custom.

Moisés Ville's society today is one proud of its legacy. For, while some
towns host national events like the Roast Pig with Skin Festival, the
Sheering Festival, and the Alfalfa Festival, here they set aside time for
the Festival of Cultural Integration. And, of course, they name a Queen
of Cultural Integration. But in the year of my visit, the Queen of Cultural Integration isn't Jewish. And this is hardly unusual. Around here,
until quite recently, a simple vox populi expression could be heard in
response to questions about the exodus of the Jewish descendants: "We
planted wheat and harvested doctors," said the mothers of first-, second-,

or third-generation Argentine children who left by the hundreds, heading for the big cities in search of superior education, modern commodities, and work opportunities. Then again, for immigrants who had never worked the land, life in the country was a very hard one. Of the initial colonists, two-thirds had left by the end of the nineteenth century. Later, many young Moisesvillians set out after their own ideal, the same one their ancestors had carried to the Pampas, though renewed in the reparations of history with the creation of the state of Israel.

Ingue Kanzepolsky was one of the ones who stayed, but he admits that he, too, once thought about going to Israel.

"Really, it was one of my aunts who was so insistent about it," he says now, sweeping a hand through the air.

Kanzepolsky made his living as an accountant and math teacher, and also as a farmhand. He still works the old small farm in the region of Wavelberg (twelve kilometers north of town) that belonged to his grandfather, Froim Enah Hacohen Kanzepolsky, a colonist brought from Lithuania by the JCA at the dawn of the twentieth century. Ingue lived in this very countryside as a boy: his father did the harvesting, his Ukrainian mother raised poultry, and his sister (a future mathematics professor who would settle in Buenos Aires) helped out with domestic tasks. There were cows and chickens, trees and horizons, horses and sulkies, and in addition to livestock they grew flax.

"You've never seen a harvest?" he now asks, and his face lights up. "Flax is beautiful: it blooms sky blue. Looking at a field of flax is like gazing into the heavens."

Not even in the hardest times did they run short of food on that small farm. Later, when young Ingue reached fourth grade, the family left the countryside and moved into town in order to send him to a larger school. And so Kanzepolsky grew up in Moisés Ville, a "Jewish state" as Jevel Katz sang, and attended classes taught by the colonists themselves in the synagogue.

"They weren't so religious, but the habits they brought from Europe were very deeply ingrained," he recalls now. "So it wasn't such an extraordinary thing to study: how could we not study?"

That magical town, which lingers on in this man's memory, could never have imagined the dwindling of the Jewish population today. But there was no way of avoiding it, even at its feeble pace.

"No one realized it was happening, because we were an overwhelming majority in the economy and institutions, you know?" he continues.

And he lives alone, Kanzepolsky, for his two children left as well. He resides in a house with high ceilings and spacious rooms, with a porch for drinking tea and watching the neighbors go by, the same house where his parents and grandparents lived before him.

"Things slipped by me like a story happening to someone else," he ultimately reflects, slightly amazed.

And he speaks of the girl he met at a cousin's wedding, that night when an aunt wanted to introduce her to him and he responded, "*Tía*, don't bother me, if I'm going to meet someone it will be in my own way," only to end up sitting next to the very same eligible woman by pure chance and saying to her, impishly, "Take your napkin," before starting their courtship. That eligible woman became his wife, and now, after a long marriage and a separation, she is his ex-wife and lives elsewhere, far away from the town. But Ingue doesn't feel like he's alone. Maybe because, in Moisés Ville, everyone finds out what's going on with everyone else.

The town reached its peak between the 1920s and '50s, when people used to go to the theater at the Kadima (which also screened films twice a week), where plays would pass the test of those four hundred spectators before making it to Buenos Aires, and more than once the famous Berta Singerman performed there. Back then, people read in Yiddish, Spanish, Hebrew, Russian, French, and English at two libraries: the Baron Hirsch, which held more than twenty thousand volumes and gave awards to the most voracious readers, and that of the Kadima Society, which had some ten thousand and also functioned as a night school. Two periodicals were in circulation—*El Alba* (The dawn) and *Mozesviler Lebn* (Moisesvillian life)—and people remembered those of bygone days: *Der Oifgang* (The sunrise), *Di Tribune* (The tribune), and *Zangen* (Seedlings). They lived in an atmosphere of constant ideological debate that had, for example, seen the birth of Micaela Feldman de Etchebéhère, a Marxist captain in the Spanish Civil War. They prayed in one of four synagogues: the Baron Hirsch, the Brener, the Arbeter, and the Litvishe (or Ashkenazi, demolished in 1980). Classes were taught among five schools in town and fourteen in the country, in addition to the Hebrew Teachers' Seminary, which reached enrollment of 150.

Moisés Ville was an important livestock marketplace in the north of the province, sending a thousand head of cattle to various corners of the nation every day, at the same time that they were building windmills; planting alfalfa, wheat, corn, and flax; opening dairy farms and creameries; and working in agricultural cooperatives. They struggled through droughts and floods, locusts, weeds, and pests, while also manufacturing toys, soap, soda, and candy in town. They deposited money at the local branch of the Banco Comercial Israelita. And there were two sets of parallel train tracks, running north–south: the Moisés Ville station stood on the east line, the Palacios station on the west.

In 1937 they were already beginning to welcome dozens of displaced Germans escaping from Nazism, who found themselves in Moisés Ville with seventy-five-hectare farms, houses fenced with barbed wire, fifteen milking cows, oxen, horses, carts, and seeds, all provided by the JCA. In 1942, a Campaign for the Assistance of Jewish Victims of War and Refugees was introduced with a tumultuous event at the Kadima that assembled more than a thousand people bringing provisions, clothing, and medicine; the peace of 1945 was celebrated with a huge party and a free barbecue, and the celebrations continued the following day on the property of the cooperative La Mutua Agrícola, attended by the governor of Santa Fe, even though all were mourning family members killed in devastated Europe.

They played soccer and cheered along in Yiddish. And they practiced track and field, boxing, tennis, and equestrianism at the Moisés Ville Recreation Center, or bowled and went shooting at the Federal Range. They relied on support from Mutual Aid, the Sociedad de Damas de Beneficencia, the Women's International Zionist Organization (WIZO), the Committee for Immigrant Relief, and the Rotary Club; and in summer they welcomed poor children from the Home for Jewish Seniors and Orphans in Burzaco, a suburb of Buenos Aires.

And the JCA presented the colonists with a scroll in honor of fifty years of effort, which stated in one passage: "They have created a worthy and wholesome life for themselves in the great and generous Argentina, becoming faithful citizens of their new homeland and at the same time preserving the noble traditions of Judaism."

The years come back to life with each of these recollections. But none offers more than two words in a row about the murders of Moisés Ville.

To hear anything about them, you have to ask the oldest neighbors and see how their eyes darken at the memory, have to invoke ghosts that still lurk on these silent streets, have to explore the ruins that stand in the city center or chase after some elusive legend; in short, you need to do some digging into the gaps of the official history.

Or else return to the starting point.

For, in the colony, everything accelerated in the year 1891, when the wave of migration from Russia multiplied as a result of further persecution. The misfortune the pioneers had suffered in 1889 had been left behind, but Baron de Hirsch's lands in Santa Fe and Buenos Aires were not enough, and the harvests were not strong either. Just when many farm laborers were giving up and abandoning the fields, Doctor Loewenthal was replaced, as the Baron considered him too tolerant toward the colonists' complaints. Part of the conflict was cultural: the JCA's delegation was composed of English, French, and Swedish people with inflated salaries who knew neither Yiddish nor Hebrew and had difficulty communicating with their Russian colonists, who did not know the languages they spoke either. Sometime later, the Baron gave the order to have any rebellious farmworkers, those whom the administrators considered schnorrers, or parasites, ejected from the colonies. And so, in Moisés Ville, only some fifty families remained.

Living in the colony had been no easy thing in 1891, a year of poverty and plagues of locusts. Neither had dying. In July, a twenty-one-year-old colonist named Ziml Seivick had ridden out at a gallop, searching for a cow that had strayed from the corral during the night. "Two hours later, the whole colony saw a horse returning very swiftly, carrying one person and heading toward that family's house," Mijl Hacohen Sinay wrote in the article "The First Jewish Victims in Moisés Ville."

> When it drew near, the horse stopped still and the rider, who was the young Ziml, collapsed onto the ground. The neighbors ran toward him and, filled with fear, watched as young Ziml lost consciousness. When they tried to pick him up, they realized his chest was completely covered in blood. They quickly called the doctor, who was already there in the colony, but all his help was in vain for Ziml perished that night. At some point the boy managed to return to his senses for a few moments, and he told them that a gaucho had approached him while he was out riding in search of the cow and had asked for money. Since he wouldn't give him any, the gaucho had attacked him with a knife, running him through before making off for his hideout.

Shortly before the summer of that same year, 1891, another crime shook the small society of colonists. Mijl Hacohen Sinay writes:

> One of the Podoliers, Kantor, was a young man who was unmarried and had not yet been colonized. Although able to stay in the colony, he had not been authorized to cultivate the land and was working as a shopkeeper. He was in the custom of opening his business very early, before any other household was awake. One morning, his shop still remained closed after all the others had risen. This did not draw any attention at first, but later the neighbors approached and started calling at the door. On one side there was a voice, but no one answered from the other. They knocked harder and harder, but it was no use: only silence came from within. All of them knew that Kantor had not left the colony, and their fear turned contagious. When they broke through the door and entered the bedroom, they stood frozen before the scene: Kantor was dead, on his cot, lying in a pool of blood already nearly dry. His belly lay open, and his face was slashed through: it looked like a cabbage sliced open. Everyone

wondered how the murderer had gotten into a room that had no windows. The only entrance was through the door of the shop, and it was well sealed. But they realized at once that the boards of the fireplace had been torn out. As for the motive behind the murder, there could be no doubt: it was a robbery. There was no way to know if any merchandise missing, but not a single cent was left inside his room.

The following year, many laborers decided to leave the colony and make their way elsewhere, whether in other fields (farther north, toward Tucumán, or farther south, toward Rosario), on railway construction, or in the city. The majority still lived in tents and mud huts, and they had a shortage of tools, though they did receive a monetary allowance from the JCA that allowed them to live modestly. Although agriculture was growing nationally, the harvests were not yielding well in Moisés Ville, and Argentina was seeming less and less like the promised land. The JCA's plan of moving 25,000 Russians during that first year of existence had been blown to smithereens. One-tenth of that, barely, was the number that had made the journey. On the other hand, as reported in the June 9, 1892, issue of *La Unión*, a newspaper from the colony of Esperanza, Moisés Ville was "awful terrain for colonization."

Three years after settling in these harsh lands, many of the Russians decided to go out in search of work, unaware that the provincial roads were hazardous and beset with bandits. "Only the women and the elderly were left in the colony," Mijl Hacohen Sinay noted in his article.

Of those who went away to work, another six fell victim. How they were killed is unknown, for there were no witnesses and no one could speak for them. As I have said, they were murdered far from Moisés Ville and on different roads: two were middle-aged family men, Zvi Wainer and Jaim Schmucler. The other four were young men and still unmarried, Shmuel Bersanker, Reuben Kristal, and the two Finkelstein brothers.

And 1892 would turn out to be the bloodiest year in Moisés Ville's history.

The horror began in January, when, in a remote area known as Monigotes, a fellow called Tejedor and his friend stopped to buy a bottle of gin at a shop run by a Frenchman named Tissieres. Whether or not they had a plan, history has forgotten. But from there they made for the house of the Jewish Tuchman brothers, who'd arrived from Russia not long before. The visitors knocked, and, when the door opened, they fired their guns. "The head of the household's brother, overwhelmed with fear, threw himself onto a bed to feign sleep, believing the murderers would not kill him," the newspaper *La Unión* noted in its issue from January 31, 1892. "Seeing the man there, they fired on him as well, leaving him dead on the spot."

The wife and several of the children begged for their lives. And by grace or good luck they were saved. The criollos left with all of the money and the few possessions they believed to be valuable. The next day, a familiar story, they were captured. "The things happening in our colonies are alarming," stated the newspaper *La Unión*. "Barely a day goes by when we are not shocked by details of another hideous crime. The guilt rests entirely on the inconceivable negligence of our criminal justice system, which allows individuals charged with crimes and misdemeanors to walk around with total impunity."

The Tuchman brothers' terrible killing led the Monigotes colonists, who were few in number and terrified, to organize a nightly patrol. But not much time would pass before they would decide to abandon those lands and move toward Moisés Ville or anywhere else. In fact, the locality that exists today under the name of Monigotes is located close to the place where the Tuchmans were slain but not on the exact same site. That first Monigotes became depopulated, and today the precise location is unknown: historical maps refer to it as "Old Monigotes" and situate it imprecisely, like an Atlantis on the Pampas.

3

Definitely Endangered

One day, in the margin of an old document, I scrawl: "This is an investigation into the forgotten crimes of a language now gone."

Another day, I find my scrawl and cross it out: neither are the crimes forgotten (and that's why I keep hammering away at this inquiry) nor is the language gone (and it seems even less so now that I have my own Yiddish–Spanish dictionary, an old book from 1931 that I borrowed from my grandmother's library—against her will, for she told me to leave there empty-handed).

But if I want to work with my great-grandfather's article, which consists of twenty-seven pages in Yiddish, I need to procure more tools. Because it starts like this:

דער אויפֿבוי פֿונעם ערשטן ייִדישן אַגראַר־ייִשובֿ אין אַרגענטינע—מאָזעסװיל—
האָט געקאָסט אַ סך בלוט, און די ייִדישע פּיאָנערן־קאָלאָניסטן האָבן דעם דאָזיקן
בלוט־אָפּצאָל געמוזט געבן.

And I understand nothing.

As a popular Yiddish saying goes, "*es iz shver tsu zayn a yid*": it is hard to be a Jew. I haven't heard anyone use the phrase, but I read it in an anthology of proverbs compiled by Graciela Lewitan de Eidelsztein, *Pu, pu, pu*. I'll say now that speaking like a Jew from the East is also hard.

Like the text by Mijl Hacohen Sinay, a large portion of the bibliographic sources I need are written in Yiddish as well. At times it would seem as though everything is in Yiddish: texts, documents, newspapers, magazines, theater plays, essays, yearbooks, gravestones, letters, songs, poems, epigraphs, unpublished manuscripts, rough drafts, biographies. Everything. A publication frenzy ran through the Jewish intelligentsia in the first half of the twentieth century, when cultural affiliation held value in itself and anyone who had anything to say would set it down on paper. "If you have a hand and a foot, then write," the saying went. In this setting, the IWO yearbooks, where "The First Jewish Victims in Moisés Ville" was published, resonate.

My battle against the language is hand-to-hand and ill-matched. The pages I'm writing now are also part of this zealous charge against a language, an assault in which the major episodes take place in the fields of Moisés Ville, in the city of Santa Fe archives, in the corners of Rosario, on the streets of Buenos Aires, and on the bookshelves of the IWO Institute, which is becoming a frequent destination in my efforts, for, as I pursue the traces of those century-old homicides in the present, the shadow of Yiddish is a constant.

At the outset, I know that reading Mijl Hacohen Sinay's original text straight through will be impossible within a short period of time and I will need a translator, but I also know that I have to at least try to grasp those first lines and all the others, whatever it takes, because that first version I read—posted online—is not complete, and I will need to refer to the original.

And so I involve myself completely and get started with classes: for several months, I go to the institute every Tuesday morning to attend a Yiddish language class. The goal is to learn how to read, but, despite the pragmatism promised, the teacher Débora Kacowicz tells us other things as well.

"What defines a language, and what defines a dialect?" she asks at one of our sessions, bringing up one of the great assertions made by Jewish linguists: that Yiddish should be considered a language. Meanwhile, she writes out a few letters from the Hebrew alphabet, which Yiddish also uses even though it has Germanic roots.

Every time I go to class it is early, and I struggle to focus. My eyes stray around, onto the walls of the room where the course is taught. It is, in reality, an assembly room of which we occupy only one corner. Old posters line the walls: they advertise performances and community activities from an era in which no one needed to come here and study Yiddish in order to experience this world. I share the class with three other students: opposite me are Iván Cherjovsky, an anthropologist specializing in Jewish immigration in Argentina; Mónica Szurmuk, who is making steady progress with her biographical studies on the writer Alberto Gerchunoff; and my friend Andrés Kilstein, a sociologist and TV journalist who's keen on the singer Jevel Katz.

We all have our reading and writing booklets open on the table: for the first few pages, the instructions are simple (copying letters, spelling out words), but then the matter grows more complex. Outside the classroom, in the entrance hall, a young man is inspecting a few books. It's Ezequiel Semo, who works for the institute as a librarian and is about to earn his degree in visual arts, and who never ceases to be amazed by the tenacity for speaking and writing in Yiddish that once existed in this country. Over the course of my research, Semo will save me on several occasions by discovering some minimal page, lost among the shelves, which will turn out to be crucial for me.

One day, the professor informs us that the first letter in the Yiddish alphabet is *alef*. Its dynamics confound me: א. Like a child using crayons, I practice the shape over and over on the paper yet never manage to break out of the bad habit of writing it as an X. Clumsily, I trace its slopes, practice its composition. The *alef* can also be used as a silent letter, taking on the sound of the vowel that accompanies it; that's how it works in the word איידיש, which reads from right to left and can be transliterated as "Yiddish," which is to say, "Jewish." With a bar underneath—אַ—the *alef* becomes *pasekh alef*, which is the letter *a*. And with a T-shaped bar underneath—אָ—it becomes *komets alef*, or the letter *o*. But in most printed texts only one *alef* appears, without any kind of bar underneath, and the reader must infer whether it's an *a* or an *o*.

This popular Jewish language matured at a slow pace: the linguistic baggage that the Israelites carried with them from Jerusalem in their migration toward the Rhine River (where they would establish the region of Ashkenaz) did not allow them to communicate with their neighbors, and, at the same time, the language of this new world did not satisfy their own spiritual needs. In this way, bilingualism became identity: Hebrew for the consecrated duties, and nascent Yiddish, in combination with medieval German, for worldly matters. At other latitudes, different languages—variations of each local tongue—were developing alongside Yiddish. But Hebrew was always present and, according to the linguist Cyril Aslanov, became a "substitute sanctuary," a moveable sanctuary that compensated for the loss of the Land of Israel.

Starting from the first class I already have homework. The exercise is to write and rewrite the sentence *Mame, nemt a mate*: מאַמע, נעמט אַ מאַטע.

Another day, I take advantage of a break during class to go downstairs. Behind the institute's glass displays, alongside the books, echoes of the wonder years still ring. I find myself examining Jevel Katz's mandolin when Silvia Hansman, director of the library and archives, and Abraham Lichtenbaum, director-general of the institute, appear behind me. The latter takes a step forward when he finds out about my investigation.

"Mijl Hacohen Sinay? But I met him! I saw him once, when I was a boy, at the IWO library. He was a man of enormous substance . . . a major figure," he says.

Lichtenbaum—a longtime IWO member—smiles from behind his thick glasses, collects a few books, and disappears.

To comb through the mystery of the crimes of Moisés Ville, one has to delve equally into that colony in Santa Fe and this corner of the city of Buenos Aires, which stands at 483 Calle Ayacucho. And that was why, when this door opened before me for the first time, I encountered the most significant time machine among all those that this investigation could provide: overflowing with books, Latin America's most important Jewish library operates in a luminous square building, its three levels connected by an ancient elevator. Open space is scarce in every direction: the paper multiplies endlessly. Today, the institute's appearance is completely different from what it was not so many years ago. True, it still houses thousands of volumes; an archive of publications, manuscripts, documents, and correspondence; a museum bearing the name of the painter Maurycy Minkowski; and spaces for hosting lectures, exhibitions, and courses on Yiddish, Hebrew, and Jewish culture. But the aged charm of its shelves and the pride of its collections were all blown through the air on the morning of July 18, 1994, at 9:53 a.m. Back then the institute occupied the fourth floor of the AMIA building: the terrorist attack that destroyed that structure reduced this library to rubble as well.

Today, at its headquarters on Calle Ayacucho, the institute possesses several thousand volumes: here, the world is retold. It is sketched out and explored. It is interpreted through a particular lens, with elements from folklore to scientific theory, from classical narrative to the Argentine story, from biblical history to the horror of World War II, from advanced pedagogy to universal problems, from views of the Jewish Right to news from the Jewish presses, from the Polish novel to the Moroccan pentagram, from basic psychology to modern Yiddish literature.

The library reflects the world, but it must do so with a kind of organization the world does not possess. And making it so is the task of the archivist Silvia Hansman, a dynamic and methodical woman for whom order is, quite rightly, a working practice: she is exactly the kind of person they need at the IWO, where, nearly twenty years after the attack, they are still trying to recreate the order that was lost.

When Silvia arrived at the beginning of the 2000s, after stints working as an archivist in the United States and Israel, she took on responsibility for a library in which it was so difficult to track down a title that each query—even if the request was about something as basic as the Jewish gauchos—would lead her to examine every corner and leave her on the edge of a nervous breakdown.

"Imposing order was no easy thing, so I had to set myself both short- and long-term goals. If I couldn't identify the funds, the collections, and the provenance of the collections within two years, I would leave," she says.

Before long Hansman achieved her mission. But even so—and this is one of the primary issues for an investigation like mine—the collection (the same one destroyed in the 1994 attack) is still yet to be completely restored. Silvia estimates that, between the books, hardbound periodicals, archival documents, and other materials, there are ten thousand units in the IWO Institute's current building, but the amount rescued from the rubble at AMIA's building is much greater: there are currently sixty thousand "items"—as the library and archives director calls them—stored inside three depositories, in boxes labeled with yellow or blue tags depending on the category of the material. In each depository there are a series of duplicated books, cataloged books, uncataloged and unduplicated books, and religious books, as well as books in the lengthy collections *Musterverk fun der Idisher Literatur* (Masterpieces of Yiddish literature), and *Dos Poilishe Idntum* (Polish Judaism).

One of these depositories—a house in which one hundred vacuum-sealed boxes are being held—is still yet to be processed, and so the exact contents remain unknown.

"There most likely aren't any manuscripts or archival collections," Silvia explains, "because those were always stored in special boxes. But there may be some periodicals that were hardbound, which could have been misidentified as books and placed there."

One day the sixty thousand items in storage will be assembled together once more. That day will come with the inauguration of the Casa de la Cultura Judeo-Argentina, a community center that is slowly being built as I write these lines, which will house the institute so it can move out of its headquarters on Calle Ayacucho, which grow more overburdened by the day.

Under these circumstances, my first inquiry meets with no response. I want to see *Der Viderkol*, the periodical my great-grandfather published in 1898: I have a feeling there will be some news story within its pages alluding to the killings at Moisés Ville. But my attempts to confirm this are in vain. *Der Viderkol* is not available for examination; it isn't even listed in the institute's registries. The fact that at least one copy was salvaged after the AMIA attack is certain: in 1997, the IWO displayed its collections at the National Library as part of an exhibition on the rebuilding that followed the attack, and the newspaper was featured— its antique condition required that it be mounted on washi paper. But later, amid the anarchy throwing everything into disarray at the time, its trail was lost.

Over the course of my investigation, *Der Viderkol* will become an obsession for me: I search for it in every archive and library possible, but it never turns up. In the end, I even go as far as to hire a book detective.

It is Elena Padín Olinik, owner of the bookstore Helena in Buenos Aires, who recommends him to me.

"We have an investigator who finds out everything about certain books or manuscripts for us before we put them up for sale," she says one day, as I'm interviewing her about forgeries in the world of antiquarian books.

Over our two steaming coffees, Elena has just struck a very sensitive nerve with me: I need someone who can take the name "Viderkol" and launch themselves into the search, a bookworm whose meal could take the shape of a timeworn nineteenth-century newspaper.

"You'll recognize me: I look more like Danny DeVito than Schwarzenegger," the detective tells me over the phone a few days later. We're about to meet at one of his favorite outposts, La Ópera, a bar on Corrientes and Callao. He prefers to speak face to face. "You'll tell me what you're looking for and buy me a coffee, that's how I do business."

It is easy to recognize the detective in the doorway: as he said himself, he's no Schwarzenegger. Danny DeVito, yes, it could be. But he is gray-haired and maybe a bit skinnier and younger than the actor. He wears large round glasses; his name is Ricardo Zavadivker. He is also a Jew, but the Jewish press he's familiar with comes later than *Der Viderkol*. The detective sits at the table and talks without pause, displaying a level of *tertulia* conversation embellished with an infinity of details learned through his readings and commissions. He tells me that he and his wife used to run a secondhand bookstore but also that his own personal research is centered around music brought over by the Spanish in the sixteenth century.

While our coffee grows cold, he takes notes on a pad to supplement the ones I leave him with. His hands have turned through thousands of musty pages. His fingernails have been gnawed by millions of dust mites. And my only wish is for the mites from *Der Viderkol* to set upon him as well. The success of those mites will be our success.

"We'll try searching in the major institutions, neighborhood libraries, United States universities, and among local collectors," he says.

He brings up the University of Texas, which collects books from Argentina and has a first edition of *Martín Fierro*, and mentions a millionaire collector in New York who has an Argentine tracker send him old Jewish tchotchkes from time to time when they go up for auction.

"If a cigarette lighter from 1905 with a Star of David on it turns up, that one will buy it," he adds.

And I dream of being a collector and having a vault with every issue of my great-grandfather's paper inside.

Der Viderkol's erratic fate, like that of many other lost publications, is owed to the fact that the catalog of the institute's old library disappeared in the attack, leaving the place mired in a Borgesian nightmare. That catalog was two meters wide and made of wood and iron, with dozens of little drawers and thousands of cards typed up in Yiddish, Spanish, Hebrew, English, or whichever language might be the case: file cards in yellow, green, and pale blue for searching by author, title, or subject in the main library, and green and pink ones for searching by author or title in the lending library.

"When the original catalog was lost in the attack, we drew a blank," admits Silvia Hansman. "So we cleaned up the salvaged material, stabilizing it, drying it, and removing dust and mold, then organizing it into groups and starting to catalog it over again. During our stay in the AMIA building, up until 2005, we managed to catalog seven thousand books and a significant number of periodicals, which are now in storage."

But my problem is not to do with a missing catalog. After all, I have one. What, if not that, is the text of "The First Jewish Victims in Moisés Ville"? Within the article, twenty-two homicides occur one after the other, but not everything that might be said about them is contained there; and so, in my case, unlike the institute with its thousands of items, what I need is more information.

That's why this investigation into such a distant series of murders is keeping me awake. On the route traced by my great-grandfather, the colonists' luck is abysmal: they fall victim to bandits who rob them, assault the women, slit the children's throats, and finish by killing them off one and all. A dark side of European immigration, agricultural colonization, and the racial melting pot is put on display. That's twenty-two good reasons right there to doubt the official version of Argentinian history, the one that tells a story of happy immigrants arriving from all four points of the compass. That such people existed, there can be no doubt. That they were a majority, it's quite possible. But the idea that this was the case for everyone, that idea, after reading this inventory entitled "The First Jewish Victims in Moisés Ville," is no longer so easy to believe.

However, between the initial publication of "The First Jewish Victims in Moisés Ville" in the IWO yearbook and its translation on the website where I encountered it, there is a link: *Toldot*, the magazine of the Association of Jewish Genealogy in Argentina. Its director, Paul Armony—a trailblazer who has assembled more than 220,000 files related to immigrants in the last two centuries—was the one who received Mijl Hacohen Sinay's original 1947 text from the hands of a contributor and decided to publish it. But Armony couldn't read Yiddish. He had enlisted his friend Nejama Barad to translate it for publication in the twenty-first issue of his magazine, in November 2003.

When I meet Nejama, she tells me she's a retired Hebrew instructor who still continues to teach at the institute. We meet there, among several people crowding together in the hall to attend a tribute to the writer César Tiempo. Nejama teaches Yiddish classes for students at the IWO and the University of Buenos Aires Language Center with the same dedication she had back in the 1950s, when—newly graduated from the AMIA Teachers' Seminary—she worked as a Yiddish teacher at a primary school. In those days, a famous professor named Shmuel Rollansky had asked her to join the institute, but she stepped away and chose to devote her free time to her family. Fifty years later, Nejama put together a workbook for Yiddish-language students, turned her attention completely over to the institute, and settled the score.

"Paul Armony found that article by Mijl Hacohen Sinay here," she continues. "I told him I'd already translated lots of material about the colonization, but he was adamant because this text was special."

When she finally saw the text, she thought there was something different about it as well: she had never read anything to do with the killings. She knew some problems existed and life had not been easy then,
but she'd never heard about twenty-two murders in a row. Her fasci-
nation was such that every day she ended up translating more than the
proposed number of pages. And when she had the translation ready, she
gave Armony one copy and kept another to add to her course on farming
immigration with fifth- and sixth-year students at the ORT school. In
the classroom, the kids were amazed at their ancestors' perseverance in
in the face of violence, asking: "And they stayed there all the same?"

4

Krisis Disco, Moisesvishe

It is, perhaps, that famous police instinct: on my second day in Moisés Ville, the blue uniforms already know I've come about the crimes, and they surprise me midmorning in the street, on my way out of the Leshanto bar, by slamming on the brakes of their Chevrolet S-10 patrol car. Two get out: one woman and one man.

"Where are you going?" asks the man, a tall and wiry type, his gaze obscured by dark glasses.

Around here, any outsider is a prospect for interrogation: whatever goes on in town, they know about it in the Moisés Ville police station. It turns out that the authorities remember the robberies suffered by a few residents and are suspicious of unknown visitors. But when I invoke the name of Señora Sofía, the woman whose house I'm staying in, and the reason that brings me to Moisés Ville, the officer cools down. I search through my bag and pull out a copy of my great-grandfather's article, which I show him. He has no idea what I'm talking about: he's never heard of anything resembling the murder of a colonist. In a certain way, our roles become reversed as his companion looks on, as if at a ping-pong match, and I'm the one who starts to act as interrogator. The policeman tells me he's been in the jurisdiction of San Cristóbal for eight years and two in Moisés Ville; he's never seen a homicide around here. Then I ask him about crime in the present, and he brings up livestock theft.

"Sometimes they'll butcher an animal right there in the field and leave the rib cage lying there, like the gauchos used to do," he says. He looks uneasy.

In this Moisés Ville, Moisesvishe, the sign of violence is something different; it's unlikely that any killing has happened in recent times. Sometime after my run-in with the police, Diego, the boy who tends bar at Leshanto—and one of the few young adults to be seen in this town—thinks back and shakes his head.

"Someone told me about a case from before, right, about some guy who turned up with a stab wound . . . But I don't remember any during my lifetime, not here or in any of the areas nearby."

Today, Diego occupies the place of the violinist Shie Godl Kleiman, who tended this very bar in the 1940s and used to deal out cones of sunflower seeds left and right to people as they went out to walk in the evenings. In that era, perhaps, someone could still have remembered the crimes I have listed in my notebook. Not so today. The question about crime rings strange.

But something seeps in through the cracks in the present.

The police have been ultimately unable to shed light on the sins of a recent killer from Moisés Ville: the one who killed a hundred dogs and cats. In the first half of 2009, an unknown person set about poisoning pets, always at night, by setting out laced meatballs. With each sunrise another five or six dogs would turn up dead. The Society for the Protection of Animals was on the warpath, but its efforts seemed useless: the poisoning was random and terrible. "There will be no more games with children now, no understanding laughter, their loving and faithful eyes are gone, they are gone," the teacher Lorena Maryniv wrote in a letter to the editor published on February 18 in *La Opinión*, a newspaper from the city of Rafaela. Her brother, Cristian, was the owner of Sansón and Wilson, a boxer and a German shepherd that fell victim to this psychopath.

"When I saw Wilson lying there, I noticed the smell and realized he'd been poisoned. It was a chemical smell, like Gamexane or Raid," recalls Cristian, a big moreno guy who works as an operator at the San-Cor factory in the town of Sunchales, turning sad as a boy when he speaks of the subject. Wilson lay on the ground, his mouth purpled and bloody. Youth, inoculations, and a careful diet had not been enough to save him. The man grows upset: "The dog went as though he was blowing out bit by bit."

It is night when we speak. Cristian asked me to meet him at his house, on Calle Barón Hirsch, but I arrive there before him. I wait until he appears, along with his whole family: several children clamber down from a purring Renault 12, and the man himself, who seems too big to get into this car and travel to the factory every day, gets out last. His large hand closes around mine; a cap hangs over his fringe of hair. The Marynivs' grandfather was a Polish man who came to the Chaco after World War I to work on the railway construction and somehow—though he himself was Christian—ended up in a Jewish town. Today, these grandchildren are typical inhabitants of "Moisesvishe": humble, hardworking, proud of the native soil that came to be theirs.

That very morning of February 13, 2009, when Wilson and Sansón were killed, another four animals turned up "blown out," to borrow Cristian's phrase. So Lorena sat down at the computer, opened her text editor, and made up her mind to tell the whole thing: "I'm writing as a last resort, as I want to shed light on a sinister event that is happening with horrifying frequency in the area of Moisés Ville," she began.

"I wrote that letter without any intention of sending it to the newspapers, but later I decided I should send it so that people would find out what had been going on, and because children playing in the street were at risk too," she tells me now, holding her son in her arms while sitting beside Cristian in the dining room, a setting of peeling walls enlivened by a TV. A photo of Sansón and Wilson stands out on the table.

Her letter spread the story around the region, and calls from Rafaela and Sunchales, the two nearest cities, started pouring in. Lorena and Cristian went out collecting signatures so as to expose the number of animals that were poisoned: on the three tally sheets they show me now—which register sixty-seven cases—I read that Chiquito, a ten-year-old sheepdog, was poisoned at night; that Amigo, another sheepdog, was lost at barely four months old; that a greyhound named Baldemiro, a Pekinese named Bucky, and a cat named Lisa fared no better.

. . .

In spite of everything, it's evident that Moisés Ville is coming more and more to resemble an open-air museum.

At the UNESCO World Heritage Committee's thirty-sixth session, held in 2012, the Simon Wiesenthal Center put the town forward as a candidate to be added to its list of World Heritage Sites. The Brener Synagogue, which has been declared a National Historical Monument, was restored with all of its original components and reinaugurated by President Cristina Fernández de Kirchner. In the year 1999, the site was named a National Historical Town due to its singular features: its settlement, which was developed along a line, in a communal block manner, following the characteristic design of Eastern European shtetls rather than the checkerboard pattern typical of Argentine villages; its cemetery, the first Jewish one in the country; its rabbi, Aharon Halevi Goldman, the first one among the Russian rabbis to arrive in the Pampas; its agricultural cooperative, La Mutua Agrícola, the first of its kind in Santa Fe province; and its rural schools, the first ones in the region.

"The concept of an open-air museum is lovely and poetic, but it has dangerous connotations for the future, namely the belief that this is a natural site and can maintain itself on its own," says Elio Kapszuk, director and producer of *Shalom Argentina: Huellas de la colonización judía*, a guide for touring the colonies of seven provinces, which was part of the program "Argentina, Mosaic of Identities," by the Ministry of Tourism, Culture, and Sports under Fernando de la Rúa's government.

Kapszuk, who has an office in the bustling Tribunales district of Buenos Aires, leans back in his chair and rests feet clad in a pair of orange Adidas on the desk; he is the director of the art space and special projects for the AMIA, the programming coordinator in visual arts and curation for the Recoleta Cultural Center, and the head of his own production company. In his office, pictures and caricatures by Miguel Rep mix together with photos of Kapszuk's ancestors.

He prefers to say that he's simply a madrich, or group leader, and that he received the first tools for realizing projects—ones that still underpin his work—at the Hebraica's madrichim school here and at the Machon L'Madrichim in Israel.

"Moisés Ville is a cultural asset," he continues, "and if it is an open-air museum, it's because seeing the names on the streets and shops is enough to amaze you. But accordingly, if this heritage isn't cared for, and there's no systematic transmission of history, a protection and a valuation, it's over. The city tells a history, but the work of memory needs to be done all the same."

Shalom Argentina, the project Kapszuk directed, still points out sites in Moisés Ville and its surroundings with signs and maps placed in the streets: after a decade, its itinerary continues to direct the steps of tourists. He returned there in 2007, this time to produce a program with joint involvement from the AMIA and the Fundación Ideas del Sur (presided over by the TV animator Marcelo Tinelli), which provided computer labs for ten schools in ten provinces.

"Tinelli and I would show up in a plane and revolutionize the town," he recalls enthusiastically.

But some Moisesvillians never saw him except on television: for example, the former residents who are now scattered in cities all over the country. Many of them take part in the annual dinners of the Moisés Ville Foundation in Buenos Aires. And at one of these gatherings—held in the assembly hall at the Sociedad Hebraica on a recent November Friday—I meet the clerk Isaac Waxemberg, a man who's taken part in all of the meetings and has already passed the milestone of eighty years yet still has not lost his drive. Waxemberg excuses himself from a group of friends and comes over, smiling. We talk loudly over the racket of several dozen Moisesvillians, and he mentions that he's been trying to bring in more young people:

"Around twenty kids showed up to the last dinner, most of them raised outside of Moisés Ville, and they were very welcome."

Waxemberg left the town in 1943 to study at a secondary school in Buenos Aires. Now far from Moisés Ville, he took part in the first dinner for former residents, organized in 1947: just 15 men attended. Today the figure averages at 65 diners and reached 105 on the fiftieth edition, the best attended yet. Over the course of more than sixty years, these Moisesvillians in exile have made their way through a score of Buenos Aires restaurants, also mounting cultural events and commemorations for the arrival of the steamship *Weser*. And it was from these dinners that the Moisés Ville Foundation arose, proposed after the centenary in 1989 and registered in 1992 with the social objective of sending back money for the museum, hospital, and Jewish community in the town.

After my encounter with the police, I pause in Moisés Ville's town square: I want to sit and rest before making my appointment to see an old sergeant with a good memory. I settle down on a wooden bench; it's siesta time on a Monday. I imagine that six hundred kilometers away, in the city where I live, the anthill is abuzz. Here, on the other hand, there's no one. In this long park, festooned in the center with a bust of General San Martín, I grow bored, baking in the sunlight.

On an equally sunny morning, in a corner of this very plaza, one of the great chapters in Moisés Ville's dark history began with the robbery of the Banco Comercial Israelita. It happened on Monday, October 25, 1971: five gangsters armed with heavy machinery took the bank floor by force, ready to make off with everything down to the last coin. At 7:45 there were twelve customers and seven employees inside, all of whom were thrown to the ground and held at gunpoint. However, the thieves were not aware that an alarm connected to the police station would be activated as soon as the door to the treasury and the vault was opened.

Today, many of the crimes Mijl Hacohen Sinay wrote about seem like child's play compared with the bank attack.

Subordinate Officer Oscar Chazarreta and First Corporal Eliseo Duarte were the first ones on the scene: they showed up running while the assailants were grabbing banknotes by the handful. "Give it to them!" the ringleader said when he saw them, and welcomed them in with a thorough round of bullets. Although two more officers quickly joined Chazarreta and Duarte, it was obvious that they were outmatched in both number and caliber. The new arrivals took cover behind the trees in Moisés Ville's main square and, returning fire, retreated a few steps toward the patio of the post office, scattered with trees. In the pale blue sky of the town at morning, the music of bullets made a strange reveille.

The assailants knew they had to escape at the earliest opportunity. They already had a haul of 3,967,000 pesos in hand, Chazarreta and

Duarte had already been sent out of the action—both had fallen with injuries—and they could hear more sirens approaching. In no time at all, they would have Moisés Ville's entire police force on top of them, ready to hold their baptism by fire. And so they made a run for their cars—a pale Ford Falcon and another black car—and sped off, firing bursts of grapeshot back toward the police. Not many hours later, the newspaper *El Litoral* spoke of a "spectacular assault."

One of the thieves, however, was left there on the bank floor, lying in a pool of blood and surrounded by scorched banknotes. The man was Zenón Menéndez, the son of a policeman, and he'd already been given a taste of the Santa Fe prison system. He had regained his liberty only a month before, and now, smelling like gunpowder and frenzy, he breathed with a rising whistle: he had one wound in his jaw and another in his chest. Around him an uproar of neighbors and police had assembled, and somehow the injured man ended up inside the V8 Ford truck of Ingue Kanzepolsky, the math teacher, who'd left his fourth-year class at the National High School to come over and see what was going on (and whose young son had just returned home from kindergarten, warning, rather reluctantly: "Mami, there's a shootout in the plaza").

Kanzepolsky took the fallen thief to the Baron Hirsch hospital. Beside him rode the police medic, who, in addition to that role, was headmaster of the National High School. Zenón Menéndez, the man with the bleeding chest, had been pulled in due to his fame as a hired gun: the head of the gang had gone looking for the man in the Rosario underworld, to have him act as their gunman in case of a confrontation that seemed unlikely, almost impossible. But, against all their plans, the hired gun would die in the Rafaela city hospital a few hours later.

"The gang had been assembled by an old prison guard based in the region of Rosario, where he commanded it from," says Alberto Lind, the policeman with the good memory, when I visit him at his bicycle shop, Lili, on Calle Barón Hirsch, a long and wide street that spans the town from east to west.

A child of Russian immigrants (his mother had arrived from Kiev; his father from Chernobyl), Lind stares out from behind large glasses that hang over his attentive eyes. Aged sixty-five, he's a robust moreno man who was educated in the local schools, both the Hebrew school and the technical one, from which he emerged with skills as a machinist and went on to continue his studies in the city of Santa Fe before returning to work in the cooperative La Mutua Agrícola. Bicycles were his thing even back in those days: Lind was the one who fixed them up for all of his neighbors, and he made his way far enough up in the business to open his own tire repair shop for cars and trucks. Everything went along fine for a few years, but then the great floods of 1973 destroyed all his work, a meter of water and mud covering Calle Barón Hirsch, the very place where he still runs this bright workshop with its cracking walls, replete with bicycle tubes, frames, and wheels.

"This all became a sea, mayhem, something beyond belief!" Lind says in horror, recalling the floods.

In the fields only the wire fences were visible, and the rest became the bed of a sea that plunged Moisés Ville into deep economic depression. When the water abated, farmland and dairy yards made way for greenhouses and cattle raising, and large planters began absorbing the smaller ones.

"Then the town turned to stone," laments the bicycle repairman.

Was the 1973 crisis the beginning of something that still has yet to reach its culmination? Half a block from Lind's bicycle shop, one business's iron shutter has been left hanging halfway. It's hard to imagine a line of young people crowding forward amid laughter and jokes on a Saturday night to get into this nightclub. But such a line did exist, once. Two words on its façade take on a disturbing timeliness: "KRISIS Disco." (The letters look drunk; painted on by hand, their informality seems outrageous.)

Lind made it through the 1973 crisis by entering the police force: it wasn't uncommon for a Jew to join the institution in a place like this, where, as Jevel Katz once sang, even the chief of police was Jewish. For his part, Lind says he was one of the kind who enforced the law.

"I was born and raised in this town," he explains. "But if I had to go after someone who'd screwed up, friend or otherwise . . . Well, he does his business and I do mine!"

Times changed: there aren't even any gangsters left today, despite the notoriety enjoyed by the district of La Salamanca, the most destitute section of Moisés Ville.

Lind, holding the inner tube from a bicycle wheel in his hands, explains that he retired at the rank of sergeant in 2000, during an era when advancement was no simple thing. "Are you crazy?" one of his friends rebuked him when he found out about the decision. "What's a monkey like you doing, leaving the police? What's Moisés Ville going to do?" But he didn't hesitate: he was tired of the infinite red tape day in and day out and wanted to go fix bicycles instead. Then, just like in the movies, he turned in his badge and gun: the last Jewish policeman went away quietly.

"That gang made lots of attacks," he continues now, back on the robbery at the Banco Comercial Israelita. "They worked with a plane waiting for them twenty kilometers away to pick them up after the attack. That's how they would escape. I found out that after the Moisés Ville robbery there was another one in Entre Ríos, where they'd broken into several banks already, but the thing was over before long . . . After they left that one gunman here, they started dropping one by one."

In Moisés Ville, you move as though on a chessboard: the maneuvers are short, but significant. The town's important points are concentrated within eight blocks and, if you wanted to be even stricter about it, only three. To be a reporter here is to tour around the same coordinates again and again, as though on a stage set, believing you have finally made it a bit farther only to realize that was just one more loop around the same block. And it's impossible for an outsider-reporter to try to go unnoticed: "We saw you pass," "You were walking around the library," "You went to see Kanzepolsky," et cetera . . . The Moisesvillians know wherever you go.

Three and a half blocks from Alberto Lind's bicycle shop, two from Ingue Kanzepolsky's place, two and a half from the Leshanto bar, and one and a half from the plaza—in other words, too close to everything else—lies the nerve center of the local government: the Moisés Ville Commune. There, inside a modern office, runs a government with five sitting members, headed by a president and voted in by the townsfolk every two years.

The community president I meet, Osvaldo Angeletti, is a Peronist who aligns himself with Kirchnerism and is up for a second term at the time of my visit. Historically, the list of community presidents has known few non-Jewish names: Angeletti is one of them. This country man, descended from Italian immigrants, took seventy percent of the vote to beat out his opponents, a group from the Radical Civic Union (a party that arose after the national economic and political crash of 1890) who had recently defeated the socialists in the primary elections. But the taste of victory and growth is fleeting in the governance of Moisés Ville; after one year of work, politicians already begin preparing the next electoral campaign, which takes with it the second half of a two-year term. In this way, government projects usually aren't thought through in the longer term because there isn't enough time. Some ideas, however, are introduced in provincial and national spheres, seeking more resources. At the time of my visit in Moisés Ville, there are twenty-seven projects on file with the national government, of which only five are ongoing. Many of these are related to social welfare and housing. In that sense, the term *Fonavi*—referring to monotonous low-rise houses made by the National Housing Fund—became normalized in the town some time ago.

"We have a high population level with very limited resources, not only in the district of La Salamanca but also within the town itself," Angeletti explains from behind a short desk flanked by the provincial flag. "As the people residing downtown disappear, whether because they're deceased or have moved away, there are many people coming in to pick up houses. Around eighty percent of the population is of limited means, though they are working, and the remaining twenty percent make a decent living off agriculture or livestock. Of this twenty percent, sixty percent or more are elderly."

Moisés Ville is growing old: many of the children from Jewish and Italian colonization have left, and their lands have been rented out or sold to larger players. Some of the remaining inhabitants don't seem much better off than the pioneers who sought refuge inside the railway sheds back in 1889. Not even the factory producing mayonnaise, salsa, and dressing, opened by SanCor in 1981, which was producing thirty thousand liters per day with fifty operators on staff at the beginning of the 1990s, could remain unscathed in the face of collapse: following the crisis in 2002, it shut its doors.

"The factory was welcomed in our town, but things weren't handled well," the community president explains, "because the eggs were supplied from Entre Ríos and the oil from Avellaneda. Then everything was produced here and taken to Sunchales, to the original SanCor plant, where it was distributed. No one took the risk of putting in a chicken hatchery to provide supply locally and decrease the expenses."

But in the last few years the plant has reopened its doors to become a small supplier, with just twenty workers, for a few food companies based in Buenos Aires.

However, the town's young people, who surely number more than twenty, make their own exoduses as soon as they finish their secondary studies—as Angeletti's own children have done. SanCor, for its part, had to lower the price of rent at the request of the commune: it was the only way the factory could keep its doors open. Under these circumstances, the soil remains the town's sustenance, just as it was in the days of its founding. Soybeans supplanted wheat, corn, sorghum, and alfalfa. Today, the livestock breeders—old royalty in the fields of Moisés Ville— lease their properties to soy farmers who come from far away.

"The numbers dictate," pronounces the community president, noting that only two dairy farms still survive out of more than forty that once existed, and he resigns himself with a sigh. "But even so, we have to offer a mea culpa ourselves."

In Moisés Ville, the routine of the countryside leads to more countryside, and it's been a while since anyone has thought seriously about industry. Neither has cultural tourism become the goose with the golden eggs that many purported to see in it: the lack of investment in the hospitality industry and the distance away from larger urban centers have threatened its development. And so, the Mordechai Goldman complex—an accommodation for groups of up to one hundred people, opened five blocks from the town square by the founding rabbi's own great-grandson—seems to have turned out too big in light of the actual number of visitors. And an option like Señora Sofía's house, where I am staying, appears to be the only alternative for solo tourists.

For the future, the community president predicts more agriculture and more livestock. And maybe, if luck comes back to Moisés Ville's side, some investment will finally arrive.

"It's a challenge managing to get anyone to put in a peso," he says. "We've had a few ventures. One, for example, was to make biodiesel. But it didn't succeed, and now they have the plant rented out as a warehouse."

Although not everyone in Moisés Ville has been seduced by soy. "Around here you can get lucky with a harvest and make good money, but one hailstorm and everything you have is destroyed," Luis Liebenbuk, the ba'al tefillah who hosted the Kabbalat Shabbat ceremony at the Baron Hirsch Synagogue, had explained to me in the temple. Liebenbuk is a typical Moisesvillian country man and doesn't even like to hear talk of soy, a crop that moves millions of dollars and led some of his fellows to take on the risk of planting it, even knowing that the most fertile lands were farther south. "I'd like to see what they're going to plant in their fields around here a few years down the line, because the crop dusting burns everything, and the chemical products they scatter on the ground are very nasty: they kill the topsoil and the fertility," he'd said. "I'm no agricultural engineer, but I'm telling you these lands won't be worth a thing in ten years."

Just like his father did, just like his grandfather, Liebenbuk works with his cows from dusk to dawn. "A cow's day comes, and she goes into labor: I watch her, feed her, and know that she'll always be salable. A cow is a cow, end of story, and they'll sell because they're raised for meat, and everybody eats meat," he assures me. His father and grandfather were colonists from the JCA. Or the "Iévich," as many people say, himself included, for "Jewish." Liebenbuk, who did a stint as a volunteer in the Israeli kibbutzim of Revadim, Ga'ash, and Mesilot several decades back, is now the last one in the line: his two children have moved away from Moisés Ville, his daughter to teach English classes in Israel, his son to study in Córdoba.

For many of those who have stayed, the land continues to be a choice of lifestyle that extends Baron de Hirsch's redemptive dream. And that is what makes Argentina's Jewish community unique: its agrarian origins, which still continue in some measure, have no match in the diaspora.

The short walk through Moisés Ville ends at the newest of its institutions, the Rabbi Aarón Halevi Goldman Museum of Community History and Jewish Colonization, founded in 1985. After its inauguration, the museum settled in a building that used to house the post office: a spacious old house that today unfolds into five exhibition halls, and which is perhaps the strongest link between Moisés Ville and the world outside. Over the course of 2011, for example, it welcomed six thousand visitors: more than double the local population.

Before sunset, I decide to take a guided tour in which I am the sole visitor. Hilda, one of the museum's docents, leads me through its shelves bristling with documents, tools, and photographs. She shows me German refugees' passports; a banknote issued for the Czech Theresienstadt Ghetto; the original yoke that Chiaffredo Giovanni Cuniglio, a Piedmontese man, used to mark a furrow for the Podoliers so they wouldn't lose their way; a lantern that once hung from Rabbi Aharon Halevi Goldman's carriage; a portrait of Baron de Hirsch and one of Wilhelm Loewenthal, the Romanian doctor who was his envoy; a map of the large Moisés Ville colony and a flamethrower for burning locusts; a public agency's founding charter and a Royal book of cake recipes in Yiddish. All enchanting, all still holding the life of those first people.

And I peer into the glass displays expecting to find a trace of the killings. But it isn't so easy. That history—the one I am pursuing—does not seem so deeply rooted in the memory of Moisés Ville. But it is at this precise moment that Eva Guelbert de Rosenthal, the director of the museum, appears. This tall woman, who has sharp features, short curly hair, a forceful presence, and a diploma in museology, is the engine that has been driving this local museum for several years. Her entrance, at a firm pace, takes me by surprise.

"Hello," she says, with a friendly smile, and extends her hand an instant later. "I'd like to know exactly what it is you need."

I tell her about the murders and mention my great-grandfather's article. Eva nods in silence.

"I am quite familiar with the text of 'The First Jewish Victims in Moisés Ville' as well. It's been turning over in my head for some time."

5

Memory and Myth in the Cemetery

A single place holds me absolutely enthralled during my walks through Moisés Ville: the cemetery, a field of sunlit eternity that has stored its denizens' remains for over a century. I come on the advice of the museum director, who told me about it at great length, and, pausing before the granite headstones, confirm that the wind has already erased the names of some of their lodgers buried in their shrouds after the ancient way, without coffins, in direct contact with the earth. The wind that blows here is the very passage of time.

And then there is the moss. A fine green layer covers everything, life sprouting from among the cracks in death and bringing with it ants that mark their paths on the serene tombstones. Of course, some gravestones still remain carved with the fine detail of their first days. Most of the names and their circumstances are composed in Hebrew letters (even the years are usually listed according to the Hebrew calendar), and the symbols decorating them repeat: Stars of David, seven-lamp menorahs, sacred books for eminent figures, pitchers for the charitable, tree stumps for those whose lives were cut short before their time.

On the short landing that opens behind the portico of its entrance (in the middle of a dirt road called Nicasio Sánchez, fifteen blocks northeast of the town square—or, to put it another way, in the middle of nowhere) there are two instructions written in plain view. The first is of an earthly order, administrative: "Respect the tradition of wearing a head covering to enter. The Commission." The second, of a divine order, gratifies and sends shivers through those of us who believe cemeteries are also sites that guard the secret of life (in the sense that the end is part of everything): "לא במותו יקח הכל—Cuando muera nada llevará consigo. Salmo 49." (For when he dies he will carry nothing away. Psalm 49.)

Two steps farther along stands the enclosure where the old hearse rests with its carved wood and beveled glass. Along the side it reads: צדק לפניו יהלך (Tzedek lefanav yelech: Righteousness shall go before Him.) It bore its final coffin in 1979, but it would be able to go this very day, drawn by horses, and lead a funeral procession just as it did for nearly sixty years: the coach has outlived all of its dead.

"Making the transfers is always complicated, especially if they're coming from another province," sighs Emilio Hoffman, a pale, bald man who looks after the cemetery and now stands contemplating the hearse beside me.

That Moisés Ville has scattered its children around the world is as certain as the fact that many of them want to return here to rest in this soil for eternity. And just as one of the primary aspirations for devout Jews is to die in Israel, for Moisesvillians the preference is to come back here to die. I ask Emilio about who—among the living—comes here to visit. He makes a face.

"Not many, maybe some distant relation, a grandchild or great-grandchild . . . and otherwise the tourists."

Like in any cemetery that takes pride in itself, here, too, the town's heroes lie at rest: Rabbi Aharon Halevi Goldman; the colonist and founder of several local organizations Noé Cociovich (or Noaj Katzovitch, according to another possible transliteration of his Yiddish name); and the millionaires of the Weisburd family, held inside a mausoleum erected in 1937—a shrine in overblown proportions for the size of things here, and very deteriorated after the floods that engulfed Moisés Ville between 1972 and 1983.

There are, in total, more than 2,400 graves looking out to the east, toward Jerusalem. Some, in granite and marble or with colonnades, shine more than others, in brick and dry stone. The most ornate ones date back to the 1920s and 1930s, a period of prosperity. In the center of the cemetery—where its two main pathways intersect—rises the Monument in Homage to the Victims of the Holocaust. There is also another monument, installed in 1964 near a few extremely ancient graves, in memory of the children of the first colonists who fell to fever in the railway sheds:

HOMAGE TO THE CHILDREN!
OF THE FIRST IMMIGRANTS
DEPARTED BEFORE THEIR TIME
ON THIS LAND OF COLONIZATION
COMMUNITY OF MOISÉS VILLE AND COLONIES

But one section of the cemetery shows no honor or glory.

Its nineteen tombs are humble, most covered over by moss and oblivion, and some have lost their names forever. Today, now that the cemetery has earned a historical value in itself and the one-and-a-half-hectare plot it occupies has been divided into thirteen parts, this section is given number five: it belongs to victims of murder. And several of the wretched number whose fates are related by my great-grandfather in "The First Jewish Victims in Moisés Ville" are in here.

The people at rest in this area suffered violent deaths (in the form of homicide, accidents, or suicide) and cannot lie next to those deceased due to natural causes. The religious mandate is clear: man must die as he was born. And that means dying alone, without the aid of any other. God gave life, and God would take it away. For those who'd been unable to abide by that precept, there was section five.

For several years it was believed that the cemetery had originated with one of these nineteen tombs of presumed impurity: that of Noaj (or Noé) Horovitz, who in the present grid occupies section five, row eight, grave nine. In this cemetery—as in the majority of Jewish cemeteries—the tombs stand above the earth rather than below; they are stone cells (some rectangular, others tubular) that rest on the ground and hold within them the remains of a deceased person who is indeed buried. Many have their headstones at the back, so that you have to stand on the other side of the tombs to read them. Noaj Horovitz's grave is engraved on its upper face: it is a sarcophagus in matte gray stone, isolated and carved in bas-relief with Hebrew and Latin characters, a Star of David, and the stump of a tree. It says:

פ"נ

הבחור החשוב הקדוש

נח זכריהו

בר שלמה זלמן

הוראוויץ

נפל על ידי בני עבלה

ביום ה יג ניסן ה תרנ"ג

הובל לקברות אור ליום

ב א דחוהמ פסח

תנצב"ה

Which can be translated from the Hebrew as: Here lies / the honorable and blessed young man / Noaj Zehariahu / son of Shlomo Zalmen / Horovitz / who fell into evil hands / on the 13th day of Nisan in the year 5653. / He was brought to the grave in the light of / the first day of Chol HaMoed Passover / May his soul be bound up in the bond of life.

And then, in Spanish:

NOE HOROVITZ

FALLECIO EL 31 DE MARZO

1893

A LA EDAD DE 23 AÑOS

In his article, Mijl Hacohen Sinay reports that in 1892—the year in which he situates this case, though it actually occurred in 1893—several colonists were lost. He says, in Yiddish:

The first victim was an administrator for the Jewish Colonization Association, Hurvitz, or Horovitz, as he wrote his name. Only a few months after having been selected, he fell victim at the hands of a gaucho. Some had predicted as much, for he was too friendly with the gauchos, though it may be that he grew close with them in order to avoid just this kind of event. Whatever the case, he paid for that decision with his life. One evening, Hurvitz went out on his horse for a ride around the colony and never came back. The next morning, quite early, his friends roused the townsfolk: they formed a group to go out looking for him in some nearby fields, only to find him among the tall grass, his neck severed, half a kilometer from the colony. Hurvitz's body was discovered at some distance from his head, which had been cut clean off. Such savagery triggered a state of terrible shock among all the inhabitants of Moisés Ville.

It was said that the bereaved Horovitz family had donated a plot from their own small farm—which by 1893 was already cultivated colony land—to initiate the necropolis with this supposed first deceased (and it is true, as Mijl Hacohen Sinay notes, that the man's real name had been Hurvitz before he'd changed it to Horovitz, likely seeking a certain refinement through that German reformulation).

It was also told that, in accordance with another rite, a few friends had stayed at the foot of the grave, day and night, to keep young Noaj company: they didn't want to leave him on his own. While there, they would tell him, perhaps, about the progress in the colony, or how strange they still found this foreign landscape that was now their home. And they didn't leave until someone else was buried at his side and they could finally judge that Noaj Horovitz, that first one to fall, had his rightful company.

The anecdote is lovely, but, in point of fact, the cemetery was already well populated with dead by the time Horovitz arrived, in the days of Passover (or Easter), 1893. It turns out that, over its first four years, Moisés Ville had progressed sufficiently to have buried, also, several of its pioneers. Including, for example, a certain Seivick, someone called Kantor, and a few others still.

One might suppose that, having come to Moisés Ville in 1894 and left in 1897, Mijl Hacohen Sinay would not have visited the cemetery very often. I wonder if my great-grandfather ever stood before Noaj

Horovitz's grave, on which it reads plainly that the murder occurred in 1893 and not 1892, as he identified it in his text. In fact, Mijl himself gives a disclaimer: "Some of the details about these crimes were told to me by the Podoliers and colonists, and others are known to me through my own experience from the time, some fifty years ago, when I lived in Moisés Ville."

A woman known as Hinde Fisztl (though she was registered aboard the steamship *Weser* as "Ende Fistel," alongside her husband and two children) was the one who related several of these details to him. She'd been twenty-four years old at the time of her arrival with the pioneers. When the article was published in the IWO, Señora Fisztl was eighty-two. Half a century or more had elapsed since the critical period. Mijl Hacohen Sinay, a teacher and journalist, seems to have trusted more in his own memories and those of colonists like Señora Fisztl than in documents associated with the murders. (On the other hand, where could he have gone looking for such documents in those days?) As a result, it isn't strange to find that the text contains several errors.

Soon I have my own contributor who, like Hinde Fisztl, brings me into the crimes of Moisés Ville: she's Jana Powazek de Breitman, the Yiddish translator who will accompany me through the investigation as my linguistic guide. Jana is a music teacher, trained in music therapy, who completed her education in Israel and, in her fifties, enlisted as a volunteer at the IWO Institute. There, the only place in the world where finding a Yiddish translator is an easy task, we meet. Her card says "Reference Librarian," but the work she undertakes with me goes much further. Jana translates and explains, she finds pathways and travels down them, she learns and remembers, she pauses over details and delights in the discoveries.

But before turning to her, I made attempts with other translators. In the early days, my friend Andrés Kilstein would come over equipped with his Yiddish–Spanish dictionary and his goodwill. He was the first to lend his help, but the texts rebelled against us. Then I tried my grandmother Mañe, who at her age of eighty-nine could pick up a manuscript by my great-grandfather—her father-in-law—and progress through it without difficulty. The issue with my grandmother was time: each page had to wait its turn between the ritual episodes of the meal and table talk. I'd leave her house thinking how she, who had as much mastery over the Hebrew alphabet as she did over the use of lekach cake, would sooner choose to present herself as an affectionate cook than a pragmatic translator.

For a while the one helping me was Mendel, a rabbi from Chabad-Lubavitch—one of the largest Jewish organizations in the world—who generously opened the doors of his home to me, already at night, and would read out the texts I'd brought him while his wife was putting their several children to bed. Orthodox Jews usually speak in Yiddish so as not to sully the sacred tongue of Hebrew with their everyday affairs, and while the rabbi would be sailing swiftly through the rushing waters of those texts, I would also be examining the portraits of his distant ancestors, framed along the walls, and trying to explore his vast collection of books with Hebrew lettering on their spines.

These nighttime meetings followed one after the other until I started to feel like a pupil in a heder, the Jewish primary schools of old Europe. One night I took part in a strange and beautiful ceremony: the children lit candles, the rabbi prayed, and I looked on, disconcerted perhaps, too secular or even too profane to understand. Yet even then it was a ceremony for Hanukkah, one of the most emblematic of the faith. Later, very gradually, something pulled me away from the wise rabbi, his kind family, those pleasant readings.

I thought, then, about my own hypothetical bar mitzvah ceremony: if it had existed in any form, there were no religious protocols, no rabbi, no prayers. Instead there was an old hardback tome of more than six hundred pages, written by Leon Uris and entitled "Exodus," which narrated the dangerous journey of some Jewish refugees on a ship bound for Palestine and went into each of its protagonists' pasts, forever marked by the horrors of World War II. The foundation of the state of Israel was the epic underlying those six hundred pages of war and suspense that I found in my home library and read during vacations: at age thirteen, that was my bar mitzvah.

. . .

I had already heard from Alberto Lind, the ex-policeman from Calle Barón Hirsch in Moisés Ville, that the cemetery also provided a source of work and was, in that sense, a living place. Even he, in his bicycle shop, had another job as well: he devoted part of his time to engraving headstones and had even sculpted a few memorials in white marble for the synagogue. After telling me about the town's criminal life and the Banco Comercial Israelita robbery, Lind moved on to the graves.

"I've engraved six this month and there are another three coming in: I have one from a nearby town, for a woman who worked there as a midwife; there's another for a resident from the town of San Cristóbal; and a few others from right here," he said.

It was nothing new for him; he was used to writing the final period on the lives of acquaintances and even family members.

Bicycles hung from the walls of Lind's workshop, but in its boxes there were, as well, all of the tools necessary for that other labor some-how bound up in eternity. The ex-policeman, his hands on a gravestone (a half-finished job), told me that he always asked people to bring him the marble unfinished and would then begin a slow, artisanal process, very different from the rapid automation of the machines used to etch the epitaphs in Buenos Aires.

"Nearly all the stones made there become illegible before long. These, on the other hand, will last from here to three thousand years," he boasted, caressing the marble. And he told me that his works had traveled thousands of miles to reach Jewish cemeteries in Tucumán, La Plata, Rosario, Santa Fe, and even Israel.

Then, enthusiastically, he gave me a step-by-step explanation of how he chiseled his gravestones. He said he would add a layer of industrial chalk using liquid rubber. Then he would mix a little pot of white paint, which he would use to paint over the whole thing. Once it was dry, he would trace out what he was going to inscribe, diagramming it as well as possible to make the letters all fit and be legible. For that purpose, he worked using a ruler to mark out all the lines. Then he would set up little boxes, drawing a letter inside each one, to be marked and traced out with the diamond blade. Once he had done a pass, he would wash off the stone and remove the liquid rubber. At that point the marble would be marked, and he could begin the work of sculpting.

"It can be in Spanish or Hebrew, with a Magen David or any other symbol," he said. "But mind you: it's all done by hand!" Lind fell silent and took up his hammer and chisel: tic-tic-tic-tic. His words were culminating in a direct demonstration. After a while, he lifted a grayish stone slab, turned it toward me, and voilà! I was reading the epitaph of a woman who'd passed away at age sixty-three, in the Hebrew year of 5772, and whose soul, the inscription declared, would live on forever.

Back in the cemetery, it's easy to prove that the myth around Horovitz is false and he was not the first to be buried. Likewise, the land for this necropolis had not been donated by his family either: although it did lie adjacent to the Horovitz farm, by 1891 the land already belonged to the Jewish Colonization Association, Baron de Hirsch's colonial enterprise. Despite what many believe, the oldest known gravesite is not, then, that of Noaj Horovitz, but one that stands in a section of old tombs, beneath a wide headstone well populated with words in Hebrew and Spanish. It belongs to Jacobo Nirenstein, born in 1837, dead on August 4, 1890, and lacking in any record beyond that of having left his name on this first tomb.

In any case, it was a privilege for Horovitz, Nirenstein, and any of the others to lie at rest in this soil: after the makeshift burial grounds in Palacios and Monigotes were abandoned, the cemetery in Moisés Ville became the first one for Jews in Argentina—inaugurated twenty years before that of Buenos Aires, even. But there's nothing unusual about the alternate version being more interesting than the truth: myths, in Moisés Ville, are numerous.

"In the course of this research, we're stripping the legends bare. Things become clearer through this work and, in a way, it's about doing some historical revisionism," considers Eva Guelbert de Rosenthal, the museum director.

Sitting at a computer, she arranges things so she can talk with me in one of the museum's exhibition spaces while giving instructions to her coworkers. She tells me, almost apologetically, that it's getting close to the date when she has to appear at a regional museology conference and the work is piling up. Even so, she doesn't lose her concentration.

The subject of myths seems to hold as much interest for her as it does for me: "Aside from the Horovitz matter, there were several legends around here. It was said that the cemetery held five thousand graves, when in reality there are less than half that. And we always wondered which of the small graves hold the children who died in Palacios, because they aren't actually buried there, their graves were moved. But were all of them moved? My father used to say there were a few small graves in the back of the cemetery, level with the ground, which were then raised so no one would step on them. Some have names, others no. Do they belong to dead children? Or is the monument to them built over a mass grave? There are so many things we don't know and would like to find out . . . Around one hundred thirty-six families came; around fifty settled. What about the others? Three returned to Europe, but which? Paradoxically, the fact of having lost their children rooted some to the land. So these people, the ones who refused to leave, were they only the parents of lost children? And why is one group of graves at a different angle in relation to the rest? All those things stand out like a sore thumb."

Eva refers to "The First Jewish Victims in Moisés Ville" in much the same way. As she told me when we met, it is a text she knows well: she read the article over and over again, wondering if the murders had really been so many. Because, out of that score of crimes, Eva can only certify the existence of four or five.

"I do believe Sinay lived through some of the things himself and had others told to him by the colonists, as he says . . . but they may well have told him too much. I think some of the cases have been legends and, as long as we're unable to prove them, will remain so."

Using a copy of the text, we go through name after name. To confirm the events Eva is deploying her entire arsenal: books, documents, and the computer. There, on the monitor, she's running a program that cross-checks several different registers at the same time (including people who arrived on the steamship *Weser*, students in the schools, names mentioned in the newspaper *El Alba*, and people buried in the cemetery,

among other sources) and can accept wildcard characters to account for
different spellings of the same name. It is the Goldman System, which
was programmed in 2001 specially for this museum.

But there are some names that do not appear anywhere, or whose
death dates do not match those in my great-grandfather's text, particularly in the string of murders from 1892.

While Eva searches, I feel a mixture of fear and trepidation. Fear that
the whole thing will fall apart, that after all this the museum director
will tell me what I'm doing amounts to nothing. Trepidation that something will turn up, any single detail: something truly revelatory.

Meanwhile, she, dead set on this text—this enigma—picks up the
phone and makes a call: "Hi, how are you, I'm going to give you a few people's names, to see if they show up in the cemetery. The first one is David
Lander . . . You don't have any Lander, but there is a Langer . . . And
what year is . . . Make a note, yes. Anyone who might have died in 1889
or '90? No? No one . . . I'll keep going: Ziml Seivick, S-E-I-V-I-C-K,
age twenty-one . . . The thing is, I have Sinay's great-grandson here
looking for the truth behind this text. And the text has passed through
my hands several times before. I'm reading it again, I don't know how
many times I've been through it, yes, I even had a friend call asking
me the same question once, if it was true there really were that many
victims. Okay, I'll give you one more: Kantor, from 1891 . . . He's one
who wasn't colonized, died in Palacios. There is somebody from 1891? A
bachelor? Not colonized? Yes, a small shop . . . Aha, 1914 . . . Okay, we
don't know the name here . . . There's one here that says Kantor, which
could be the same . . . I have a Hurvitz in 1893 . . .

"Hurvitz, Horovitz? . . . T-Z . . . Yes, you have him, I'm sure of it,
in 1893: they used to say they took out part of the Horovitz farm to set
up the cemetery, another of the many legends . . . Yes, I remember that;
we always make a note of it . . . Then there's another one named Tzvi
Wainer . . . And there are a good few who were lost far away from the
colony, in 1892, all of them Podoliers . . . Two were householders: Jaim
Schmucler and Shmuel Bersanker . . . Others: Reuben Kristal and the
two Finkelstein brothers . . . If you find anything, let us know. Thanks."

. . .

Is the murder of David Lander, the first of all the victims, just one more myth? The cemetery's records know nothing of his name, but if his death did occur in October or November of 1889, as Mijl Hacohen Sinay estimates based on testimonies he collected (as he himself only arrived in the colony five years later), it's possible that David Lander would have been buried near the Palacios railway sheds. His clues are eluding me, and no one in Moisés Ville seems to have ever heard anything about the man.

Did David Lander really exist?

In the town, like a kind of founding document, they keep a list of 815 travelers who arrived on the steamship *Weser*. It may not be the complete list, but it is the official one. And in it there is no David Lander to be found. Only one single Lander is there, first name Isaak. According to the directory, Isaak Lander was fifty years old at the time of his arrival in Argentina. And it is worth pausing over that detail: "The first victim to die at the hands of a gaucho was a middle-aged Jewish man, some fifty years old, whose name was David Lander," my great-grandfather notes in his text. The age is the same. On the other hand, "David" and "Isaak" are both very typical names for a turn-of-the-century Jewish man: couldn't it be, perhaps, that the Podolier who described the case to my great-grandfather mixed up this rather negligible detail? I suspect it's quite possible, but there's no way to prove it.

The Moisés Ville cemetery bears no record of any Isaak Lander either. But by the same token, it can't account for two out of every three of the pioneers who came on the *Weser*. What was this Lander's fate? Was he part of the outflow of three to four hundred people who quickly abandoned the precarious Palacios settlements, seeking work, support, and sustenance elsewhere? In that vein, Mijl Hacohen Sinay wrote in his article that Loewenthal, Baron de Hirsch's envoy, was initially able to select only twenty families for colonization.

Most of those who did not meet the requirements for working in the country went to the cities of Rosario, Santa Fe, or Buenos

Aires, where many Podoliers found work as *cambalecheros* [*sic*;
sellers of used items]. Five of these families settled in the town
of Sunchales and opened *verdulerías* [produce markets; Spanish
in the original] and *almacendlej* [*sic*; denoting small shops]. And
they did well with these businesses. A few other families stayed
in Moisés Ville and opened their own *almacendlej* as well.

But perhaps Isaak Lander was not lost in the Argentine territories but
returned to Europe, overwhelmed, like many others, by all he had seen
within a short spell at this southern latitude.

Mijl Hacohen Sinay tells us that the Lander affair did not end there;
that the lynching of the gaucho who'd killed him brought about serious
consequences. "A few weeks later," the article continues,

> midway through the month of November and three and a half
> months after their arrival in Moisés Ville, three Podoliers were
> slaughtered all at once: the three Iegelnitzer brothers. They had
> gone looking to find any available work for themselves with the
> Italians, but the next morning they were found dead in the high
> grass, not so far from the colony. All three of their throats had
> been cut. How did this massacre come about? It was impossi-
> ble to know. And the burial for the three murdered men was
> heartbreaking. It could be, and indeed everyone took it to be so,
> that this treacherous killing had come about as revenge for the
> previous gaucho. In this way, over a period of only a few weeks,
> four people in Moisés Ville had fallen. That would only be the
> beginning.

Just as with Lander, there aren't any Iegelnitzers in the Moisés Ville
cemetery. Where were the three brothers buried? And what were their
first names? The roster of passengers from the steamship *Weser* is the
only clue. Several Iegelnitzers appear on it, and the victims, no doubt,
number among them. The family comprises eleven members: the father,
Moses, aged fifty; the eldest son, Samuel, aged twenty-five, and his wife,
Chane (or Jane), aged twenty-two; a son, Isaak, aged twenty-four; a son,

Fischel, aged twenty-three, and his wife, Keyle, aged twenty; a daughter, Divora, aged eleven and a half; a daughter, Braina, aged eleven and a half; a son, Leybe, age seven; and a son, Manasse (or Menasche), aged three. The murdered men are the three brothers at working age: Samuel, Isaak, and Fischel. The trail of the case seems to end there.

But a couple years later, the whole story seems to collapse: Fischel and Samuel have been recorded on the 1895 census, one of two censuses performed in Argentina that included first and last names. Only Isaak was lost along the way. The others, more living than dead, provided their details to the census taker, who marked them down as "Igolnitzer."

So, who were those three dead men, cut down in revenge for the lynched gaucho?

Whatever the case may be, Lander's killing has a touch of a founding myth about it. A myth that with brutal violence reveals the difficult encounter between two cultures; a collision, rather, that ended in death on both sides.

This conflict was not new but had come from long before. On February 9, 1870, a columnist for Rosario's newspaper *La Capital* estimated that some five hundred English people had been murdered in the few years prior. He was, of course, referring to agriculturists. After several dozen armed conflicts, the fields of Santa Fe had turned into a no-man's-land. Between 1871 and 1884 the border line had been extended farther and farther toward the north, which also meant the addition of large expanses of untouched countryside and widening distances between army troops. This land, which quickly became annexed into the agro-export grain boom, was traversed by brave men with Winchester rifles slung over their shoulders, and these gringos were viewed as easy targets by bandits, who frequently acted with protection from authorities—policemen and magistrates often drafted from among the thieves' own ranks.

But the gauchos, in their own way, were facing their end as well: the emergence of a new economic and social order was not without cost to them. In the 1860s, foreign trade—and particularly the exportation of wool—shot through the roof. The fields of Santa Fe Province filled with sheep in the south, cows in the north, and grains in the center; within a few short years, the train connected everything, and Rosario, the port of shipment for the output, became the most populous city in the province.

A few decades before, the gauchos' routine had been bucolic and celebratory. Between 1879 and 1889, Eduardo Gutiérrez—who wrote thirty-one novels in ten years—published one of his most famous sagas, *Juan Moreira*, as a serial in the newspaper *La Patria Argentina*. In this story, that of a man with a "great generosity of spirit" who is led by the injustices of the authorities to become a grim gaucho outlaw (and who actually did exist, dying at the hands of a police posse in 1874), Gutiérrez describes the event where Moreira celebrates his son's baptism: "The party lasted for two whole nights, including the day between, and the collective enthusiasm never flagged. When a guest started seeing double and was unable to dance he went to sleep it off in the high grass and, when he woke up, returned to the party."

None of that could exist in a productive environment. None of that must exist in a powerful capitalist country.

The disciplinarian effort, then, was blatant and successful: gauchos committed the sin of being too idle and profligate, with or without any will of their own. They had to show transit papers in order to move and receive payments, and they were forbidden from renouncing their patrons. And any who rejected the system was automatically left on the margins. Every gaucho became a fugitive, an insurgent, a bandit. These, and many more besides, were the words used to describe the defiant state whereby they came to live as nomads, often seeking refuge among the indigenous people who lived on the other side of the border, accompanying them on their raids or else joining the bands of cruel thieves who appeared and disappeared like pirates on the Pampas, sowing terror through the fields now fenced and foreign, fields that once had been their own. Criminals sprang up like mushrooms in rain; they were learning, in one final desperate gesture, to kill in order to live.

Even today, a thousand stories were woven around the mass poisoning of dogs in Moisés Ville. And a number of myths. As before, as always.

Some residents recalled the far-off days when municipal administrations around the region would take it into their own hands to kill stray dogs, and a rumor started running around that the Moisés Ville Commune itself was responsible for the poisonings. Maybe that was the reason community president Osvaldo Angeletti took energetic action: police patrols on the streets at night were a counterstrike made to show his hands weren't stained with canine blood. At the same time—and in a year when elections were being held—there were comments that the undertone was political and the opposition was trying to pin a hundred dead dogs on Angeletti to prevent him from remaining in power. People said that the greatest vices of the nation's political system were being reproduced in local politics.

But perhaps the most toxic allegation was one hurled at Rubén Holmgren, one of three veterinarians in Moisés Ville and the only one who worked with dogs and cats, as the other two took cows and horses. "That vet is poisoning them to bring in work and make more cash," someone said. Today, Holmgren laughs. At his clinic, Los Gurises, he brews yerba mate and tells me that 2009 was the year he came to Moisés Ville from Esperanza, where he'd pursued his degree.

"Whatever they say, there were already poisonings before that year, and they're still happening today," asserts the vet, the son of a Swedish man and a Brazilian woman, who is originally from a town in Misiones Province called Colonia Aurora.

In 95 percent of the cases he treated, the poison was an organophosphorus pesticide. Possibly the same kind used to kill off parrots, which are declared pests in the country.

"The medical signs are straightforward," he explains. "The toxin will cause a dog to have seizures, muscle contractions, and bronchoconstriction, which leads to a decrease in blood oxygen levels, and a cyanosis causing the animal to discharge liquid from the bronchi in the form of foam. When the dog starts asphyxiating and tries to take in air, its mouth will turn purple, cyanotic. Some also vomit, urinate, or have diarrhea."

This image of a purple mouth is the same one the Maryniv brothers described seeing in their two dogs, Wilson and Sansón.

In those critical days when the dawn light would reveal several dead animals, Holmgren had to make diagnoses on the bases of what he could see, with no more tools than trial and error.

"What had they actually been given? The answer to that would tell you the treatment, but if you wanted an accurate analysis it would have to be done in the lab. And there isn't a single one in Santa Fe Province," he continues.

The fact is that his atropine injections did yield results, provided they were delivered in time. The drug was one the veterinarian used in surgeries as a preanesthetic, to decrease salivation and prevent vomiting, and during that time it became an anchor to life for Moisés Ville's pets.

"Atropine causes a bronchodilation, allowing the tissue to become oxygenated, but the true antidote for an organophosphate is actually pralidoxime, which acts at the cell level and blocks it," Holmgren explains.

The veterinarian never let himself be affected by that fatal series: some dogs would become poisoned simply by smelling some poisoned vomit; others would die in ten minutes. As a veterinarian, he knew he had to act without becoming too emotionally involved, but he couldn't help himself from falling into the toxic wave when Chito, his son's mutt, fell ill. At the time, the veterinarian was living across from his business, where he'd left three poisoned dogs in care. Maybe Chito had sniffed the vomit of one of those animals. That night Holmgren ran out to look for atropine, but he'd used up all his doses on other animals, and Chito's fate appeared to be sealed. When he started to foam at the mouth, the doctor applied corticosteroids to stabilize membranes and stimulate his heart. Anything was worth trying if it meant saving Chito's life.

But the dog was unresponsive.

"My son wasn't there, and I thought it was better to tell him Chito ran off and took up with another dog," says the veterinarian. And he sucks on the mate straw down to the last sip.

The young Noaj Horovitz—the future victim in Moisés Ville—had reached Argentina in the 1870s along with two brothers, Abraham Itzjak and David. The three were originally from Grodno, the same snow-covered city in Belarus where my great-grandfather Mijl Haco-hen Sinay came from. Because of this, the latter referenced them in one of his final articles, entitled "Di dray hurvitses" (The three Hurvitzes) and published in 1955's issue VIII–IX of the *Grodner Opklangen/* גראָדנער אָפּקלאַנגען (or Echoes from Grodno), a voluminous magazine edited by Mijl Hacohen Sinay himself and published in Buenos Aires by the Union of Residents from Grodno and Its Surroundings.

The three Hurvitz brothers had been among the first Jews to arrive in Argentina, long before the Podoliers on the steamship *Weser*. Mijl Hacohen Sinay writes: "All three brothers were very intelligent young men, masters of a very important culture. Particularly the eldest [Abraham Itzjak], who was extremely knowledgeable about Hebrew and very proficient in anything related to Judaic culture."

This brother, Abraham Itzjak Hurvitz, had changed his last name to Horovitz, and the others followed suit. Of the three, he was the one who triumphed as an agricultural businessman, and he eventually became a well-known figure in the countryside of Santa Fe. This could be confirmed by all he had written a few years before, filled with hope, as a local correspondent for the newspaper *Ha-Tzfira/*הצפירה (or The alarm, in Hebrew), published in Warsaw and read widely in the East—so much so that a street in Jerusalem bears its name in tribute.

The second of the brothers was David. If not the most renowned, he at least made his way into history as having been the translator for Rabbi Aharon Halevi Goldman when that man first pronounced the colony's name before the landowner Palacios. His linguistic gifts also enabled him to sign his name on the *Manual of Spanish–Yiddish Conversation*, published in 1906 by the printing house Wolf Zeitlin in Buenos Aires. During 1890 he acted as an initial administrator for Moisés Ville, but it was no easy task: the colony lay empty, as empty as its people's stomachs. He was later able to play a larger role in Entre Ríos, though his inflexibility did not serve to earn him friends, and he would certainly not be the only leader forced to face a conflict in the lands of the JCA.

Noaj was ten years younger than Abraham Itzjak, whom he looked up to. Mijl Hacohen Sinay says:

> The third brother, the youngest, was also taken on as an administrator in Moisés Ville during the period before the second group of Podoliers had yet arrived. This third brother was a fine

administrator, well loved by the colonists, but he ended up murdered by gauchos after going out, at night, to ride around the
colony.

The two brothers traded glances then, a bit uneasy. Inside the house,
the tea was steaming. Outside the sun was slowly setting and already
the crickets were chirping. The absence of Noaj—who had left in the
morning—had already stretched on for too long.

And so, they decided to saddle up and ride out to search for him. They
suspected trouble and rode in silence for a long stretch, until they reached
the home of an Italian colonist. The second Horovitz, who knew that
language well, asked the man if he'd seen or heard anyone on horseback.
The Italian first answered no, but before seeing them off he remembered
that a rider had stopped at his house a few hours before to take some
water with his horse. When the man dismounted, he was weary and
sweaty. The Horovitz brothers exchanged looks. They thought this man
could have been Noaj, in trouble. They rode on toward another farmer's
house, cut off from the Italian's and mired in an area of swamps and
lagoons, as they knew the horses their missing brother took out riding
could sometimes get lost in those lands. But he hadn't been seen passing
there either. Sundown caught them far from home and, preferring to
avoid ending up as a bad piece of news themselves, they turned back.

Upon reaching the center of the village, they summoned the neighbors to ask for help. Seven young men on horseback joined their search
and headed out into the vast countryside for another three hours, trying
to catch a glimpse of something in the lagoons and swamps under the
light of the moon, but it came to nothing. They returned to their homes
in distress, waiting for sunrise so that they could go on with the task.
And before the sun came out several other colonists had already set out,
but they spent all day following the wrong paths. They questioned everyone they crossed paths with but obtained no answer: the missing man
was still unwilling to show himself.

The inquest was later related in the pages of *Ha-Tzfira*, the newspaper
from Warsaw. Abraham Itzjak Horovitz (this time spelling his name
as "Hurvitz") took up the pen to lay bare an open wound, writing in

Hebrew of the desperation of the women and the fury of the men, the pain, the uncertainty, and the cruelty of the dreaded discovery. His letter was published in issue 154 of the periodical, on Monday, July 24, 1893:

> Kiriath Moshe, May 27. Today I am not a man bearing good news, for I am here to remember the soul of my dead brother, lost in a terrible murder that brought much sorrow to our Jewish brothers here, especially those of our own village. Such was the event: on the fifth day in the week, on the thirteenth day in the month of Nisan, at nine in the morning, my youngest brother, aged twenty-two, went out into the countryside, riding his horse in search of three lost horses that had escaped the day before. As the prophecy says, no one should go out into the fields alone at morning, but this was not the first time that my poor unfortunate brother had been on a horse. No one had ever told him that such misfortune could befall him on the road. But the thing we had never imagined came to pass!

Horovitz wrote, disconsolately, that his brother had said he would return for lunch when he left the house, but at two in the afternoon it was his horse that showed up. He came alone. "Seeing this, we steeled our hearts for some tragedy that might have happened on the road," the eldest wrote. The two brothers got on their horses and rode like the wind. They wanted to think that the other horse could have thrown its rider to the ground, and the man could have been left too weak to return on foot. But it was difficult, even for them, to believe the story.

A week before Horovitz's death there had been a murder of another colonist, Pinjas Fainman, a Romanian man, aged thirty-eight, who, like Noaj, had met his death away from home. His ghost eludes me: I can't even find his name engraved on the stones in the Moisés Ville cemetery, though I know from my great-grandfather's account that Fainman was discovered not long after his disappearance. "The very day they found him he was already dead: his belly had been cut open with a knife," Mijl Hacohen Sinay wrote. Of his horse, no tracks remained: it was assumed that the killers had stolen it from him.

As the search stretched on, pain weighed on the faces of everyone in the village. "From youngest to oldest, from children to women, all were asking if we had found the missing man," wrote the eldest brother.

> "Have you heard any news?" they would say, and with sorrow and pity our brethren's souls joined us in our misfortune, as if it had touched them in their very flesh, and on the next day, Holy Saturday and the first day of Passover, the honorable Rabbi Goldman told us to ride out on horseback with fifty or even sixty riders, all together, into the fields.

But they returned, once more, empty-handed. In the face of those who had already lost hope of finding the body, a large band of colonists went out the next day to comb through the most distant pastures on foot and on horseback, in group after group, in several lines, keeping no more than five meters of distance between them.

So it was that they finally came to the location of the dead man.

They found Noaj Horovitz lying among the reeds, with a slit through his throat and three stab wounds. The scoundrels had stolen his shoes and discarded his clothing. He had gone without any money but had been carrying a few tools for recognizing his horses: they were found two kilometers farther on. The oldest of the three wrote from his home in Moisés Ville:

> We do not yet know the murderer's face, but someone did witness a fight between my brother and the man from afar. Later, a few pursued and captured the criminal. Unfortunately, my brother had not taken the rifle from our house. He carried no weapon because he expected no evil.

Very close to the Horovitz farm—which remains cultivated land to this day—stands the neighborhood of La Salamanca, in which is concentrated the town's population of least means: bricklayers and field laborers. La Salamanca is a long strip that stretches east until won over by countryside, and it is a place where you can still hear the word "gringo" in a contemptuous tone, a bad aftertaste from distant times. The houses are of exposed or plastered brick, or simply adobe and sheet metal; a few altars erected to Gauchito Gil crown street corners.

Don Tanasio Acosta, an old criollo man who wears a beret on his head and bears one of the most widespread last names in Moisés Ville, greets Ingue Kanzepolsky when he sees him appear:

"Taking a walk?"

Don Tanasio's son, a beefy guy of thirty, was the first to poke his head out.

"He must be here looking for me to do some work," he said to his father.

But he was mistaken. I was the one who had asked Ingue, while we were out driving in his truck, if we could get out and try to talk.

The roosters move a bit farther along while Ingue and Don Tanasio share memories of old acquaintances. The criollo recalls anecdotes from back when he was a young man and brings up his father:

"He spent all his life driving cattle to Rafaela," he says. "We were all born on the back of a horse."

Don Tanasio carried on in the same trade: a cattle drover and farm-hand, he spent eleven years in an agricultural post overseeing 1,200 hectares and more than a thousand head of cattle.

"You've got to put your back in the sun, like an iguana!" he laughs, midway through his story, turning his little folding chair so the sunlight won't hit him in the face.

Memories emerge and accumulate, and I ask Don Tanasio if he ever met a gaucho. Or if his father or grandfather considered themselves as such. But the man just stares at me. This question of an outsider from the city seems to amuse him.

"No, what do you mean 'gauchos,' they were civilized people, just like us," he says.

It turns out he's never heard stories about the murders of Moisés Ville, nor does he recall country outlaws passing through this area. He knows still less about the homicide of Noaj Horovitz. On the contrary, Don Tanasio says and repeats that life in Moisés Ville was once peaceful but is no longer.

"These days, the young people, not to offend anyone, are more rebellious. It would seem like a different world!"

A long time ago there was another Acosta, first name Antonio, who worked with the livestock, and he had a Jewish employer. He counted the animals and rounded them up; his wife worked in the house, washing clothes and cooking pastries. Now, one of their daughters remembers them well and recaptures, in her own right, the respect they commanded:

"If they caught wind of you saying any bad word, they'd tell you off straight away."

Her name is Rosa Acosta, and out of eight siblings she is the only surviving one. Her wrinkled face and compassionate eyes tell Moisés Ville's history more than her words: she is 103 years old when I visit her at the care home of the Baron Hirsch Hospital. She is the town's oldest resident.

She followed in her mother's footsteps and worked as a domestic in the house of a family of Jewish colonists.

"Those paisanos of mine never complained," she says and repeats it. And she still remembers the Hebrew words they taught her: Rosa is living proof that criollo people Judaized, perhaps as much as those Russians adapted to the Pampas.

"I knew what they would avoid so as not to eat like a goy, things like that," she continues. "As for bread, I knew which kind was for Passover too. And the dates of their holidays. So, I was wise to everything and used to attend the Shabbos. I still remember a few things now," Rosa says, with a proud smile.

But when called on to talk about gauchos and bandits, she doesn't remember them either.

"There used to be parties and we'd dance, but there weren't any gauchos. A lot of people came from outside, from posts out in the fields. But very few would get into fights."

For her, as for Don Tanasio, "gaucho" is synonymous with "idle and profligate."

· · ·

Apart from the newspaper *Ha-Tzfira*, there was another far-reaching publication in the European Jewish world at the turn of the century: the newspaper *Ha-Melitz*/המליץ, whose Hebrew name can be translated as "the interpreter" or "the advocate"; it, too, can be seen on a street in Jerusalem, one block away from the street paying homage to *Ha-Tzfira*. Founded in Odessa in 1860 and relocated to Saint Petersburg ten years later, its pages, which were fertile ground for the debates of the age, had been the beginning of Hebrew journalism in the East.

In its August 1, 1893, issue, *Ha-Melitz* delivered news, also in Hebrew, of these murders in Moisés Ville. Its Argentine correspondent was a professional journalist named Abraham Vermont, who was twenty-five years old at the time and who, before falling upon Argentina (and that's the right word for it), had gotten a taste for ink in periodicals from Russia and the Balkans, where he began writing while barely an adolescent. Within a few years, Vermont had developed an irreverent, high-impact style, with a proto-sensationalist pen destined to make history in gringo Argentina. Already in this letter from *Ha-Melitz*, dated June 30, 1893, the young journalist seems to be practicing the tone of his forceful cries:

Five months have passed since an article titled 'Emet meretz atzemaj' ['The truth about a flourishing country'] came out in issue 28 of *Ha-Melitz*, and our brethren in Moisés Ville still have not learned to take knives in their hands for war. Instead, with revolvers, the gauchos have already killed three. [Administrator Michel] Cohan wrote elsewhere that 'the Jews know how to rise to face their soul.' But between Passover and the present two men were murdered: one of the Hurvitz brothers and Pinjas Fainman, originally Bessarabia, who represents the well-known Fainman family here. Maybe they were not warned in advance that Santa Fe is a cradle of murderers and thieves, for in this colony of five hundred souls, within the last year and a half, five Jews and three Italians have already been murdered, and three Jews were gravely injured.

Back again in the cemetery, the guardian stares at me in surprise. Thinking about Noaj Horovitz's grave, I've just asked him about ghosts.

"It's been eleven years I've worked here, and I never saw a thing," Emilio says. "It's just that it isn't a subject for everyone: certain people have to see them, and others don't."

We're all alone in a cemetery, yet no shiver passes through this place. Here, green countryside and full sky filter in from every side; it's the kind of place where all of us should come to spend a spell of eternity.

The morning is crystal clear and cold, luminous.

We walk toward the exit, and I ask the guardian if he'd really never seen a lost soul in section five, where the murdered lie at rest. I want to know if Noaj Horovitz's soul ever gave a sign, even once. "But no . . . !" he insists. (I find it hard to believe: could it be that the caretaker of a cemetery has never come across an apparition?)

"Though if I had to come at night, I wouldn't do it. These aren't places to be disturbed," the man explains.

Emilio, who is originally from Entre Ríos and is of Russo-Christian ancestry, lives in Moisés Ville with his family. And he admits that he did have a paranormal experience once, though it wasn't in the cemetery but the Brener Synagogue, the one that now shines after a restoration. It was on a very hot day, not too long ago, when some children broke one of the high windows with a slingshot and Emilio got called in to repair it.

"The panes of glass that were still left had been attached to the frame on the outside, so the whole thing had to be removed before it could be fixed. I got it down and set to work over that window with its six little panes, using tiny nails. I was bent over, setting the filler . . . and in an instant one of those long benches lifts up and the backrest comes crashing into me! The bench came down, threw all the glass down to the floor, the dust flew up inside the synagogue . . . if you could have seen it, I was left chewing on sand!"

I watch his face. I look for a sign, a wink to follow his joke. There isn't one: Emilio is speaking in complete seriousness.

"There's something there in that temple, something . . ." he shivers. "Lots of people tried taking photos and saw a large crowd before them, and later, when they developed the reel, it was black."

Emilio told his story about the synagogue in every corner of town, but people invariably laughed. For his part, he resolved to finish the maintenance task from the outside and not enter again.

An answer to his experience arrived sometime later, when an old neighbor told him a story and asked him not to repeat it until after he was dead. Now the man is at rest inside one of the graves that Emilio himself cares for, and I can listen to his tale:

"Children used to play on the roof of that temple, and one time one was pushed, fell to the ground, and was killed. Afterward, the others, to cover it up, said that he'd fallen on his own. But that's not how it happened, and this neighbor told me the truth. And right there we get into an injustice . . . If it's true, and I believe it's true because that neighbor was not the kind to tell you a lie, then there was an injustice. And the soul of that poor boy, who is left forgotten, awakens so that someone will be touched by that injustice."

But more harmful than a ghost, Emilio tells me, is the rascal who broke the locks of the little administrative office in the cemetery some time ago to steal what little they had in the collection box.

After my initial visit to the cemetery, I return a couple more times. It is, possibly, the site that should be most important to me regarding the murders of Moisés Ville. Or at least the place where I can have direct contact, or the most direct contact possible, with several of the histories that are keeping me awake at night. I walk with the guardian along the main road of the necropolis, and we come out at a monument to the victims of the Holocaust. No one is there but the two of us and the songs of birds.

Emilio thinks for a while and says the last name Sinay doesn't ring a bell to him. Then he looks through the records—a filing cabinet holding several pages of names, dates, and coordinates—and, with a bit of luck, finds one reference: Sara F. de Sinay.

"I don't know who she is," I say.

All the same, Emilio leads me to her grave, a classic black stone from the 1950s, shiny and polished. There, next to the image of a menorah with five branches, is a photograph of Señora Sara giving a half smile beneath a head of snowy hair. Like most of the gravestones, it has words remembering her both in Hebrew and Spanish. "An important and distinguished woman," read the first. And they ask that "Her soul may be joined into the chain of life." The lines in Spanish run with a more informative cast:

SARA F. DE SINAY

DIED APRIL 25, 1954

YOUR SISTER AND BROTHER-IN-LAW

WHERE YOU SPENT THE FINAL YEARS

OF YOUR OLD AGE

DEDICATE THIS MEMORY TO YOU

Today, her grave is the only one that alludes in any way to Mijl Hacohen Sinay in Moisés Ville, the town he had dreamt so much about at the turn of the century, when he traveled halfway around the world with his own kind to live free. But despite the negligible traces that remain of him there, Moisés Ville and its situation remained part of Mijl Hacohen Sinay's obsessions throughout his life. A short time later, I find a box in archives of the IWO Institute with some papers that had belonged to my great-grandfather. Inside there are letters in his own handwriting, drafts of a few works, and newspaper clippings. I also discover a few references to the colony. Later, more will appear in other places.

As I write these lines, I have several of his works spread out before me. All are in Yiddish: "A Theme on the Subject of Moisés Ville's History (for the Right to a Free Debate)," which came out in the January 30, 1942, issue of the periodical *Undzer Tzait*; "Memories from the First Years of Jewish Colonization around Moisés Ville," in the May 1950 issue of the magazine *Colonist Cooperator*; "Lithuanians from Grodno and Its Surroundings in the Jewish Colonies of Argentina," published in issue VII, from November 1953, of *Grodner Opklangen*; "On the History of Local Jewish Colonization," also from *Grodner Opklangen*, appearing in issue X, from December 1956; and "The Difficult Situation of Our Colonization and the Reasons Behind It," from the December 1957 issue of the magazine *Der Shpigl* (The mirror). To this list must also be added his text about the murders.

With all that, Moisés Ville returns again and again in his articles, like a promised land with an unfulfilled promise. Or like the tree stump that adorns the graves of so many lives cut short in the cemetery. Yet, for some reason, nothing now remains of my great-grandfather in the colony beyond his last name carved on a gravestone of little relevance.

Mijl had left no further traces.

That day, when I stopped before the grave of Sara F. de Sinay, that perfect stranger, I wondered why.

6

Rebellion in the Colony

Once upon a time.

One of the possible beginnings to this story could be: Once upon a time there was a rabbi who, along with his family and a few hundred compatriots, wished to live in America and forget the ill-fated world of Russia forever. On November 11, 1894, in Grodno, that man—whose name was Mordejai Reuben Hacohen Sinay, the father of young Mijl—boarded a train that would deposit him several hundred kilometers away, in a port city, where he would board the ship that would bear him across the ocean.

To understand why nothing is left of Mijl Hacohen Sinay in Moisés Ville, it is necessary to go back to the previous link in the generational chain, to take a look into the history of his own father, my great-great-grandfather, a strict and well-respected man according to the recollections that have made their way to me.

On the day that he and his family left Grodno behind, a correspondent for the Polish newspaper *Ha-Tzfira* was present. He wrote:

> Three hours have passed since I returned from the station, and my soul is still touched by the surprising and agreeable vision that met my eyes as I bid farewell to the group of emigrants from our city, setting out on their way to Argentina. You could hear the great murmuring of the many who had come to join the

company of travelers. Herr Fainberg, the leader of this mission, came from Saint Petersburg and settled in our city for the last week, awaiting the party. Forty-two families departed at seven this morning, very early, escorted to the train station to later board a ship.

Among those traveling are two distinguished scholars who will take charge of guiding the sacred spiritual life of the village Kiriath Moshe in Argentina and the forty-two families who are leaving Grodno. Into Rabbi Mordejai Reuben Hacohen Sinay's hands were given two Sifrei Torah and a new Aron HaKodesh, provided by a group of envoys led by the honorable Herr Abraham Frumkin from the central organization for Argentina. Herr Sinay has also gathered many books, which were provided to him and his family, as well as the rest of the travelers, on behalf of local millionaires. This gentleman and his family have been given not only the responsibility of working the land but also that of directing matters regarding religious life and taking charge over the Shabbat sermons. At the moment of the departure, Herr Frumkin sent a special telegram to Herr Sinay to fortify his heart, give a blessing to all in the group, and extend his sentiments, as it was impossible for him to be present at their farewell. This general scene caused a strong impression in my heart and those of all gathered there.

The newspaper published the story, such as it appears in the citation above, on the following day. It was a time of reverie. With the pioneering Podoliers now settled in Moisés Ville, and their stomachs now filled, Baron de Hirsch had decided to send a second large group to Santa Fe. Moreover, it would be the tenth such group to set out for Argentina. Nine other contingents had already traveled to colonies in the provinces of Buenos Aires and Entre Ríos. In 1894, the number of immigrants who entered the country was 107,104, an average figure for the period. Of these, 2,890 were Jews—in the ten years following, there were never as many.

I know very little of the journey aboard the ship. In its issue from December 9, 1894, the newspaper *Ha-Tzfira* noted that the collection of books being brought by Reuben Sinay had increased to 120 *pudi*. The "pood" is a Russian unit of mass, and converting this gives us an incredible figure of two metric tons. Additionally, he brought 2 pudi (32 kilos) of items necessary for worship: tefillin, or phylacteries, to be wrapped around the arms, and mezuzot, to be hung in doorframes. Moisés Ville was a desert, then, onto which material as well as spiritual and cultural structures had to be erected.

The ship was called *Corania*, and it set out on November 11 from the port of Liepāja (or Libau), four hundred kilometers north of Grodno in the present-day territory of Latvia. This was the largest port in the Baltic Sea and that with the greatest traffic of Russian immigrants headed for America: the people from Grodno were camouflaged there, lost in a human avalanche swirling together to board the ocean liners, shoals of little children crying and holding tight to their mothers' hands, fathers carrying trunks and knotted sacks, keeping sight of each of their baskets, suitcases, bundles, canary cages, even rope-tied cows, and all of them dreaming of the unknown that lay across the seas, of New York riches or the Pampas around Buenos Aires. Of a radically new life.

As I write this, I bring out another article by Mijl Hacohen Sinay, "Harab Reuben Hacohen Sinay" (where "Harab" is another way of saying "Rabbi"), a short biography that my great-grandfather dedicated to his own father and published in issue III of the *Argentiner IWO Shriftn* in 1945. "In 1894, my father abandoned Russia and came to Argentina," he wrote. "He was impelled to leave by the difficulties that Jews were enduring in Russia and by an aspiration for his children (five male and one female) to become workers of the land and lead a productive life."

They spent a month and a half at sea. The Ambasch, Radovitzky, Bloch, Epstein, Singer, Skidelsky, Katzovitz, Kaller, Kaplan, Teitelbaum, Kohn, and Trumper families were some of those who, day after day, shared a horizon with the Sinays: all of them would forever be *shifbrider*, ship brothers, united by a slow journey of over ten thousand kilometers. A distant—very distant—cousin once told me that the voyage had been marked by tragedy. She, an elderly woman named Silvia, lived in a suburb of the city of Rosario, where she ran a produce market, and where I had gone specifically to listen to her tales.

I went to visit on a sunny November day and waited a while in the doorway before she turned up, on a moped. We stared at each other in surprise: we didn't look like we came from the same family—she was a bit closer to criollo, hardened by the Paraná sun; I still bore the pallor of the East. Silvia invited me in, and we entered a house with construction at the back. After offering me a soda, she produced a briefcase from somewhere:

"It's is the only thing I have left of my dad," she said as she opened it.

There wasn't much inside. Only an appointment book, a notepad, a few family photos, some papers. All seemed to have been left just as it was the last time her father put it away.

We chatted for a long time; our small families had never come in contact despite the fact that all of us were Sinays. Her great-grandfather's name was Aharon Leib (or León), and he was one of Mijl's brothers. There beside her father's flattened briefcase, Silvia told me we shared the same great-great-grandfather. She couldn't remember Mordejai Reuben Hacohen Sinay's name, but she was sure that he'd been the first rabbi in Argentina. And that his wife had met a tragic fate: that of dying at sea.

"One of the donkeys in the hold kicked her, and she died," she told me. "It also kicked Leib, one of her sons, and he was taken for dead, but then later, when they were holding a vigil for him, they realized he was still breathing."

It wasn't rare for an immigrant to bring their donkey when they traveled or for the animal to grow restless inside the hold of an ocean liner—a hold that, what's more, must have been packed not only with donkeys but also horses, cows, oxen, and all manner of baggage, as well as passengers whom I imagine being reduced, after several months on the ocean, to their purest animal nature.

However, sometime later, I confirmed that the incident was a myth: Rifka (or Rebeca) Rakhil Skibelsky de Sinay had been punctiliously recorded in the 1895 Argentine census as "Reina Sinay." Apart from that, there was yet another myth: Mordejai Reuben Hacohen Sinay was not the first rabbi in the country. At least two others had preceded him:

the Englishman Henry Joseph and the Podolier pioneer Aharon Halevi Goldman. Just as it is in Moisés Ville, in the heart of the Sinay family— even to the present day, as with any family of immigrants—there seems to be an indefinite number of myths floating around.

In reality, the journey across the ocean had been ordinary. Of course, when the sea's fury made the heavy ship *Corania* dance about like a nut-shell, panic did infect the 277 immigrants. But when the sun came out, everything took on the calm of a postcard. At long last, on Thursday, December 27, 1894, my ancestors arrived in Buenos Aires.

The Hotel de Inmigrantes, standing at the river's edge, was the first gate into a country eager for hands ready to work. When the Sinay family arrived, around 1,195,000 European immigrants had already landed in the country, and many had stayed in that hotel. My great-great-grand-father was lucky: he spent only a single night there, along with his chil-dren (five sons: Joseph Mijl or Miguel, Jaim Zeev or Jaime, Aharon Leib or León, Moshe Zalmen or Moisés, and Abraham Shmuel or Samuel; and one daughter: Jaia Lea or Leontina) and his wife, Rifka Rakhil (or Rebeca) Skibelsky. The next morning they set out again, this time on board a train headed for Palacios, the station nearest Moisés Ville, the colony they had heard so much about.

All day long the track advanced sluggishly; in a way, the Pampas were yet another ocean.

They arrived on a Saturday and were lodged for the night in one of the railway sheds their Podolier brethren had come to know so well. Five years along, there was no longer hardship but food and embraces, there beneath the battering of an intense nocturnal storm. Michel Cohan, the administrator appointed by the JCA to command the fates of the forty-nine families now being duplicated, was also waiting for them at the end of the line, along with his entourage. (And the next morn-ing, that of Sunday, December 30, 1894, he would guide them on the eighteen-kilometer stretch from Palacios to the center of the Moisés Ville colony.) Cohan was a robust and vigorous sort, originally from Białystok despite his French name. His figure remained steady against the storm that buffeted the scene; while the new arrivals were running for shelter, their leader stood firm as if the rain did not exist.

Over the nine years he spent in Moisés Ville, from 1893 to 1902, Cohan laid the foundations for the growth that was to come, but he also left a mark of iron discipline. For a long time, his name had repercussions in the hearts of my family: my great-grandfather Mijl took it upon himself, even until his final days, to question the man's achievements and point out his cruelties. For, at the turn of that century, Michel Cohan had become my great-great-grandfather Rabbi Mordejai Reuben Hacohen Sinay's worst enemy, excluding him from a simple life in the colony.

Grodno, the place that had been left behind, comes back to me again and again. Like the writer Alberto Gerchunoff, who at the beginning of *The Jewish Gauchos* describes Tulchin—the distant Ukrainian origin he brings his colonists from—as a "sordid" and "snow-covered" metropolis, I wonder how dark and cold Grodno must have been. That city, almost as far north as Moscow or Copenhagen (and, for that matter, equidistant between the two), would surely let the sun's rays touch it only rarely.

Today, Grodno is one of the larger urban centers of the country known as Belarus or Byelorussia or White Russia, which as I write these lines is governed by Aleksandr Lukashenko, a president friendly with Russia, Cuba, and Venezuela. Since his ascent to power in 1994, he has been, according to his supporters, the only man in Eastern Europe to have created a capitalist system incorporating the best elements of Soviet socialism, or, according to his detractors, simply Europe's last dictator.

Although it has a cathedral named for Saint Francis Xavier and a church of Saints Boris and Gleb, in the 1890s Grodno was a city of Jews: they were the major leaders in commercial, industrial, and educational endeavors. The Great Synagogue—erected in the sixteenth century—was famous throughout the East. And the Haskalah (the enlightenment that permeated Eastern Judaism) and the newly arisen Zionism had many supporters in Grodno.

I read, in the biographical sketch of my great-great-grandfather written by his son, that this was the setting where Mordejai Reuben Hacohen Sinay—in turn the son of another rabbi, Aharon—grew up. The latter died in 1853, leaving his son an orphan. One of the boy's uncles, Zeev Skibelsky (the father of Rifka Rakhil, Mordejai Reuben's cousin and future wife), took charge of him. And one of their cousins discerned in him the qualities needed for a religious life and sent the boy to a yeshiva in Kaunas, from which Mordejai Reuben emerged at age eighteen transformed into a rabbi. My great-great-grandfather then returned to Grodno but, influenced by the winds of enlightenment, chose instead to make his way as a teacher, giving private Hebrew and Bible lessons.

His son—my great-grandfather—was born on December 3, 1877, in the neighboring town of Zabłudów. In an autobiographical piece entitled "Vegn main eigener vinikait" (On my personal conscience), published in issue III–IV of the magazine *Grodner Opklangen* from September 1950, my great-grandfather recalled how he was educated from a young age in Grodno. They lived in a house that contained a library packed full of books in Hebrew and Yiddish, and they received nearly all the Jewish and Russian periodicals of that era. Mordejai Reuben was also a frequent contributor to several publications and followed the news about Zionism and American immigration with great interest. Between 1881 and 1900, some 770,000 Jews—one-fifth of the inhabitants of the Pale of Settlement—would depart.

The majority of Russian Jews believed that the solution to their problems lay outside the czarist empire, but part of the issue was where to go. In 1895, Doctor Theodor Herzl and Baron de Hirsch held a meeting in Paris. In a letter, the Zionist leader had been so bold as to inform the millionaire that he didn't believe in charities and had offered him a new plan, more in line with the actions of Baron Edmond James de Rothschild, who was financing the people emigrating to Israel, forerunners in the practice of real Zionism.

With little enthusiasm, Hirsch agreed to receive him. Herzl, awed by the figure of the magnate, had bought himself a new pair of gloves and then rumpled them so it wouldn't be noticeable: he wanted to be more of a snob than the magnate himself. Seeking support for his plans, he very quickly solicited the same thing of him as he had of other wealthy people: a sum of several million to buy lands close to Jerusalem. "Delusions!" Hirsch raged. "Rich Jews don't just hand over . . . I bet Rothschild signs for less than five hundred francs!" Doctor Herzl was surprised: "You speak as if you were a socialist!" "And so I am," the other responded.

"I'm ready to give it all away . . . if and when the other rich people do the same."

But Herzl left empty-handed.

There was no turning back: Hirsch had already started up the machinery of the JCA, which was building its bridges toward Argentina. Between colonization and Zionism, between Hirsch and Herzl, between Russia and Palestine, between Argentina and the United States, between the newspapers *Ha-Melitz* and *Ha-Tzfira*: it was one of those moments when everything seemed to be up for debate.

For his part, Mordejai Reuben Hacohen Sinay, who occupied the position of a community leader in Grodno given that he had founded a Zionist center in 1884, sensed the call drawing closer. A well-off cousin of his, one Abraham Frumkin, who was the central committee's representative in that city and needed to assemble an initial group of colonists to send to Argentina, was the one who convinced him to board the ship. Finally, in 1894, the bells of destiny rang for my great-great-grandfather.

Santa Fe Province had little or nothing in common with that city frozen in Slavic ice that today seems mythical.

By the time the Sinay family set foot in one of the farming colonies, around 350 had already been founded. Santa Fe had transformed into a major producer of flax, corn, and wheat, surpassed only by Buenos Aires Province in wealth and power. However, the prosperity that had propelled the colonies began to weaken in 1893, when low prices in the international market caused a domino effect and resistance to the tax on grains spurred armed rebellions throughout the countryside, all Remingtons blazing, with support from the Radical Civic Union.

In the same period, the province's population quadrupled, and the number of rural settlements grew five times over. The 1895 Argentine census—which registered 4,094,011 inhabitants in the country—established that 46 percent of Santa Fe's inhabitants were of foreign origin, with the majority coming from Italy, Switzerland, Germany, and France. In 1894, in addition to the eight members of the Sinay family, another 18,545 immigrants entered the province.

My ancestors as well as several of Moisés Ville's founders appear in that 1895 census, listed on tally sheets that were completed by hand in a meticulous and rather baroque script: the handwriting of a prestigious community member (the fact is, only a person in such a position was able to make the register). In Moisés Ville there were five volunteers for the census, among them the administrator Michel Cohan and the businessman and community activist Abraham Itzjak Horovitz. As for the Sinays, Mordejai Reuben is listed as "Marcus" and his wife as "Reina"— none of those strange Russian names! In the records, both are fifty-nine years of age, have been married for thirty-five, have seven children, own real estate, are farmers, are Jewish, and are educated. Among the children there is "Migue," nineteen, single, Russian, Jewish, farmer, educated. That is my great-grandfather. The report exhibits a strange and repeated error with regard to the numbers: neither fifty-nine nor nineteen was anyone's age, nor were there seven children. Did the census taker falsify these records? Did they give an eyeball figure? Or did the people registered lie on purpose to obtain some kind of benefit? I can't be sure. In other respects, it represents a valuable document for understanding what sort of life the Sinays were leading when the survey was conducted, on Sunday, May 10, 1895, five months after they first landed in the country.

On one of my trips through the town, schoolchildren stare at me blankly but smile. The national hero Manuel Belgrano surveys the whole scene from a portrait, and the classroom walls look crowded with cut-out letters and colorful numbers. In one of the classrooms of the Vicente López Provincial School No. 6054, Eva Guelbert de Rosenthal, the director of the Moisés Ville museum, aims a camera at me and I smile.

"I'd like you to know the school where your grandparents worked," she'd told me the day before, at the museum.

Of course, nothing of the original remains. But this school is the heir to Moisés Ville's first, founded in 1895 with the arrival of the group from Grodno. It was also the first in the JCA's network of seventy-eight rural schools, an investment that no other colonizing enterprise developed. The classes in the national curriculum were taught by Sephardic teachers whom the alliance sent from Europe, and those in religion and Jewish culture by teachers from the colony itself, among whom the Sinays were the first. Just as he had been in Grodno, Mordejai Reuben was tasked with establishing the school, using support from the association. Young Mijl, who had worked the land for his first few months there, would join his father and, at age seventeen, become a teacher as well.

The first year in Moisés Ville went by fairly uneventfully for my ancestors, between the land and the classroom. However, the harvests were meager. Noé Cociovich, who arrived in Moisés Ville as a pioneer among the Grodners and quickly became a leading colonial figure and a founder of cooperatives, schools, and community institutions, wrote his memoirs between 1930 and 1931 and published them in the periodical *Mozesviler Lebn*. In them, he recalled how the failure of agriculture in the colony created a somber atmosphere of epidemics, floods, droughts, and locusts (which were bold enough to infiltrate the houses and eat all of the paper and cloth they could find).

In 1895, so as to stay afloat, the administrator Michel Cohan proposed incorporating mixed agriculture. Cultivating alfalfa, the plant eaten by horses throughout the region as well as those in the large cities—as they were used at the time to pull trams, coaches, and cargo trolleys—meant a swift success that was followed by the arrival of purebred cows and plans to install a cheese and cream processing plant: the very foundations of the colony's economic progress.

But when everything seemed to be improving and the colonists had already been informed of a future visit from the baron (who would be coming along with a hundred journalists to show the world what Jewish people were capable of doing when they were free), the unexpected happened: Hirsch died.

It was on April 21, 1896, while the baron was lodging at the country house of one of his wealthy friends in the Hungarian town of Komárom. He had arrived from Vienna the day before and gone from one social gathering to the next until, at eleven, he turned in for the night. The next day, when they went to wake him, they found him pale, his tongue hanging gray from his mouth.

The news flew by telegraph.

At a mourning ceremony in Moisés Ville, my great-great-grandfather Mordejai Reuben preached from eight in the morning until six in the evening: even before that, people called him *hamagid*, orator. All of the colonists fasted that day, and they remained inside the temple, listening to the rabbi and crying.

They had been left so alone in the world.

After the baron's death, everything changed. His wife, Baroness Clara Bischoffsheim, well known for her generosity, was left at the project's helm, but three years later she, too, was dead. The JCA did not collapse—as its founder's money seemed inexhaustible and the work was already underway—but before the new century began the association had transformed into a cold, faceless organization.

It seems like a twist of fate—a sad joke—that in 1896, one of the few years in which the colonists did not experience a murder, their patron would have died. On the other hand, before that wicked year could end, the affairs of Santa Fe politics would once again strike the baron's already wounded orphans, who on December 21 would present a letter in Spanish to the provincial governor, Luciano Leiva, asking for someone to protect them. Their clumsy words, in looping calligraphy, relate that the commissioner Don Idelfonso Coria had been arrested a month before at the police headquarters of the town of Monigotes; it would not be unusual for such a thing to happen as a result of some quarrel over power. The colonists explained that "the absence of an authority in this district does considerable damage in our interests as the nearest authority is at a distance of ten leagues away," and they asked that the man be released. There are 145 signatures—the majority in unsteady writing by strong and clumsy hands; among them are those of Israel Weisburd, Salomón Alexenicer (Zalmen Aliksenitzer), Noé Cociovich, as well as Marcos (Mordejai Reuben) and Miguel Sinay (Mijl Hacohen Sinay).

A commissioner arrested in the Argentine Republic? Even while writing the letter, the colonists must have known this was nothing new. Four years before, Caraciolo Sayago, the commissioner from the town of Sunchales—twenty-five kilometers south of Moisés Ville—had also been arrested on charges of theft and abuse of authority. The fact that the colonists would defend Commissioner Coria in their letter doesn't mean the man was clean; the fact that they would cast votes because of the prosperity of Leiva's government doesn't mean they would support him either. The only thing beyond doubt is that those 145 people felt they were in God's hands, and it was not strange that some would go out to sow their fields with a Schneider rifle slung over one shoulder, a weapon the JCA itself had given them.

In a different century, a new collective letter would unite the inhabitants of Moisés Ville once again. It was in the winter of 2009, 113 years later, and it was addressed, once again, to an authority figure. This time it was to Judge Aldo Precerutti, head of the criminal trial court for Judicial District number 10 in San Cristóbal (the department capital), requesting his intervention in an investigation the police had already opened due to the dog poisonings,

> which has been occurring successively for three years to date incurring a total of eighty-three dogs poisoned and highlighting the fact that high-toxicity poisons are discarded in the public streets, more specifically in the central urban area, this being an obvious public safety concern for the children who on several occasions were playing in and/or traveling through the same places where the criminal events took place.

Lili Graff, a woman with long features who listens to a symphony of barking each time she arrives home, was the one who organized the matter. Her love for pets was well known: a member of the Society for the Protection of Animals, Lili would—and continues to—bring home animals she was able to rescue from the streets, and since the beginning of this wave of poisonings the people have turned to her, sometimes in desperation.

"I've seen children crying over the loss of their dogs and big men crying like children," she says.

Lili Graff still has a clear memory of the day when her dog Corbatita—a bristly mutt with a dark back and white stomach that she'd rescued from the street—slipped out after her and barely made it back. That day was rendered in "Letter from my Dog Corbatita," from June 12, 2009, in which Lili took on the voice of her pet:

> Today I got up and felt inside me the same happiness I always feel every time I go out, free to run around the neighborhood and play with my friends. But even being a dog, with all the abilities that define me, I couldn't sense the danger that lay in wait for me. And so, in the middle of siesta, I followed my innate instinct and ate something I found next to a tree.
>
> It took no more than a few minutes for me to notice that my body was shaking, and I was running out of air. When I saw the tear-filled eyes of someone who one day, simply by valuing my company, my faithfulness, and my signs of affection, came to love me, I understood what was happening to me. She was crying, and I was barely breathing! And she took me in her arms and said: 'My love, they've poisoned you! But I'm begging you to hold on because I need you by my side!' And she went to the vet, holding me in her arms. Someone who knows from personal experience how to understand the pain and helplessness this causes in us.
>
> And once I managed to stabilize, I wondered: WHY? WHY ARE THEY KILLING US? And I couldn't find any answer that made sense, so I am asking whoever is doing it, no more deaths! now, no more tears! If nothing else to make up for the pain, the despair, the anger, the hate, the wickedness of the people who are mercilessly killing us!
>
> And please ask yourself, what will happen when this all gets out of your hands? And the division becomes an ABYSS because even TODAY there are CHILDREN PLAYING in the SAME PLACE where I was POISONED!

Today, Lili Graff smiles:

"Corbatita was in a very bad place for four days, but little by little he started to recover and now he's here with me."

And just at hearing the sound of his name he appears, playful and a bit nervous, a little dog who stood at the door of death.

In Moisés Ville of old, 1897 was no better than the previous year: the colony had transformed into a collection of wills without any common objectives.

While the administrator Michel Cohan had tightened his relationship with the colonists (enforcing payments of the fixed installments from their contract and threatening to expel anyone who did not comply), they responded by conspiring and nicknaming him "The Second Haman," in reference to a biblical villain. Later, when Cohan pushed the improvement of cattle breeding, the planting of chinaberry trees, the fencing-in of farmland, and the expansion of alfalfa, the complaints grew: forced to demonstrate their productivity, to reeducate themselves under the paternalistic ideas of the baron, the colonists felt their hands were tied against growing rich. The JCA would never permit it: they could not lose sight of the goal of demonstrating the agricultural nature of the Jewish people; forming a rich colony wasn't part of the plan. Then there started to be talk of slavery and feudal philanthropy.

Not long after, the disgruntled colonists went to request help from a powerful man who could counteract the administrator: the rabbi and teacher Mordejai Reuben Hacohen Sinay, who was similarly convinced that freedoms in the colony were rather scant.

In his recollections of the conflict—later collected in the book *Génesis de Moisés Ville*—the colonist Noé Cociovich, an ally of Cohan's, says that my great-great-grandfather "confused minds with his skill as an orator and provoked a maelstrom in the colony." There, my ancestor occupies the role of villainous agitator, but his son—my great-grandfather—tried until the end of his days to disprove that account.

When everything seemed irremediable, the conspirators held an assembly and swore on a Torah scroll to send a delegation to Paris, where the highest leaders in the JCA were to be found. After March 1897, Mordejai Reuben made for Buenos Aires to seek economic support, and by the time he returned his two companions had already been chosen, the silent Note Grauer and Abraham Braunstein, from Bessarabia. A mandate in Hebrew, signed by several colonists, certified their mission.

My great-great-grandfather and his companions set out early on a cold April morning, still in the dark. Passover, the celebration of freedom, had just ended.

Moisés Sinay made a life for himself in the United States, where he arrived while still quite young after passing through Peru and Mexico. Now a well-regarded neonatologist with three children and two grandchildren, he lives in Palos Verdes Estates, not far from Los Angeles. In a way, he, being one of Mijl Hacohen Sinay's grandchildren—and my father's cousin—is the one who holds the living memory of this branch of the family, and, over email, he shares some of his memories with me. He never knew Mordejai Reuben, but he was Mijl's closest grandson.

"My *zeide*'s dad was very religious and very strict, as well as being conservative," he writes one day.

My uncle Sergio tells me something similar when I visit him at his house, where I've come to get a few of Mijl's old papers that he says he has for me. But when he brings them out, I discover they are a real treasure, saved for generations and passed from hand to hand: there are even papers from Mordejai Reuben. And several hundred clippings, letters, photos, and drafts. My uncle gives them to me with the utmost generosity, and when he sees that I've recovered my breath before this treasure trove of paper, he brings me a cup of coffee. Sergio, like most of us who bear this last name today, knows little about his great-grandfather Mordejai Reuben. But he says the man was a rebel, that he wasn't afraid of the rich, and if he did stand up against the JCA, it was because he saw that what was being received did not match what had been promised.

"He traveled to France to lodge a complaint with the directors, but when he arrived there he found himself on his own," he tells me. "It seems that his companions in the revolt had been bought off. And that meanwhile, in Moisés Ville, his house had mysteriously burned down, with his wife and children only surviving by a miracle."

Later that night, I spread out the articles and papers my uncle had given me and understood Mijl's life a bit better: I had the remnants of his labor right before me. I saw the evolution of his sinuous work and how he had gone from a more or less sensible young pioneer to the old witness of a foundational era. I fought hand-to-hand against the Yiddish: only two articles were written in Spanish. I armed myself with my dictionary and the notes I'd taken in class, wished myself good luck, and launched myself into an arduous, cryptic, anxious reading.

The mystery of Yiddish always remains seductive.

In the days that followed I couldn't stop thinking about my great-great-grandfather and the impossible adventure of his journey, with the scarce funds of a rural life, from Moisés Ville to Paris.

Again the ship.

Again the shifbrider.

Again Europe.

Though this time, not quite so naive.

On the way out of my Yiddish class, I mention it to the anthropologist Iván Cherjovsky, one of my classmates in the small weekly course. As we walk along Lavalle toward Junín, he explains to me that some colonies were more contentious than others. He had visited several of the ones that still remain.

"In Mauricio, which was the most contentious, there were several cases against the JCA in the 1910s, though it won them in the end."

Fittingly, Iván graduated with a thesis on these conflicts, in which the most significant cause was that of children who'd been denied the possibility of settling along with their parents as colonists, since the new lands must be reserved for new immigrants. When he began his thesis, Iván did not understand how, in an enterprise where there was so much money and such a rush to emigrate, the conflicts turned out so vicious.

"That's how I came to the issue of productivity," he explains, "an ideological issue that placed a great deal of pressure on the project and prevented the colonists from growing in an ultra-capitalist environment like the gringo Pampas. The Jews were not permitted to profiteer: the JCA's economy was a moral one; tension arose between the desire for progress and the rigid guidelines of the company."

"And how did you do on the thesis?"

"I got a ten," he says, but makes a gesture to cast off the laurels: "Everybody gets a ten . . ."

Around the middle of 1897, the director-general of the JCA in Paris, Sigismund Sonnenfeld, met the three delegates thanks to the influence of Judah Lubetzky, the Russians' rabbi in the City of Lights and a distant cousin of Mordejai Reuben. But he didn't want to hear any of the complaints they were bringing.

The whole thing fell apart in an instant.

And the decline was violent. Noé Cociovich says in the book *Génesis de Moisés Ville* that the three envoys fought among themselves and pressure from a charitable society made Grauer and Braunstein change their tune. "And Sinay?" he wonders. "The lovely praise he'd received led to an attack that would keep him bound to a hospital for a long time"—and it seems clear that he was assaulted by goons from the JCA, or what else could it have been?

It would be several months before my great-great-grandfather's return to Argentina. In a newspaper from the period, the *Krakowier Yiddishe Zaitung*, a group of Jews from Buenos Aires published a letter on July 12, 1898, condemning Cohan's abuses, and they mentioned the misfortune of Rabbi Sinay's family during his absence: "When his wife requested tools for plowing, only so as not to die of hunger along with her children, they beat her until she was left ill and bedridden." (A matter that reveals something of my character in the presence of my investigation: if I had a high representative of the JCA before me, some gentleman of fine manners and strict rules, I would bitterly hold it against him.)

The colonists learned of the failure before the envoys' return, but they stood by their complaints. For that reason, in September 1897, le Petit Tsar (as some called the administrator Michel Cohan) began a wave of evictions and traveled to San Cristóbal to bring the police, under the pretext that there were plans to rob the administration's bank. Bent on imposing order, no matter the cost, he had the most rebellious colonists arrested, and, once transferred to the jail in San Cristóbal, they endured torture and unexpected abuse. While the scandal was making it into the pages of the capital city newspapers *La Prensa* and *La Nación* in November 1897, many left the colony and took refuge in Sunchales and Rosario or ended up living in two Buenos Aires tenements, at 1419 Sarmiento and 1365 Cerrito. The city-dwelling Jews referred to them as "castaways."

To Roberto Schopflocher, the last living administrator from the JCA in Argentina, the conflicts between administrators and colonists are an old story. At eighty-nine, he spends his days in a warm apartment with a view overlooking the boulevard in the neighborhood of Belgrano. Certainly a very different landscape from the one he used to see every morning in Avigdor and the other colonies around Entre Ríos where, from 1943 to 1952, he worked and rose to become one of the youngest leaders in the JCA.

"An administrator, I know from personal experience, had a lot of power. But I was a bit immune to that, maybe because I was young," he recalls, adjusting his heavy glasses. "There were some administrators who let the power go to their heads a bit, and others who were arrogant. Maybe the temptation did exist. I don't know. What I can say is that the administrator was also the lightning rod for all of the colonists' discontent."

In the 1950s, during Schopflocher's time in Entre Ríos, there were seven administrators. Quite far from the style of a cruel ruler, this bulky man, who invites me to talk in a small room with bookshelves rising up to the ceiling, is an agronomist, historian, sculptural artist, old subscriber to philosophy courses, disseminator of agriculture and livestock, and well-regarded writer of novels, plays, and short stories published both in Argentina (where he was awarded the Faja de Honor by the Argentine Society of Writers) and Germany, the land where he was born and from which he emigrated while still an adolescent, along with his family, in 1937.

We talk for a long while. Schopflocher speaks without pause, in a low voice, telling me that in his era the administrators could do nothing about many of the problems that arose. In the same way, there were exaggerated reactions from both the colonists and the administration as well.

Finally he leads me to the door. And as I press the button to call the elevator, he shakes himself up with a memory:

"Do you want to hear an anecdote? I'll tell it to you because I'm a fellow writer and I know you're going to need juicy stories . . . It's nothing new, but it will help you to understand the bureaucracy in the JCA that the colonists complained so much about. It goes like this: an administrator sees that the townspeople have gathered in front of a well, so he goes over, and when he gets there they tell him a young calf has fallen in. One colonist tells him that they'd need a lasso to pull it up from the depths. So the administrator pulls out his pad and says, 'A very good idea!' and makes a note: 'Write to Paris to request approval for the acquisition of one lasso' . . . That's a very well-known anecdote, don't write about it and act like you've discovered something new! . . . On the other hand, I don't think it could have been true. We were bureaucrats, but not like that!"

In spite of everything, Michel Cohan passed on into history as a good administrator.

And Mordejai Reuben had to endure exile from the colony and disperse his family along the coast. It turns out that Cohan's economic successes carried more weight than his cruelties: he built a school, a ritual bathhouse, two boulevards, a creamery, and a hospital, and he laid the tracks for two train stations, one in the center of the colony and the other on the San Cristóbal line. His numbers were irreproachable: he assumed the position in 1893, with a population of 47 families and close to nine thousand hectares, and he left it in 1902, with 251 families and more than one hundred thousand hectares, purchasing land at 19 pesos per hectare and seeing its value rise to 250 pesos within the next twenty years.

On the other hand, I have no doubt that the colonist Noé Cociovich must have had something to do with the purification of the administrator's image. At the end of the day, Cohan was his protector. But even the editors of his book of memoirs point out in the prologue that Cociovich idealized the administrator and lost his way with regard to Mordejai Reuben. His son Mijl Hacohen Sinay recognizes in his autobiography for the magazine *Der Shpigl* that his relationship with the great colonial leader had been friendly, since he had respect for his extensive work in Moisés Ville and his Judaic culture. But he also relates that, having read the man's words about the Cohan–Sinay affair, he had the chance to confront him in Buenos Aires.

I imagine the episode in the hall of some cultural institution, against the backdrop of some ceremony. "I know that they were enemies and bore a grudge, but I never would have believed you could write something so base and vulgar about my father," Mijl said to him. "Don't you know? Those of us who study the Torah are as vengeful as snakes," Cociovich challenged back. "Can words be so lawless? Can you just write anything about anyone? Everything you've written about my father is a lie!" my great-grandfather insisted. "You know what? Why don't you go and defend him," said the other, in conclusion.

That, in short, is all.

And that is why nothing has remained of the Sinay family in Moisés Ville, apart from the grave of a woman unknown to me.

But be that as it may, while the colony was struggling through the revolt and my ancestors were gambling with their fate, in an isolated house at the far end of the fields, the worst murder to have stained the dirt of the colony took place. A massacre that, most certainly, caught everyone by surprise.

7

The Killing of the Waisman Family
(and Remembrance as Duty)

On the winter night of July 28, 1897, as the atmosphere in the colony was growing tense and Mordejai Reuben Hacohen Sinay's delegation in Paris was crashing against a wave of denials from the JCA, a group of horsemen arrived at the door of Joseph Waisman's house, in the vicinity of Moisés Ville.

Inside lived a Russian family that had expanded on Argentine soil with the births of four children—the last, only twenty-two days old—but made itself seem smaller in this ramshackle brick house in the middle of the countryside, which also housed a shop run by Joseph himself, a man of around thirty who was already showing signs of age.

The horsemen's leader knocked on the door and waited, holding his breath.

Five years before, Joseph Waisman's father had made the decision to leave Kamenetz-Podolosk along with his family: Froim Zalmen Waisman was his name, and he had feared for his four children and his grandchildren. On the steppes of the czar, it was well known that military service fell on the Jews as a special punishment, ever since an 1827 law promulgated by Nicholas I had imposed a twenty-five year conscription on them. The czar, who believed this was the only way he could force the assimilation of this strange people, assembled a special corps of *khapers* or official kidnappers, who would snatch children and send them off to be raised in child battalions.

Influenced by the "Argentinists" scattered around the shtetls—and very familiar with the experience of the Podoliers, who had departed from the same city—old Froim Zalmen boarded a ship in 1892 to leave the czarist cruelties behind. With him he brought his wife and three of their children, and on a different ship he sent his oldest son, Joseph, along with his wife, Gitl, and their three children. In addition to trunks full of tools, suitcases of clothing, and baskets of food, Froim Zalmen brought a cushion, which drew considerable attention to him as he wouldn't let it out of his sight. Some weeks later, the dockworkers in the port of Buenos Aires were startled by the care this man devoted to his cushion—they didn't know that gold ingots were hidden inside its down filling: it was everything Froim Zalmen had left over from the sale of his flour mill in Kamenetz-Podolosk. Now, all of his fortune and future was contained within that unassuming vessel.

When he reached Moisés Ville, having been changed into "Fermín Salomón" after passing through customs and immigration, old Waisman found himself with several of his old Russian neighbors once again. Using his savings in gold, he opened up a shop in Moisés Ville and helped his son Joseph set up his own farther out in the countryside, on the way to Palacios. His son lived in that ramshackle brick house for a few years, keeping his shop and listening in disbelief to the history of the colony's foundation and the hunger in the railway sheds. It had all happened right there, in Palacios, in a recent time that nevertheless seemed like a rarefied past. Once the two businesses had been opened, the remaining gold ingots were carefully wrapped and buried, to be planted over.

In this way, things proceeded well. For a time.

But then came the night of July 28, 1897, irremediable, irreparable.

"That was a horrible night, the drunks wanted wine . . . and my grandfather Joseph refused to let them in!" recalls Juana Waisman, the daughter of Marcos (or Meyer) Waisman, one of Joseph Waisman's sons.

That boy, Marcos—eight years old at the time—was lucky: he was with his brother Bernardo (or Bani, age ten) at his grandfather Froim

Zalmen's house in Moisés Ville, the town where he attended classes. They were the eldest of the seven siblings and the only family members who were not at the shop for the arrival of those "savage, malicious, criminal people" now being described by his daughter, Juana Waisman. She is the closest person to the event whom I'm able speak to: she is ninety-five when I visit the retirement home where she spends her days, a large house with creaky wooden floors where the seniors stare at visitors in surprise, a short walk from downtown in the city of Rosario.

Juana has never read the text of "The First Jewish Victims in Moisés Ville," but she isn't surprised when I tell her that Mijl Hacohen Sinay devoted two pages—no small amount—to her family's case, the one that brought the most profound horror to the colony. "When night was approaching, the head of the household, Joseph Waisman, was preparing to close up shop while his wife, Gitl, was in one of the rooms putting their four children to bed," my great-grandfather wrote.

> The oldest was a boy of thirteen, and there were also two twin sisters as well as a boy of six. After Waisman locked the door, he heard people knocking very loudly outside. He went back to open it again and saw a group of gauchos, who leapt upon him, giving him a stab to the heart at once. Hearing her husband's death cries, his wife came running from the bedroom into the shop, and the gauchos buried a knife in her chest as well. The woman fell to the floor and lay dying beside him.
>
> The next scene occurred in the other room, where the gauchos killed the children. The oldest brother tried to face them, but in an instant he was thrown to the floor, his body cut in pieces. The two girls were gunned down on their beds: they shot them through the heart and then slit their throats. While the gauchos were busy with the massacre, the youngest boy silently slipped out of his bed, made it clear of the house, and hid among the high grass of the fields.
>
> Once they had finished with the massacre, the gauchos stole everything and disappeared without a trace. The neighbors only

found out about the event the following morning. Although there had been cries, wails, and calls for help during the tragedy, no one had heard a thing, for the seven little houses that formed the community of Palacios were all separated by a considerable distance. It was impossible for the neighbors to hear the victims' cries and groans. When the inhabitants of Moisés Ville went to Palacios—all as one: adults, seniors, young people, children, women—having just received news of the tragedy, and they saw the grim scene that was left in the Waisman home, they took it with great distress: it was a universal lament of men and women.

The home, like the small shop, looked like a pogrom. Everything the gauchos had not taken lay strewn on the floor, broken and trampled beside the lifeless bodies of the husband and wife, whose faces were a horrifying sight. Even worse was the bedroom, which looked like a slaughterhouse. The floor and windows near where the children slept were covered with blood. The mattress was drenched. The oldest boy lay on the floor, his body ruined. The twins, their throats slit like two chickens, lay sprawled on their beds and painted with their own blood.

The victims were taken to Moisés Ville, where they were given a burial in the cemetery. At the funeral, moans and hysterical sobs could be heard rising up to the heavens, from women and men who could not help but lose heart.

The grave where the Waismans are buried is the largest in Moisés Ville's cemetery. An unsuspecting visitor might think a giant lies there, but actually the father, mother, daughter, and son were all placed in a straight line, the feet of one touching the head of the next. For some reason, there are not five victims, as represented in Mijl Hacohen Sinay's text, but four. And they are not located in section five, that of the murder victims, but in another section of ancient graves, number six, where they occupy grave six, row two. More than 120 years later, the Waisman grave has come to be a reference point, perhaps for tourists: "Past the long grave," someone will say to indicate a location.

But their headstone still tells a poem of fear, terse as a bleak haiku in Hebrew: "Here lie the blessed / Herr Mordejai Joseph son of / Froim Zalmen his wife / Gitl daughter of Moshe / their maiden daughter Perl / their young son Baruj / who were killed at the hands of murderers" (nothing about "Waisman" on the stone: their Hebrew names are more than enough for setting forth on the final journey).

Today, Juana Waisman's blue eyes—already beginning to gray—look out with the serenity of a calm sea while her words carry a distant echo of Yiddish, the same Yiddish she grew up with in an Argentine home where prayers were held at morning and night.

"They never figured out anything," she says. "There was fear! Because there was a forest in Monigotes where criminals sheltered, and no one could give them away without running the risk of death. But everyone knew what was going on. Because they, those animals, had also killed someone named Kantor in town . . . And in those days there was a great deal of fear about bandits."

Since she was born in 1916, Juana has lived through the peak and decline of Moisés Ville, which she retired from forty years ago at the point when she started to find herself alone, with little company beyond her husband, Santiago, the manager of the town's power plant. Proudly, she tells me how her husband started working at the plant at age seventeen as a minor clerk and ended up as its accountant, with a fifty-gram gold medal, as well as being an honorary administrator at the hospital for fifteen years and a member of the bank's board of directors for two terms. Small-town things.

At the retirement home, Joseph Waisman's long-lived granddaughter is often entertained by her children and their own grandchildren these days. But she thinks about Moisés Ville, or "Moisesvishe," as she, too, pronounces it.

"There are loads of us here in Rosario, but back there we used to be somebody. Every time we left to travel they'd throw us a goodbye party: going on a trip was like a miracle, but they let us leave on the condition that we'd tell them about everything when we returned. We went to Israel, Hawaii, the Caribbean . . . There are such beautiful things that haven't been written! And later, when we weren't living there anymore but would still visit, all the doors would open to greet us. But now there's almost no one left. No, not anymore . . . That's the history of my town and I've gotten used to it now. After so many years . . . that's the way it is. It's all the truth. I've lived through it, and I wasn't born yesterday."

The Moisés Ville that Juana Waisman grew up in was no longer as dangerous as the town that had seen her grandfather's death. In the 1920s, the modest shop-home where the multiple killing took place had started to turn into a ruin that the murder victims' descendants would, sometimes, point out from afar. Everything had changed by then: gauchos and Jewish colonists maintained a friendly and cooperative relationship from which emerged the Jewish gaucho, so famous around the Pampas.

"The criollos spoke Yiddish better than we did; there wasn't any discrimination or fear," Juana recalls. "And they'd sing Hebrew songs phonetically on the guitar: *in-cre-í-ble!*"

Could Juana's father be the "little orphan" that Noé Cociovich calls up in his memoirs? The great colonial leader didn't like to speak about the murders of Moisés Ville: in his recollections he barely mentions one or two events, as if in passing. He doesn't even go over the Waisman killing, though he does reference it when describing a mysterious traveler who arrived at the end of 1897, "an older gentleman of a fine appearance, robust, stout, extravagantly dressed, who could speak several languages including Spanish." The man introduced himself as a JCA stockholder, claiming to be Dr. Klein, from London, and requested kosher food. But the administrator Michel Cohan, who had welcomed him respectfully, became suspicious when he saw him drink several toasts of *caña* rum and smack his lips without hesitation. "You can recognize a man, as our sages used to say, by his glass," notes Cociovich. The next day, Dr. Klein went around the cultivated fields, visited Rabbi Aharon Halevi Goldman, and "went to see the young orphan of the recently murdered Waisman family, gave him a kiss, and presented him with a five-centavo note . . . claiming that people knew of the tragedy in Paris and he had resolved to look after the boy."

(Of course, the whole thing was a scam: Dr. Klein was a swindler who was neither a doctor nor a JCA shareholder. He just wanted to get some money out of the farmers by offering them false plans for colonization in Montevideo.)

But, aside from the fraud, it may be that Marcos Waisman—Juana's father—was the little orphan boy. Juana doesn't know about that matter, but she can still say that her father carried on and was raised with the love of his grandparents, far from the shadow of the tragedy. He didn't look backward. He couldn't. Instead, he had to work in the fields and at a general store, supporting five children and raising them with good memories like the ones Juana calls up when she describes getting up at five in the morning and drinking fresh warm milk, or already being able to ride a horse at age six.

The children of Joseph Waisman who survived the crime, Juana tells me, all forged their lives in the same way. By not looking back. By not letting the massacre drag on through the generations. But there was one moment in which the past became present. It was not long after 1897, when one of Joseph's brothers—who plied his way through the Santa Fe fields in a horse cart, selling clothing—stopped at a ranch to take shelter in the middle of a cold night. The man tied up his horses and gave them water, but when he entered the house he was troubled by the sight, in one corner, of a fur-lined coat—a classic Russian overcoat, just like the one that had been stolen from Joseph Waisman on the night of his death. "I forgot, I have to visit someone else around here," he said. And he never went back.

"It was the killers' house!" Juana shudders.

When the cake from a Yiddish recipe that she greeted me with is nothing but crumbs, Juana shows me that, unlike her father, she was able to look back. And she compiled a long family tree with the history of the entire family, which she copied and sent to fifty relatives scattered across Argentina, the United States, and Israel. She was also the one who had the idea to put up a plaque on the Waisman family's long grave in the Moisés Ville cemetery:

IN MEMORY OF OUR DEAR GRANDPARENTS MURDERED IN 1897
JOSE WAISMAN AND GUITEL PERELMUTER
AND THEIR DAUGHTERS PERLA AND BABY
R.I.P.
AUGUST 1994.

"We knew who was in there, but the letters were already getting faint," she tells me, as though having to justify it. "And I felt that we needed to put up that plaque, because I went to the Moisés Ville cemetery as a duty, every year, between *Rosh Heshune* and *Yom Kiper*"—and she doesn't say "Rosh Hashanah" or "Yom Kippur" but follows the pronunciation of her region in the East, just as I once heard from my own grandmother's mouth a very plain "*Yom Kiper.*"

In a way, Juana took on the responsibility for passing on her family's legacy into the future. If the letters were fading away with the wind, the absence of Yiddish or the difficulty of reading a gravestone in Hebrew, she made the contrary decision to help history endure. To pass it down to others who someday, in the years to come, could take it over.

Juana then sought and received support from the whole family. She had always been a woman to take initiative: while living in Moisés Ville she had invented a men's suit bag and gotten a patent for it in Rosario, and for a while she had manufactured them in her home with three seamstresses, making the local office of the Argentine Automobile Club her primary customer. So she couldn't have had much trouble putting up a plaque. And only once it was there could she feel at peace, as if she'd settled a debt for those grandparents slaughtered in vain. There, standing before that four-person grave, she used to clear her head and pray that her ancestors could rest in peace.

"I'd pray for them to answer us, to watch over us," she explains. "Though they're dead, dead and in the grave, I still got it off my chest. And although it's been a while since I've gone to the Moisés Ville cemetery, I already have the plot next to my husband. My children were worried and bought it for me. Such good kids I have, eh?"

There is another record that dates from the period, almost as brief and terrible as that of the gravestone. And Eva Guelbert de Rosenthal, the director of the Moisés Ville Museum, has it in her hands. In the museum offices she looks through it again and again. It is a spiral binder of photocopies, taken from a minute book handwritten in Hebrew, and she reads inch by inch, struggling against a manuscript on the edge of indecipherability:

"1897

"July 28. At the Palacios Station four souls were murdered:

"Joseph son of Zalmen Waisman age 32 - -

"his wife Gitl, daughter of Leib Braunstein, age 32 - -

"their daughter Perl age 8 - -

"Their son Baruj 22 days old. The name of

"Joseph's mother: Jana and the name of

"Gitl's mother: Shaia Braunstein

"who resides in the city of Kamenetz-Podolsk."

After this reading, Eva seems exhausted. For several years, this binder of photocopies has become a valuable key to open the door, usually sealed, to the past: its original is a fragile civil register where a traveler aboard the steamship *Weser* named Pinjas Glasberg recorded births, marriages, and deaths. And also crimes. For that reason, Eva and her collaborators have been notating and expanding a code to decipher the book's contents, written in a terrible scrawl, a stretched and slanted cursive, overlapping and unsteady. Its author's Hebrew, very antiquated, resembles that of biblical times. For each of Glasberg's letters, the code offers three or four variants. In this way, Eva can take a word from the original and check it against her code to decipher its meaning letter by letter, as if she were an archaeologist examining a papyrus scroll.

"In his earliest notes, Glasberg would write the bare-minimum details for each event: what happened, who it happened to, when it happened," she explains. "Later, he started to write down more details. By the end, each event would take him several lines."

Pinjas Glasberg's original record is exhibited in one of the museum's glass displays. It is a large and well-worn Russian accounting book, with columns headed by strange Cyrillic words that become meaningless under its redefinition as a Hebrew civil register. Starting in 1890—and for nearly a decade—Glasberg also used it to record a chart of animal

slaughter and dairy yield, an inventory of tools and equipment, as well as
the first cattle brands.

Two portraits of the colonist Glasberg watch over the book. In one
he sports a long white beard and a little square cap to cover his head in
the traditional way, and he is holding a book (this book?) on his lap and
a pen in his right hand. In the second one, framed, Señor Glasberg is
now old and is shown alongside his wife, Mariem, and two of their six
children, possibly the oldest: Chaskel and Pachel. All are dressed up.
Pinjas is sporting a top hat.

Glasberg was a pioneer who became directly involved in the construction of history: he performed community tasks as a magistrate, presided
over a fledgling municipal council, and organized night watches to combat the harassment of bandits and cattle thieves. His work with the civil
register-book was so meticulous that the government of Santa Fe Province accepted it as the official timeline for those initial years; therefore,
although it is exhibited in the museum today, it remains property of the
Moisés Ville Commune. Glasberg's work ended on July 11, 1899, when
the office of the Civil Registry began operations: the records from that
very day show the birth of Naum Milstein, the son of a tradesman, age
twenty-four, and a woman, twenty-three, both Russian; and the death
of Samuel Rosen, a boy, age seven, who was dragged by a horse.

There is a similar desire behind Pinjas Glasberg's effort to that which
which would inspire Mijl Hacohen Sinay to write the article "The First
Jewish Victims in Moisés Ville": the desire to tell history. It is a powerful drive, exercised by a castaway with modest delusions of being a
conquistador, marooned at the end of the earth but remembered once
in a while by the civilized world. And as I write all this, a century and
more—much more—later, his work takes on an unquestionable relevance: Glasberg, as though racing against history and oblivion, captured
the nodes of the great Moisesvillian, American, and Jewish novel that
he experienced and saw unfolding around him. On no account could he
let it be lost to memory.

On the other hand, around 1897 the massacre of a family was nothing new in the Santa Fe countryside, where there were still echoes of a

multiple killing that seemed to have presaged the fate of the Waisman family.

It had happened in 1869 in the colony of San Carlos, 120 kilometers south of the land where the Podoliers would later found Moisés Ville. San Carlos was a colony populated by Swiss, German, Italian, and French immigrants—370 families; just over two thousand people—which viewed itself as a model of the ascendent gringo Pampas. Indeed, it was a very different town from the colony of El Sauce, which stood a few leagues away and was a reservation led by Franciscan missionaries for the indigenous people who had made peace with them, where they cultivated the land, raised animals, and lived in straw huts around a chapel. Evidently, the only interest a settlement like El Sauce could hold for the Santa Fe government was its status as a military position close to territories that had belonged to the indigenous people just ten years before.

A lieutenant colonel from the Guardia Nacional was in command there. They called him "El Indio" or "El Negro," and his real name was Nicolás Denis. He was the son of a Charrúa chief and had joined the reservation quite young, going on to distinguish himself in battles against the gauchos wreaking havoc in the Santa Fe Chaco. Denis had made a career of it and, now past fifty years of age, his word was law in El Sauce. Therefore no one would reproach him for showing generosity to some outsider who might turn up in search of pity and obscurity, even if they had a bad name.

Bartolo Santa Cruz, from Corrientes, was one such man. He was married, the father of two small children, and worked at the tavern in El Sauce; in other words, he was settled. He was not a nomadic gaucho now, but he once had been, and he'd been accused of taking part in the murder of a family by the name of Guerin in the Esperanza colony. At the time, a lack of evidence had led him to freedom, and, as soon as he could, he returned to the side of his old boss, Colonel Denis.

It would seem, in the criollo world, that a tavern invokes misfortune and not just idle time. A large room with a straw roof, whitewashed mud walls, and dim light that runs on credit all year and earns big just for a couple nights; where arguments—over games, horses, contraband—are washed down with the wine the shopkeeper deals out from behind his bars; with melodies from an out-of-tune guitar and three ladies in search of money and company; and gauchos in the cots at the back, their snores as loud as the neighing of the horses outside. There is little reason to believe that Bartolo Santa Cruz's tavern would have been any different.

Bartolo owed three hundred Bolivian pesos to Henri Lefebre, a man originally from Amiens who lived in San Carlos and also ran a small shop himself. But there was no possibility of paying—or, at least, no intention of doing so: the tavern keeper knew that he was cornered by the debt and the matter was going to end the hard way.

So it was that he mustered his friends José and Mariano Alarcón, two brothers from San Lorenzo, two fierce and lanky morenos who had no fear of death (of others) and had for some time been robbing, killing, running. The Alarcóns had been held in confinement twice: the first time in prison, the second on the Northern Frontier, where they were part of a battalion and came to know discipline and hardship. They had managed to escape from each of these hellholes. When they returned home, they were greeted with food and dance by the small handful of friends they still had left, but sometime later the devil's work won: right there, in San Lorenzo, they killed again. They put the knife to two people, also stealing their money and taking their clothing to sell. But enough was enough, and their own aunt denounced them to the law. So they fled to a friendly land where they knew they could find refuge: El Sauce.

And there they were recruited by the tavern keeper, Bartolo Santa Cruz. What did he offer that convinced them to stain their hands with blood once more on the night of October 15, 1869? Wine and liquor? Money and clothes? Loyalty and protection?

Señora Julia Cornier de Rey, an old resident of San Carlos, stated at the trial that on the night of the crime she'd gone out looking for some borage to make tea for her daughter, who felt ill, and had run into her son Francisco, the blacksmith. They walked together along the dusty street and crossed paths with three gauchos on horseback near the Lefebre house. The witness related that, on her return, she saw the criollo men's horses tied in front of the house. One of the gauchos was pacing in front of the door, restless. The other two, inside, were leaning on the counter and chatting with the owner of the house. So said Señora Cornier de Rey.

The one waiting outside was Mariano Alarcón; he was eighteen years old at the time. The two who entered Lefebre's store—where he lived as well—were his brother José Alarcón, age twenty-two, and the tavern keeper from Corrientes, Bartolo Santa Cruz.

And they committed the slaughter.

They wielded their blades, using them with the precision those instruments were made for. They didn't pause before their victims' terrified eyes or the final sobs they let out when already at death's door. And then, before leaving, they stole everything they could.

A few hours later, still in the darkness of night, another French colonist discovered the scene: "Mon Dieu! Mon Dieu!" he was still screaming when the others arrived.

The doctor arrived the next morning. Everything was strewn out in a blood-drenched chaos. The bodies too. The doctor wrote, in his record:

> Enrique Lefebre, tradesman of French nationality, received four knife wounds, two on each side of the chest, one between third and 4th ribs on right anterior chest, another between 4th and 5th ribs left side, another between 5th and 6th on the right side of the chest; all of these wounds are deap [sic] but not possible to specify exactly due to inflamation [sic] of the side, death must have been almost immediate.
>
> Lefebre's wife has a stab wound slightly above her breasts wich [sic] punctures the 'sternum' and severs the main branches of the 'aorta'; she has another stab wound on the left side of the chest toward the heart, another injury on the right cheak [sic] of her face, death must have been immediate.
>
> Enrique Lefebre's son age between 7 and 9 has two stab wounds on the left and right sides of the neck that severed muscles in the neck; another stab wound on the left side of the head an inch in deapth [sic]; another on the left part of the stomach where the intestines came out; a few other injuries on the back and hands.

Next to Lefebre's son I found the corpse of a girl, 10 to 11 years of age, handmaid of the aforementioned Lefebre, of Italian nationality and called Jeroma. Has a stab wound on the left part of the stomach, it punctured the chest and exited through the back, death must have been immediate.

However, the murderers had left little Luis alive, Lefebre's seven-year-old son, and he hid himself and was later able to say that Bartolo Santa Cruz had been there along with two others.

The boy's account enraged the colonists. The Lefebres had not been the first victims to fall, and livestock thefts, assaults, and murders usually went unpunished. But when the sun peeked out the day after the crime, the gringos set out toward El Sauce with the intention of taking revenge. There were 150 men, and they went armed.

They were lucky: the fog shrouded them, and no one saw them until they were already surrounding the ranch of the tavern keeper, Bartolo Santa Cruz, in a fury. But Santa Cruz was not there. Then they made for El Negro Denis's ranch. He tried to play dumb, but the gringos would accept nothing short of the tavern keeper's head. They warned Denis that, if he didn't turn the man in, they would start something with him. And there was no turning back now. These men were determined, and the other was alone as never before; the indigenous people from the town had gone out hunting to the north, and El Sauce lay empty.

The gringos didn't hold back on resources: they lit a fire. With dry logs and fuel, they began setting bonfires to burn down the ranch of El Negro Denis, who ran, frenzied, to take refuge in the chapel, hurling sword blows at the mob as they went to cut him off. Maybe he killed one of them; once inside the sacristy he saw the blood-stained blade and heard the tumult growing outside. In the confusion, his daughter Marta took an injury to one arm and a neighbor woman was killed. Denis had taken the precaution of wearing a breastplate to protect his chest from bullets, but when the bloodthirsty gringos began setting fire to the chapel he had to come out and the breastplate could do him no good.

Surrounded by all of them, seeing the rage in their pale eyes up close and understanding that their strange howls were an inescapable song of death, Denis fell, a blow from an axe splitting open his head.

Later, standing over his desecrated body—immobile, as though bound in the dense undergrowth—the residents of the town, who had returned at sundown, swore vengeance.

In a few hours all of the region's inhabitants (gringos, indigenous people, and gauchos) seemed ready to set off a domino effect of vengeance, but on October 18, three days after the massacre of the Lefebre family, the provincial governor, Mariano Cabal, arrived at the head of six hundred soldiers to pacify the situation. There was still a bad aftertaste left over from the fight three months later, in January 1870, when Domingo Faustino Sarmiento himself, in his role as president of the nation, visited San Carlos during his tour around the colonies to uphold the peace.

Some, however, did not come to see those processions. On the same day when the governor was departing from San Carlos, early in the morning, a country police squad pursued one of Lefebre's friends who'd become the latest colonist accused in the killing of El Negro Denis— nine others had already been arrested. Michel Jérémie Magnin, born twenty-five years prior in the Swiss municipality of Charrat, tried to flee toward the south but was caught on the banks of the Carcarañá River.

Facing down the police posse that had him surrounded, Michel Jérémie Magnin could sense his fate. He sensed, too, that his brother Jean, who'd died by hanging himself from a rafter in Esperanza, had not, when all was said and done, been so wrong. And that he would be hard-pressed to escape from this wasteland where not one of his dreams was destined to come true.

"Give up!" cried the nationals, drawing closer and closer.

Michel Jérémie Magnin looked at them for one last time, raised the Lefaucheux revolver to his mouth, and pulled the trigger.

A much soberer and quieter investigation was staged in Moisés Ville in the winter of 2009. The letter that the residents had sent to a judge in San Cristóbal regarding the mass poisoning of dogs gave new breath to the timid inquiry the local police had deployed, and two plainclothes police officers, members of the investigations squad for the department capital, came to scope out the town's streets. "Two years ago now, a sinister

character, to date unknown, began dedicating his or her time to poisoning pets, primarily canines," Lorena Maryniv had written in her letter
to the newspaper *La Opinión*. Every night, without drawing attention,
the two police officers walked in circles around the few blocks of Moisés
Ville, watching out for this "dubious character," the pet murderer.

And finally he fell. Some say it was an anonymous call. Others say
they caught him while he was out distributing the poison.

In the light of day, the poisoner's identity was exposed: it was the man
who looked after the town plaza, an employee of the commune who was
friendly with everyone. Once brought to San Cristóbal, the man sang
like a bird, saying he'd been paid to do it and revealing, who knows if
with feelings of guilt or relief, the names of a pair of shopkeepers as the
ones responsible.

Those two characters, who were added into the plot as the masterminds of the killings, were a married couple of around sixty, owners of
a well-situated business, good neighbors, but key figures—particularly
the husband—in a collection of anecdotes fraught with the dead bodies
of dogs. There were rumors that he'd been poisoning animals around his
block for years and had fired his rifle on a trespassing mastiff. That he'd
hide and wait for an animal to set foot inside his house to stick it with a
pitchfork like a bale of hay. And even that his wild laughter covered up
the desperate howls of the wounded dog.

However, this alleged mastermind wasn't the one who became
acquainted with the police station, but his wife. *La Opinión*, the newspaper from Rafaela, published the story on June 21, 2009: "Moisés Ville:
the pet murderers have fallen. They had killed over fifty dogs and cats
by poisoning."

When I arrive in Palacios, searching for the history of the Waisman
family's murder, I encounter a town of a meager six hundred residents,
a sleepy village. On the trip from Moisés Ville, after passing through
a cemetery of rusty cars along the roadside, I had listened to the cab
driver complaining that this road, the same one that Italian farmers had
marked out for the first Podoliers so they wouldn't lose their way, now
needs to be paved: the accidents come one after the other and cars get

flipped. Now in the tiny town of Palacios, I find it hard to mentally recreate a quadruple murder like the one in 1897: there is such silence here, such an aroma of flowers.

Eva Guelbert de Rosenthal, the director of the Moisés Ville Museum, acts as my guide. She takes it upon herself to speak with Berenstein, the last Jewish man in town, only to discover that he is ill, bedridden. Instead she is received by his wife, who gives her the keys to both the cemetery and the synagogue. And so I get the full tour of Palacios during my visit.

We visit the temple, a building where wrought-iron Stars of David blend in with the landscape of ranches, where the doors creak when they open, and the light shakes up the dust. Inside, everything is frozen in place. I don't know when the last gathering was held here, but a book still lies open on the altar: it is written in Hebrew and Russian, and the foot of the page indicates that it was printed in Vilnius, Lithuania, in 1883.

A few meters farther on, the famous Palacios train station where the pioneers first settled is today a home occupied by three families. It's hard to believe that, after the economic boom and decline, the station should once again serve as a refuge for the needy. After passing through a few hanging clotheslines, I find myself on the platform, where grass sprouts up between the flagstones. A clock has been left stopped at just past four thirty, and a poster urges: "BE HUMANE TOWARD ANIMALS." Farther ahead, the station sign can just be glimpsed among the vegetation.

However, there is some movement across from the platform: inside an enormous metal shed, a machine is cranking, and a truck idles. Men go in and out, and one dressed in work clothes comes out to meet me. His name is Lucas Bussi, and he invites me into the shed, where a formidable mound of seeds is rising toward the roof, fed by the machine as it spits them out with great force. Bussi leads me to a cramped office where we yell back and forth over the noise of the machine. He explains that I'm in a factory for animal feed and the work here never stops. And then he surprises me by explaining that he himself is the community vice-president and a socialist loyal to the provincial governor, Hermes Binner—another descendant of colonists, born in Rafaela.

"We want to reforge the town," he says enthusiastically. "And draw in people to open a new source of employment, because there's no work: only the commune and the grain factory. But there was once even a hotel! There used to be cattle auctions and people would come from all over."

He, however, never saw it: he admits that he was told these things by his father-in-law, though he conjures them up like a golden age of his own. When we go back outside, before sending me off, Bussi greets another man who approaches on horseback. He is a long-lived gaucho with a snowy mane of hair. At a question from me, Bussi and the gaucho argue about the Podolier pioneers. This wasn't the shed where they took shelter, but one that stood some meters ahead and no longer exists, the old man says. This was the one, there's no doubt, gripes Bussi. No, it wasn't. Yes, it was.

"It was somewhere else; that's what my grandfather told me. This current shed they made in the 1920s . . . If I can remember when trains would come from the Chaco and unload here," pronounces the ancient gaucho, taking the matter as settled. It's no wonder, with his eighty-five years.

"And did your grandfather ever tell you anything about the murders?" I ask him.

"Ah, those were the early days," he says. "First the gringos came. And there were brutes among the gauchos, men who lived by raiding, riding on horseback and stealing . . . But gauchos aren't like that any longer. None of that kind are left, if there are even any gauchos! Before, there used to be men like Mate Cosido, Gauchito Gil, Vairoletto. They'd go out raiding and fighting against tyranny."

"And who was there around here?" picks up Bussi.

"There was one here called Francisco Ramírez," the other recalls after thinking for a while. But as for the case of the Waisman family, nothing. Not even after I tell him about it. On the other hand, he says: "There are lots of stories about the Jews. Look, here's a joke. The priest and the rabbi here were always going at it. If the priest bought something, the rabbi would too. If the rabbi bought something, so did the priest. The priest built a house, the rabbi built one just like it. The priest planted some trees, the rabbi did the same. Then the priest had an idea and said, 'He won't be able to copy this one!' And he bought himself a car and had it blessed. The next day the rabbi showed up with ten paisanos and a new car. The rabbi took hold of it, went, blessed it . . . and cut off the tailpipe!"

Unlike the murderers of that Lefebre family of French colonists, who were ultimately captured, the Waisman family's executioners had better luck: not even the memory of their name remains. With their countenance forever masked, we can also consider the possibility that they weren't actually gauchos, but Europeans: colonists unfaithful to their mission of sowing the land, who, instead, sowed terror. Over the phone, Etti Waisman, Joseph Waisman's great-granddaughter, suggests as much:

"My aunt Jaike told me they were Italians, who'd killed the family in a robbery."

For her, the tale of her ancestors' murder is distant, as though lost in time, and it could make little difference now if the executioners were Italians, Indian rangers, or gaucho bandits. But the history she was told said "Italians" and not a word more.

Etti's grandfather, Isaac Waisman (one of the brothers of Marcos, the father of long-lived Juana), was a one-year-old baby at the time his family was massacred. He survived by pure chance because, so they say, he remained hidden under the bed during the action. His granddaughter Etti still has warm memories of this grandfather and felt moved when, on a visit to Moisés Ville—after living in Israel for forty-eight years— she discovered his initials, "IW," painted in his old house.

"The family's murder was a story we knew, but it never pierced us too deeply," she now explains over the phone from her house in Beersheba, in southern Israel, where she immigrated as a girl. And, almost as if she'd heard Juana Waisman talking about her own father, she adds: "My grandfather Isaac was a very strong person and carried on."

Isaac Waisman left the matter in the past to such a great extent that my grandmother Mañe, who met him in Santiago del Estero, never knew of his tragedy.

"He was a popular man that one, but with character!" she accurately recalls one Sunday midday as we have lunch, a fish surrounded by potatoes, onions, carrots, and sweet potatoes.

Like him, she lived for several years in La Banda, a minute away from the provincial capital. My grandmother's father, Menajem Mendel Perelmuter—a miller from the Russian shtetl of Łanowce who once here became a furniture seller—reached Argentina in 1924 and headed straight for Santiago del Estero Province, where some of his children and friends had already settled. At the height of summer, poor Mendel believed he was in Africa: he quickly cut off his beard and put his coats away, and he found some reassurance by reading the newspaper *Di Ydische Zaitung.* My grandmother started her own family there. But in 1970, once her children were studying in Buenos Aires, she and her husband (Moisés, the son of Mijl Hacohen Sinay) decided to leave and settle in Buenos Aires as well.

Somehow, despite not being close to any colony or university, the suburb of La Banda—which today is part of the city of Santiago del Estero—had become home to a small Jewish community, and Isaac Waisman had made his way there as well. He'd been forced to pick up and move after a treacherous blow, when he discovered that his partner in Santiago del Estero, a butcher, was swindling him: Isaac was supplying the man with meat from Moisés Ville, and he was underpaying him. But the ruse didn't last long. When Waisman caught on, he decided to open his own butcher shop in that same area and moved.

"There were two groups of Jews, as always, and he was in the one opposing ours," my grandmother continues now, as though ignited. "Though I can't remember what we disagreed about now . . . must have been things about the place, the town."

"What kinds of things, grandmother?"

"Questions . . . There are always questions for fighting: seeing who was more Jewish, who was more Zionist, those things . . ."

"But he was popular all the same?"

"Yes, popular . . . but because of his character."

"And did you ever go to his butcher shop?"

"I've never eaten much meat, but I might have gone once. What I remember is that he was a perfect butcher, with his blood-stained smock and all . . . That's how he was, and popular, that Waisman."

There was no way: my grandmother wasn't going to tell me anything related to the crime. And yet, I think as I write, that may have been one of the strategies Isaac Waisman adopted to shield himself from a painful and inexplicable past.

Evidently, those fugitives from Moisés Ville have been forgotten and only their offenses remain. However, one did pass into history thanks to a writer with a long memory who condemned him for posterity. That writer was David Goldman. In his book *Di iuden in Argentine* (The Jews in Argentina), published in 1914 and notably the first work about the local Jewish community, he wrote:

> Especially feared was that famous bandit of the time, Coria, or, as he was often called, '*Coria mit di matikes*' (Coria with the mattocks). He was big boned, naturally strong. His presence alone instilled fear in all. He had twelve children, all of them murderers. And wherever a tragedy might strike it was known that they had been involved.

The relationship between this bandit and the killings at Moisés Ville is clear: Goldman mentions him immediately after reviewing a few cases. Later, I learn of another Coria, Federico by name, who on February 19, 1902—five years after the killing of the Waisman family—was sentenced by the High Court of Santa Fe Province "to a penalty of imprisonment for an unspecified term" for having caused the death of one Remigio Zárate. That, nothing more, is what appears in a brief, two-page dossier held at the General Archive of Santa Fe Province, where I go in search of any clue about the crimes of Moisés Ville and find, also, the file on the killing of the Lefebre family.

And there is little time to waste at the archive, which only opens its doors in the mornings. On my first visit I discover a bare, dark, silent place. A colonial mansion with high ceilings and vast rooms that was one inhabited by the brigadier-general Estanislao López—a caudillo who governed the province for twenty years—and today houses, on a rooftop over one of its stairways, a nest of screeching bats.

"We can't eradicate them with anything; the exterminator doesn't have the guts to get into it," one of the employees tells me on my first day. I imagine there are at least a hundred of the creatures on the other side of the wood beams of the roof. Their screeches, amplified in their masses, are magnificent even at eight in the morning.

For a few days I immerse myself in the little histories, captured on century-old paper, which form the vast history of the province. Each morning, a silent employee leaves me with several stout tomes in worn leather covers: he brings them to me on a little supermarket shopping cart and lays them out on a sturdy table. Then he leaves, not saying a word.

In the archive there are more than a thousand linear meters of documents and books, which give off a sweet intoxicating scent of damp and history. Specters dance on each of the pages I turn. I read records about the construction of a train station in Moisés Ville—a different one from that of Palacios—and discover complaints from French, English, Spanish, and Italian consuls about the maltreatment and vulnerability their subjects experienced. I study judicial records of noteworthy crimes and commercial reports on the farmers' lives.

Otherwise, Santa Fe is a quiet city where the days pass languidly, a place absorbed in administration and bureaucracy and beset by various pests: flies, cockroaches, mosquitos, offices, and signatures. Bats.

But of the murders of Moisés Ville, nothing. It seems like a curse. The judicial records from the General Archive of the Province pause in 1888, just a year before the Podolier pioneers' arrival and the first murder—that of David Lander. From there onward, and until 1915, it would seem that chance prevails: very few records are kept. The trails I'm pursuing aren't at the archive of the judiciary in Rosario either, nor at the Julio Marc Museum, in the same city, where there are different card files for jurisdictions other than the department of San Cristóbal, where Moisés Ville is situated.

My last hope is in the Courts General Archive: the very memory of the provincial judiciary, also in the capital city. There, I initiate the process, so famliar to a crime reporter, of leaving a note and giving in to the power of paperwork—indeed, opposite the courts' reception desk rises a long row of typewriters for drafting memos upon memos. One favor, at least, is granted to me: the director of the General Archive receives me in his office, a small chamber brimming with papers and folders, where damp has peeled away part of one wall and the provincial flag hangs fading in a corner.

After talking for a few minutes, I understand that the bureaucracy is implacable.

The penal jurisdiction destroys files on infractions every three years; on violations, every five; on investigations, every fifteen; and ones with sentences, every twenty; before shredding them all to a pulp, it dispatches edicts to various institutions, notifying them and inviting them to come look for papers that might have some importance. The files in this archive are cataloged according to the year they entered the record rather than the year the case began, so that even if a document for the Waisman family still existed, it might not have been registered in 1897 but whichever year it happened to be added to the archive. As if you would need to belong to a club of initiates to have access to history. The fight against oblivion at this Courts General Archive is proceeding through the digitization of lists, indices, and dossiers, as well as the preservation of documents dated from 1993 onward. On the other hand, the files leading up until 1915 have been turned over to the General Archive of the Province. After that, the question as to the whereabouts (or rather, existence) of those subsequent to 1888 but prior to 1915 is a mystery that can find its answer, though only sometimes, in Estanislao López's mansion. I leave crestfallen, struck by the apathy of a mindless state.

The file on the quadruple killing of the Waisman family—just like those on every last one of the cases I'm writing about here—seems to have been destroyed without leaving a trace.

"The problem is always space," the historian Pascualina Di Biasio, director of the General Archive of the Province, says in resignation, another time in Estanislao López's mansion.

Surrounded by portraits of the dignitaries of the province, she explains to me that the documents require a building infrastructure that is rarely considered on the agenda.

"Next to priorities and emergencies, public policies don't always conform with our needs, and so the documentation keeps getting scattered among the ministries," she says. "In Argentina, it seems that the fever for the new generates a certain disdain for the old."

Faced with this absence of files and documents, almost like another kind of massacre, I can feel only outrage and amazement.

It is the same feeling shared by Gabriel Braunstein, another of the murdered Joseph Waisman's great-grandchildren, when he stands before his ancestors' grave. Gabriel, a doctor in nuclear physics who went through the prestigious Balseiro Institute in Bariloche and has been living and working in the United States for more than thirty years, is the one who knows the most about that unfortunate family. With a passion for genealogy and a scientist's attention to detail, he has undertaken a long project in search of his origins, one he began years ago and still has not concluded, and during which he hasn't hesitated to travel through Eastern Europe or interview any relative he's been able to find. In doing so, Gabriel discovered that one of his great-grandfathers was Abraham Braunstein, the Podolier who accompanied my great-great-grandfather Mordejai Reuben on his unlucky journey to Paris, a man he learned about through reading the book *Génesis de Moisés Ville* by Noé Cociovich. And also that this colonist's youngest son, Jaime Braunstein, had inscribed his name in Moisés Ville's dark history during the 1920s when he killed a commissioner who'd become entangled with his wife, a criollo woman named Carmen Gorriz. In 1934, once out of prison—where his crime would have earned him the respect of the other offenders—Jaime committed suicide, perhaps thinking about her.

"When I stand in front of that grave, I feel a mixture of outrage and amazement," Gabriel tells me in an email.

Outrage because they were killed, and no one ever found out who did it (or they never wanted to find out). And amazement because it's almost a miracle that I should be standing here, as well as the fact that the children carried on in spite of the tragedy and led normal lives.

He knows better than anyone the Waismans' origins and the exact structure of their family: on the dark night of July 28, 1897, inside the house were found Joseph and Gitl, the father and mother, both murdered; Perl, an eight-year-old girl, murdered; Baruj, a twenty-two-day-old baby, murdered; Wolf (or Adolfo), a three-year-old boy who must have escaped into the underbrush; Isaac, one day Etti Waisman's grandfather but a one-year-old baby at the time, who was left under the bed or a blanket and survived; and Raquel, a girl of six or seven, who was injured but, unconscious or pretending to be, was ultimately saved and became Gabriel Braunstein's own great-grandmother. Away from the scene, staying at their grandfather Froim Zalmen's house in Moisés Ville, the two oldest brothers slept, ready to attend class the next day. They were Marcos (or Meyer), age eight, Juana Waisman's father; and Bernardo (or Bani), age ten.

"Raquel, who was six or seven at the time she was injured in the massacre, became a cheerful woman, with lots of personality and character," I'm told later on by Nelly Menis, Gabriel Braunstein's mother, as we're getting coffee on the way back from the AMIA, where she works as a volunteer in the library. "Raquel was my *bubbe*, she was big and tall like her brothers, and she used to make empanadas and barbecue for everyone on her birthday, every May 25."

Nelly, Gabriel Braunstein's mother, introduces herself as "a not-so-old octogenarian" and gladly invites me into a few of her memories, beginning with the best ones: vacations at her grandmother's house; her time working as a rural schoolteacher in Virginia, seventeen kilometers from Moisés Ville; her moonlit wedding night with the melody of "La cumparsita" playing in the background; and her second life in Buenos Aires, now shared with an accountant husband.

And she tells me with great affection about that grandmother named Raquel, who must have had a guardian angel inside the house of the tragedy but lost it at age forty-four when, coming to bring a sick daughter to Buenos Aires, she ended up catching a tough winter flu that would lead her to the grave. It was the first time that Nelly had confronted death. And that traumatic experience is the one she's able to talk about, much more than that quadruple murder, which, as in the cases of Juana Waisman and Etti Nachum, seems to have been left swiftly in the past thanks to her grandmother's will. Like the other survivors of the massacre, the girl Raquel had to look forward as well: she married at fourteen and had six daughters.

"Many of the things I've learned in my life, and some I thankfully never needed, she taught me," continues Nelly, her granddaughter. "For example, how to sweep in the edges and corners, because that's where you can tell if a house is clean or dirty; or how to wash the dishes thoroughly."

At a certain moment, after she finishes her coffee, a detail comes to her mind, barely a detail, which touches me and prevents me from focusing on what she says afterward:

"Even today, I can remember my bubbe's plump arm when she'd hug me, and I also remember how she had a cut on the fold of her neck, which she'd been given during the murders."

If that cut had been deeper, there would have been five victims—and the long grave in the cemetery would be longer still. Instead, the young Raquel survived. And life went on.

The scene that followed the massacre, which was no less bloody, is captured by David Goldman, son of the pioneers' rabbi, in *Di iuden in Argentine*. He puts it like this: "The next day, when they opened the door to the shop, they found the whole family slaughtered. A girl was sobbing, distraught, at her mother's breast: 'Wake up, Mamá, I'm hungry!' And they could not break her away."

8

Legacies and Sentences

In 1994, while the embers of the AMIA attack were still smoldering, Professor Ester Szwarc—who many years later would become the academic director of the IWO—assembled a team of students and friends to climb up and rescue books from the institute, which had occupied the community building's fourth floor. A few pages were still visible among the debris and in damaged areas that had not fully collapsed. In the early morning hours of Friday, July 23, five days after the explosion, the professor—slender and fair, at once delicate and agile, crowned with a jet-black bob—began the task: along with her group, she scaled up to the third level with a ladder, braced herself on a ledge, and jumped lightly to enter the fourth floor, a scene of ruins, crossing a window frame to gain entry.

Much of what I've been able to discover about the crimes of Moisés Ville thus far has emerged from a few of the books that, despite having been thrown through the air by the bomb, are now stored on the IWO's shelves as though living a second life. Some alchemy seemed to have blessed these editions: though fifty or even a hundred years had passed since their publication, they made it through the explosion intact.

Over the course of several days, Professor Ester Szwarc worked with precise organization: a group of six, ten, fifteen, or twenty would climb up to the floor the institute had occupied in the destroyed building and gather all they could from among the debris. Then, via a chain of hands extending for 120 meters, the material would be sent down to the street, where it would be collected in dump trucks that were later unloaded into an empty shop space on the corner of Scalabrini Ortiz and Corrientes provided by the father of a student. If they were short on people, they would organize themselves into two chains: the same ones who started at the top would finish on the ground floor, level with the rubble and stone.

On August 18, 1994, one month after the attack, an enormous demonstration assembled at the AMIA and marched to Tribunales, the court building. Once the people had left, Professor Szwarc set foot inside the museum hall, which hadn't entirely collapsed, and initiated the rescue of the paintings of Maurycy Minkowski, whose classic images of shtetl life lay exposed to the elements, and the musical instruments of Jevel Katz (a mandolin was salvaged when someone had the idea of improvising a fishing pole to snag it and rescue it from among the twisted irons). Until they succeeded in extracting Minkowski's paintings, Ester would climb up to a beam every night and throw down a blue tarp to protect them from the wind and rain.

"*Der Viderkol* is not turning up," I'm told, meanwhile, by Ricardo Zavadivker, the book detective I had hired.

The periodical my great-grandfather wrote in 1898, which today could shed light on this investigation into the murders, will not show itself. The institutions have no clues, nor does the sphere of collectors. The detective consoles me, at the same downtown bar where we first met, with a different item: a booklet from the play *Di kinder fun der "Pampa"* (די קינדער פון דער פּאַמפּאַ /The children of the Pampas), by Mordejai Alpersohn, which features a young character, a colonist named Beni, who has a similar love for literature and journalism. I end up buying it from him because I admire Alpersohn, the first great chronicler of Jewish agricultural colonization. But my thoughts are with *Der Viderkol*.

Zavadivker began tracking down books in 1968 as a young musicology student. Texts dedicated to music history brought up other texts, other questions, and at some point, the bibliophilia seemed to overcome the music: for several years, the detective ran a used bookstore, "Al pie

de la letra," which he founded along with his wife in a downtown Buenos Aires gallery. Eventually, Zavadivker became a supplier for other
booksellers; following the trails of lost texts was his specialty. And so, I
tell him to keep going after *Der Viderkol* and not give up the hope that
I, gradually, am losing.

The mechanical shovels that were needed to clear the crater from the
AMIA terrorist attack collected enormous piles of rubble, which were
then transferred in truckloads to Ciudad Universitaria and deposited in
the open air, creating more than five hundred mounds over a span of
several kilometers. It was only on September 7 (or nearly two months
after the attack) that Professor Szwarc received permission from a judge
to enter and search for more books among the rubble in Ciudad Universitaria. The work there was much harder, not only because the material
had been exposed to the elements and there was more space to cover (so
much so that Ester would wear a green helmet so she would be recogniz-
able from a distance), but also because vagrants had already been picking
through it to find paper for their winter fires.

Everything was jumbled together in those mounds, and the only way
to tell which section the remnants belonged to was through the most
mundane objects: a tile, a desk, or a door could orient their search among
the debris. In this way they turned up an old typewriter smashed to
pieces, a vinyl record that came back to life on the turntable, and all
manner of printed works, including some from the sixteenth and eigh-
teenth centuries and others torn, twisted, or water damaged. Many, with
no lucky solution, had to be thrown in the trash.

The collected items were cleaned and dried page by page. The work
was done—with the help of conservators from the National Library and
the United States—in the rear section of the AMIA building, which
hadn't been affected by the bomb. There, Ester and her team hung damp
pages from lines and dried out books using sacks of quicklime, which
absorbed the ambient moisture, as well as hair dryers, paintbrushes, and
cotton cloth. The volunteers worked for five months, with face masks
and gloves. The majority were young, and, altogether, they numbered
more than eight hundred.

Of the 100,000 volumes that had been in the library, some 60,000 were rescued, in addition to 32,000 newspapers and magazines, 9,000 photographs, 120 paintings, 17 musical instruments, over 2,000 musical albums, 38 sculptures, and 700 theater and film posters.

Professor Szwarc, who meets me at the institute several times to tell me about the fate of Yiddish in Argentina, speaks in a flow of serene and steady words, with a certain didactic gentleness. Ester was not in the AMIA at 9:53 a.m. on that fatal Monday because she'd been delayed, but she had been going to the institute early for some days before, putting together two music festivals and working on a reorganization project to separate books that were not in demand. The institute was starting to outgrow its space: dying people left their books behind, and their descendants would donate them. With each consignment came several common works, duplicated a thousand times: the books of a generation.

Now Ester falls silent. In critical moments someone will naturally arise to take the reins: when the attack occurred, she was teaching classes to several students and, without thinking about it too much, called on them for assistance in a salvage effort that she ended up leading.

"It seemed like the IWO was completely lost," she says. "But the rescue we carried out shows that we can never throw up our hands."

In the midst of the work, against a backdrop of death and anguish, the sense behind the actions often seemed to vanish. Why to rescue it and whom to rescue it for were two uncomfortable questions that troubled their weary and defeated spirits. But Professor Szwarc was conscious that no one could be master of knowledge, that we are scarcely more than its custodians for a time—the span of our lives—and that its legacy is a moral obligation. "Transmission" was the key word. "Future" was another. There is a concept in Yiddish that refers to that chain of generations: *di goldene keit*, the golden chain.

"When does a person cease to be remembered?" Ester asks. And she explains: "When the last person to remember them is gone as well. But that person had a life, had relationships, did something, existed. Within the collective Jewish imagination, when one generation no longer leaves a memory of its names, it goes on to form part of a chain. I am the product of all before, where each link has left something for the next. As no one can be the master of truth, I must pass on the greatest amount of information possible, all I've received and more, and the one who receives it will decide what position to adopt."

To investigate a series of crimes that occurred more than a hundred years ago is also to ask oneself about this transmission and, therefore, about the past and the future. In that sense, there may be something in common between the task of rescuing books after a terrorist attack and that of exhuming the history of some John Doe whose name has faded from his grave.

I understand now: even I am the product of this long, tragic, rough, heroic history. And this is the point at which I find a mirror in the figure of my great-grandfather Mijl Hacohen Sinay, who was there at the beginning of our family's life in Argentina and recorded (and passed down) the crimes of Moisés Ville, crimes of colonization and the cultural clash implicitly carried with it. "It was not without victims that Jewish colonization in the Argentine Republic began," declares the Spanish summary accompanying the original Yiddish text. The murders bear upon my history as well: the responsibility of redeeming the dead, of bringing them up from their eroding gravestones, is now mine.

But just as there is continuity, there is also something that causes a fracture.

Because at the same time that the crimes of Moisés Ville surface through the pages Mijl Hacohen Sinay wrote, a question also echoes as to the fate of the Yiddish language between the publication of that original text in 1947 and that of these present pages. To take up the issue of the linguistic distance that separates me from my great-grandfather (and distances me from the crimes of Moisés Ville) is also a way to consider a language that today has more history, literature, and academic prestige than it has speakers, a fact Eliahu Toker points out in *El ídish es también Latinoamérica*.

It is no accident that this should be so: the Holocaust, assimilation, the state of Israel's linguistic politics, and even the AMIA attack have all played a part.

Even in the nineteenth century, some Jews were already referring to Yiddish in a derogatory way as *zhargon*, that is, slang: the slang of the rabble. And they preferred to speak German, Polish, Russian, or French over Yiddish. The linguistic debates went on for over fifty years, well into the twentieth century, concealing—though not very well—certain clearly defined ideological positions. Hebraists wanted a new language for a new Jewish people and, at the same time, an old language for an old promised land; Yiddishists held integrationist positions in major world cities, close to those of socialism. There are nuances, of course.

But Hebrew prevailed. And politics in the brand-new Jewish state held few scruples toward Yiddish, as it was often associated with the diaspora and the Holocaust, with exile and death. Instead, Israel adopted Hebrew and Arabic as its official languages and English as a secondary language.

"The glory of Yiddish began to wane with the emergence of the state of Israel. I said as much quite plainly at a convention in Jerusalem," asserts the great veteran actor Max Berliner.

Despite his camouflage (a red scarf concealing his face and a bucket hat that still has a touch of summertime in July) I can recognize him from a distance: his sprightly walk is unmistakable. Berliner, one of Judeo-Argentine culture's prodigal sons, was born in 1919 in Warsaw under the name of Mordcha (or Mordje) and arrived with his family three years later in Buenos Aires, where today he proclaims himself "the last Yiddishist."

Right now he isn't wrapping himself up against the cold but the fame: some time ago, the old actor stumbled into the fleeting glory of a TV commercial promoting the virtues of an osteoarthritis medication. "For a certain stage in your life and joints, Reumosán . . . it's what you want!" he announced in the ad, the little medicine box in hand, before being shown running in the Palermo Woods park and, with splendid vitality, performing all manner of exercises.

"Now people know me better from that ad than eighty-five years of theater," he tells me in wonder.

Then his eyes turn back to the memory of 1982, when he traveled to participate in an international theater convention at the Hebrew

University of Jerusalem, and he still grows irritated at the memory of a man who asked him which language he would be delivering his lecture in. "What do you mean, what language?" he responded. "I'll speak in Yiddish or Spanish." "That will not work," the other said. "You need to speak in Hebrew or English." When the day arrived, Berliner skipped past the translator they'd imposed on him and made so bold as to ask the crowd if they could understand him: "*Ir farshteyt yidish?*"

"What do you want me to say!" he says with emotion now. "The hall exploded in a round of applause that shook me. I agree with having Hebrew as the language of Israel, I never say it shouldn't be, but Yiddish can't just be eliminated at the stroke of a pen."

Even so, something of the language remains. On a September night in 2006, four hundred people assembled at the National Library to sing the verses of the "Partizaner-lid," the Partisan Song, composed by the young Hirsch Glick after the first sabotage of the Nazis in the Vilna Ghetto. In the new century, those verses were still being sung with emotion, conviction, and pride in the context of this gathering, Yiddish Buenos Aires.

"Listening to that song was a great moment, a hugely important symbolic milestone in Judeo-Argentine history," the psychoanalyst Perla Sneh, who organized the event, says emotionally a few years later. She is in charge of the specialization in Judaic and Judeo-American studies at the Universidad Nacional de Tres de Febrero's Master of Cultural Diversity program.

Clearly, for her, singing those verses did not come without a cost. Her father, the well-known Simja Sneh, had been born in 1908 in the Polish city of Puławy and in 1947 came to Argentina, where he went on to develop a vast intellectual body of work, often introducing himself as "a Yiddish writer in Spanish." Simja died past age ninety, five years after surviving the AMIA attack, which wasn't even the first time he'd escaped death: two years prior he'd left the Embassy of Israel shortly before it was destroyed in a bomb explosion, and in the 1940s he'd participated in the gruesome combat of World War II, fighting against the

Nazis alongside the Red Army, the Polish Armed Forces in exile, and the British Army's Jewish Brigade.

Like old Simja, the writers and readers of an epoch argued in order to exist, and vice versa. "To read is to write and to write is to participate; one argues with the poem, thinks with the essay, battles with the lyric," Perla writes in her article "*Ídish al sur, una rama en sombras.*" And I keep thinking about my great-grandfather's text and the IWO yearbooks, which anybody could write in provided they had something to say.

"It's very concordant with Argentine culture and life, which is made of essayists and thinkers," Perla continues now, her cigarette smoking over a sidewalk table at a bar in Palermo. "The Yiddish world had that too: activism was done with writing. And reading was something more than a pastime. It had value as praxis and as a way of asserting oneself in a culture. The declaration that Yiddish is dead gets made periodically, but it's a language that no one is obligated to speak, meaning that anyone who speaks it has a strong will to do so, and that will persists."

And it seems paradoxical that, at the meeting of Yiddish Buenos Aires, there would also have been some speakers who couldn't speak Yiddish yet who were nevertheless looking after their ancestors' legacy. One of these was Ricardo Feierstein, the author of two classic works (*Historia de los judíos argentinos* and *Vida cotidiana de los judíos argentinos*) and the son of a Polish immigrant whose native tongue he never learned. What happened was that the turnover of generations accelerated Yiddish's decline.

"What do we do with the vast majority of Jews today who aren't religious? What defines their Judaism?" he asks me one day as we talk at his house, drinking yerba mate and eating a cake from an Israeli recipe. "Yiddish went from being the language of half the Jewish population to being one possible path for identifying with Jewishness. Yiddish, just as much as Zionism, secularism, or humanism."

During Nazism, on the other hand, no efforts were spared when it came to linguicide: the destruction of the headquarters of YIVO (as IWO is known outside of Argentina) in Vilnius is one easy example. Out of the eighteen million Jews who were alive on the eve of World War II, eleven million were Yiddish speakers; of these, more than half were murdered.

"None of my four grandparents was around to tell things to me in Yiddish," says Ana Weinstein, in her office at the AMIA. An elegant and precise woman, she has partnered with Eliahu Toker on some ten volumes of historical research as well as several exhibitions. Weinstein also directs the Vaad Hakehilot, which brings together Jewish communities from around the country, and the Marc Turkow Center for Documentation and Information about Argentine Judaism, another valuable informational depository for my inquiry, which has all manner of texts, photographs, recorded and transcribed oral testimonies, bibliographic indices, videos, and materials related to the attack.

This woman, who was raised by two exiled European parents in Bolivia and earned her degree in sociology at the Hebrew University of Jerusalem, has no doubt that the Holocaust, more than any other factor, was what brought an end to the language. By contrast, she considers Israel's linguistic politics to belong to another sphere: the state's nascent identity needed to be rebellious and forceful, ready to risk everything for its new ideals.

"The break with Yiddish was drastic because that was the only way to construct an identity moving forward," she explains.

The absence of Yiddish in Argentina is related, also, to the bomb that exploded in 1994 on the site where the new AMIA building now stands, a high security tower that guards its bustling inner world behind a wall of guards, metal detectors, and bulletproof doors, and whose structure, capable of resisting further explosions and fires, required a larger percentage of concrete than any other construction site. Weinstein lived through that moment as well: she was there, she experienced the horror of that morning and became one of its few survivors.

"The building I can see from my window now is the same one I saw that day, when we came out of the darkness of the rubble onto a terrace. We managed to climb onto a rooftop, and from there we were able to get down and come out onto Calle Uriburu," she now recalls.

The shock wave from the attack had several unexpected effects: the end of Yiddish instruction in schools was one of them. The only schools that were still teaching it, the Scholem Aleijem and the I. L. Peretz, took the 1995–1996 school year as an occasion to consolidate and start over with a clean slate. That's how Moshe Korin, director of the Department of Culture at the AMIA and head of the Scholem Aleijem during the 1990s, remembers it. But in his third-floor study, two levels below Ana Weinstein's office, Korin—an elegant man in a suit and tie, whose stiff white hair is swept back with discipline—believes it is too early for tears:

"No need to say a final Kaddish for Yiddish. There are eras and there are eras. These days people have fallen back to religion and the secular institutions are in decline because they've been left, generally, devoid of content. Tomorrow, we'll see . . ."

One figure: in UNESCO's Atlas of the World's Languages in Danger, Yiddish can be found at the third degree on a scale of six (where the first degree is "safe" and the last is "extinct"). The third degree, "definitely endangered," is defined as a level at which "children no longer learn the language as a mother tongue at home." Yet, according to the Jewish Museum Berlin, around three million people around the world still speak it: this has to do with a rebirth propelled by historical researchers, the nostalgic, and the Orthodox, who speak it so as not to defile Hebrew.

Now, in an office where the phone is ringing off the hook, Abraham Lichtenbaum, the general director of the IWO Institute, asserts with some resignation that the future is in Europe. No one would have believed it half a century ago: everything was in flames and the future lay here, in America. But to him it was no accident. It wasn't the Holocaust, the state of Israel, or assimilation: instead, he says the responsibility for Yiddish's absence in Argentina falls on the leadership of the community itself.

Lichtenbaum dedicated his whole life to the language he learned at home, from the mouth of Baruj, a father who'd come from Warsaw and quickly began working for the newspaper *Di Prese* as a typographer. Now, the IWO's general director carries a hundred gigabytes of digitized books in his small laptop: there are 12,000 volumes collected over the course of three years by a Polish student, and all available to anyone who wants to read and learn. The old professor confesses that what he has left of life will be devoted to preventing Yiddish from dying out.

Because of that, and for the last decade, he's been taking his sermon through Europe and the United States: in universities around the northern hemisphere, there are more than three hundred Yiddish courses. In Vilnius, students from around the world turn up to events with professors from the United States, Latvia, France, Israel . . . and Argentina.

"The issue doesn't have to do with Yiddish, but the culture. What is the community project in Argentina? There's no project that has moved more money than Jewish education in Argentina. But what good does it do? Where is there a Jewish intellectual today? Is it all a scam? I don't know, but I'd like to debate it. And I don't have the slightest doubt that if the policies were different, we'd have more people speaking and reading Yiddish in Argentina."

In "The First Jewish Victims in Moisés Ville," Mijl Hacohen Sinay tells us that in the colony of Monigotes, a neighbor of Moisés Ville, few murders took place. The Jews did not live there long: no more than five years and they left, beset by locusts and the double murder of the Tuchman brothers, which occurred in January 1892 when two bandits entered their home with intent to steal.

"In spite of everything, they were able, in the short time they spent there, to fight against the gauchos," my great-grandfather wrote. "They managed it in such a way that the others really were afraid to approach the colony. All of this was told to me by an old colonist from Monigotes, Señor Wolfsy: when the colonists noticed a gaucho approaching, they would hide in the tall grasses, and as he was galloping past toward the colony several of them together would get him off his horse, take away his knife, and beat him with a whip. Then they would put the man back on his horse and set him loose. This happened not once but several times, and by the tenth time the gaucho had warned the others to avoid the colony. 'Those colonists are murderers from Russia!' the gauchos would shudder. For that reason, there were no gauchos in Monigotes or the surrounding area, and the inhabitants lived undisturbed, without fear and without victims."

But also, without assimilating into this new country.

In any event, that would be not the case for my great-grandfather or his siblings: with their father defeated on his mission to Paris, they had to leave Moisés Ville and plunge into the vast and strange cities of Argentina.

They carried a single piece of baggage: Yiddish culture.

9

A Journalist's Dream

Mijl Hacohen Sinay was twenty years old when he set foot in Rosario. The family had decided to leave Moisés Ville after learning that the father, Mordejai Reuben, had failed on his mission to the JCA and that the administrator Michel Cohan had no intention of granting amnesty. With his father still in Europe, Mijl found work in Rosario, at a wheat business belonging to a German Jew named Sergetty. He spent two months in that city but felt the pull of Buenos Aires—that inferno, that paradise—growing ever stronger.

And in February 1898, he arrived in the nation's capital.

If I travel through the Jewish Buenos Aires of today—a scattered city, embedded inside the great metropolis, by no means limited to the textile passageways of Once, the towers of Belgrano, or the apartments of Villa Crespo—I wonder what was left over from that other Jewish city my great-grandfather knew. Very little, most likely. Only, I would say, the synagogue on Calle Libertad—inaugurated for Rosh Hashanah on September 26, 1897—which shone when my great-grandfather saw it for the first time. It was not then the place it is today, as the building was finished in 1932, but it was, indeed, this city's first great temple. Calle Libertad was still the epicenter of Jewish life in the 1930s, when the journalist and writer Roberto Arlt toured through and captured it in one of his *aguafuertes* (etchings) entitled *Merchants of Libertad, Cerrito, and*

Talcahuano: "The three streets have transformed. They have been given a fictional life, an eastern life. Someone who has never traveled imagines Gaza or Jerusalem must be the same."

In 1898, in a city that had incorporated the towns of Belgrano and Flores as neighborhoods just eleven years before, the Jewish quarter—the seed of what Arlt would later see—was already clearly delineated from Calle Libertad to Callao and from Tucumán to Cuyo (present-day Sarmiento). There, *cuenteniks*—street peddlers who went door to door, offering their wares and charging on credit—mixed together with the proletariats of the Yiddisher Arbeter Farain (or Jewish Workers Society); readers from the Russian Library mixed with the Orthodox (not so different from the Lubavitchers of today); secondhand traders from the bazaars mixed with the shadowy figures better known as *tmeiim*, or impure, who shamelessly made their money by trafficking women. Although this latter trade was well known throughout the world and would grow larger still with the Zwi Migdal—a Polish trafficking ring that involved 459 criminals and would not be brought down until 1930—some of its members had already fallen into disgrace: in that same year of 1898, the capital city's police published a Gallery of Suspects with some two hundred traffickers, recorded in the accelerating process of population surveillance (dactyloscopy, photography, anthropometry), which was also being directed at thieves, anarchists, murderers, and anyone else who, among the shapeless masses, bore the face of social ills.

They appeared head on and in profile, along with the indicated profession of pimps, in large pristine photographs that still speak volumes today: there was Herman Feytel, born in Egypt, stout and slightly brutish; Leon Mund, from Romania, with one glass eye; Anolfo Schuarst, too wimpy for the profession; Felipe Rosemberg, Austrian, with unmanageable hair; Abraham Zecler, with a clear and threatening stare; Isaac Miltz, from Paris, big and mean as an angry bear; and the only woman in the gallery, Risfka Racien, from Warsaw, a madam with a bitter glare. All had come under circumstances shrouded in darkness and walked the streets of Libertad, Cerrito, and Talcahuano; and they would likely be there again once the police set them loose. Another, one Jacobo Jacovich, earned his twelve lines in the newspaper *La Prensa* on Christmas Day of that year, 1898, when he beat and kicked one of the women he was trafficking in a tenement on Libertad and Lavalle.

The men from the Congregación Israelita de la República Argentina also walked those streets, even rubbing shoulders with the people who looked down on them, like Doctor Glow—the protagonist of the novel *La bolsa*, published by Julián Martel in 1891 as a serial in *La Nación*. In a country where one-quarter of the population was immigrant, resentment arose among the most-long-established. "The foreigner who comes to our land, naturalized or not, damned if it matters to him if we are well or badly governed," thought Glow, speaking of a dull and slow invasion, in which a character called Baron de Mackser appeared as a secret envoy for Rothschild and fueled the crash of the Argentine economy in 1890.

The Jews were the most foreign among the foreigners.

In the Jewish quarter there were refugees newly arrived from the colonies as well. Over the course of 1897—the year of the revolt in Moisés Ville and my great-great-grandfather Rabbi Mordejai Reuben Hacohen Sinay's journey to Paris—hostility, poverty, and pessimism had wreaked havoc throughout the colonies: out of the 983 families who had settled in JCA towns, close to 200 deserted. Many of the displaced Moisesvillians lived in tenements, and others slept on benches in Plaza Lavalle—a run-down plaza, which did not yet have the Teatro Colón or the Palacio de Tribunales—along with the beggars, in a city advancing in its Belle Époque glory without pausing to pick up those who were left along the way.

As I enter these streets of history, I wonder what I would do in that modern city of plazas and promenades. What would I do if I could travel in time and arrive in Buenos Aires exactly in the month of February 1898, like Mijl? I would likely walk down the dazzling new Avenida de Mayo with its art nouveau hotels, its restaurants and cafés, and would understand that the city I live in took the first step toward what it is today when several old buildings came down to give way to that rejuvenating avenue. It was a transformation not only of Buenos Aires but the whole world, the end of a century that had brought the expansion of the telephone, the automobile, the cinema, the X-ray, the gramophone, synthetic fiber, and a thousand other inventions.

At the end of Avenida de Mayo I might stop to watch the construction work at the magnificent Palacio del Congreso and then try on a suit from Gath & Chaves at 569 San Martín or a handsome silk-lined overcoat at Al Palacio de Cristal, the tailor shop on Calle Victoria (present-day Hipólito Yrigoyen), but I'd leave it, having no ship or spyglass to match. On my way out I'd take care not to be run down by a tram or knocked over by a speeding *biciclista* or even struck by the whip of a distracted coachman. And I'd watch my step so as not to fall into the massive trench that used to cleave that city where everything was being built up.

I'd have coffee at the famous Cassoulet at 710 Calle Suipacha, confirming that the members of the underworld who used to gather there had a little hidden door to escape out the back, onto Viamonte, in case of a possible raid. And I'd try to guess if one of the scarred faces of the men drinking around me could belong to the famous criminal "Rata Carcelera," or if one of the prostitutes waiting corseted in the doorway could be the famous "Parda Refucilo" or "Gringa Catalina." I'd go to the opera to see Amelia Pasi de Ferrari's Italian company do their renditions of *I Medici* by Leoncavallo and *La Dolores* by Breton. Or maybe I'd prefer *Chateau Margaux*, the zarzuela by Manuel Fernández Caballero. Perhaps I'd cross paths with the laborers carrying statues of Wagner and Verdi that would decorate the Teatro Argentino on Calle de la Piedad (today Bartolomé Mitre): would they be anarchists or socialists?

Important: I'd try not to get in the way of Mariano Castilla, a typographer who, on the warm night of March 15 in the same year, fought against eighteen police officers on his own after burying a knife in the belly of his wife's suitor. That block on Cangallo (present day Juan D. Perón), between Artes (today Carlos Pellegrini) and Cerrito, was a dark corner in those days: Avenida 9 de Julio did not yet exist.

And I'd like to get to know the park in Palermo, with its Los Abetos and Las Palmeras avenues and its thousand carriages carrying young men with walking sticks and cigars and young ladies with wide necklines and long gloves. But I wouldn't like to stumble into the muddy bog of Calle Gascón, between Costa Rica and Canning (present-day Scalabrini Ortiz), where pavement was still unknown.

Looking through the pages of the newspapers (and not the front covers, which were devoted to the classifieds in that era), I could follow the local and international events: an imminent war between the United States and Spain, a very probable war between Argentina and Chile, the upcoming Exposition Universelle in Paris being planned for 1900, the Captain Alfred Dreyfus affair—a treason scandal that stripped the first Jewish man to reach the French General Staff of his badges and provoked a wave of antisemitism. I'd try to join the students from the Facultad de Derecho who sent a letter on April 3 to salute the writer Émile Zola for his righteous and civic-minded involvement in said affair. Of course, I could read only a few of the 143 periodicals that, between ones for general information, specific communities, and political entities, were being published in that Buenos Aires.

I'd cross paths with a few of the 4,824 immigrants who, seeking the social mobility that was on everyone's lips, would arrive during that month of February 1898 (2,919 of them Italian, 1,284 Spanish, 166 French, 137 Turkish, 84 Russian, 47 Austrian, 46 German, 42 English, 35 Portuguese, 23 Swiss, 15 Belgian, 13 Morrocan, 5 North American, 4 Danish, 3 Swedish, and 1 Dutch), and if they said it felt like they were in Babel, I'd understand, for more than half of Buenos Aires's 700,000 inhabitants in 1898 were foreign nationals.

> I walked alone down the street, before noon, with measured steps, unhurried, not heading toward any place in particular, thinking about my destiny and possibly nothing else . . . And in this way, on a street crowding with pedestrians, laborers, tradesmen, everything seemed to me at once beautiful and novel. Staring at the decorated shop windows and the trams that went by carrying unknown faces, I was astonished by the loneliness and the life that drew near me, bringing so much worry in that moment as I had no work, when I suddenly saw a newspaper boy run by with a parcel of papers under his arm. Unconsciously I set my eyes on him as with an unexpected leap he rose onto

the platform of the tram, and I heard his hoarse and melodious voice: '*La Prensa! La Nación!*' I stood rooted to the spot. And like a bolt of lightning an idea shot through me.

For Mijl Hacohen Sinay, his destiny, which was to be a journalist and not a cement mixer or a carpenter (trades he'd looked for vacancies in and found none), arrived in that moment with the newspaper boy, for the idea that had shot through him was to create a periodical for the Jews in Argentina: the first one.

Only at Gedalia Schizler's shop, which sold religious articles, was it possible find an imported copy of the *Yiddishe Gazetten* from New York or the *Yiddisher Express* from Leeds. These newspapers reached Argentina at a six-month delay and didn't come cheap: Schizler asked for no less than fifty centavos (half of a laborer's daily wages) and usually saved his copies for the human traffickers, even though he would claim himself to be a God-fearing man. "What won't somebody do for a piece of bread?" he'd excuse himself.

"Could the children of Israel be unlike the rest?" my great-grandfather would wonder not long after, in the editorial for his newspaper's first issue ("An di liebe lezer!"/אָן די ליעבע לעזער!‏ or To the dear readers!), which he named *Der Viderkol* (דער ווידער־קול/The echo).

There, on the first page, he confirmed the thoughts that had been illuminated as he stood before the tram. He wrote, in Yiddish: "Could the Jews in Argentina be unlike the other peoples of the world? Each has periodicals in its language; each can make boasts with its literature . . . and only Israel does not! So many Jews live here in Argentina, and among them are found writers, sages, sophisticated people who are no strangers to the pen, yet there is no paper in Yiddish here, however small! No sooner thought than done . . . Yes, so it will be. Mijl, you will have work now!"

As soon as the tram disappeared with its newspaper boy, my great-grandfather ran to tell the idea to his friend Jacob Shimon Liachovitzky, another child of Grodno, who had come to Argentina in 1891 with the JCA and been assigned to a colony in Entre Ríos, where he hadn't lasted long before falling to Buenos Aires.

Jacob was long and lean, with a blonde beard, mustache, and wavy locks that framed his blue eyes. He was three years Mijl's senior and was his only friend: they'd met one day when Mijl, newly arrived in Buenos Aires and looking for work, had happened to walk by the Jewish school on Calle Lavalle where Jacob taught classes. It was natural for two young men from the same soil to recognize one another as friends within that Babel. From the school on Lavalle they'd gone to the Café Nacional on 974 Corrientes—then branded as "the cathedral of tango"—where, after a short talk, Jacob offered to let the unemployed Mijl, who was living in a small hotel, stay at his "house" (a room inside a tenement, shared with his wife and their baby, and furnished with a collection of Jewish books and a treadle sewing machine that did as much to pay for their bread as the classes Jacob taught). Mijl's objections were no use.

And so, the tram now gone, Jacob was the first to find out about the idea. He considered it for a few minutes and sighed. It didn't seem proper to him, nor did he have any suspicions that in time he himself would become a serial founder of periodicals. On the contrary, he explained to Mijl that a newspaper was an extravagance for so young a community, that the moment for publishing had not yet arrived.

But Mijl was determined to do it: "The idea ignited my fantasy, awoke my soul, excited me in the night. The image of becoming the first publisher of a Jewish page had me in total rhapsody: it would not only be the first such periodical in Argentina, but in all of South America," he wrote in his autobiographical series for the magazine *Der Shpigl*. "And having made the decision not to heed my friend Liachovitzky's warnings, I rose in the morning and, after breakfast of course, set about working on my idea. As no Jewish printing house existed at that time, I decided to write out the newspaper by hand myself and have it copied by lithograph."

Finding a lithography studio in Buenos Aires was no easy thing. Several neighbors had never even heard the word, but a few children playing in the street had, and they told him how to get to 136 Cerrito, to a studio called La Teatral. There, Mijl ordered a first print run of five hundred copies (a small run, considering that the following year, according to figures from the engineer Simon Weill, the number of Jews in Argentina would reach 16,000; or a large run, bearing in mind that, according to

the 1895 national census, there were 753 Jews living in the city of Buenos Aires).

The lithographed periodical was, in a way, an engraving: with very
few resources, my great-grandfather wrote out the large pages of *Der
Viderkol* using a special pen on a silken paper, which was then traced
onto a block bathed in chemicals. This would be the printing mold.
The acid would eat away all of the blank stone's surface so that what
remained standing would become a detailed relief of Hebrew letters,
images, and advertisements. In its own way, *Der Viderkol* was a work of
art as well.

When I had only just begun this investigation, I contacted the writer
and Yiddishist Eliahu Toker; he invited me to his home in Barrio Norte
and offered me a parcel of books. That hot and cramped office was
where I saw my great-grandfather's face for the first time. His portrait
appeared in *Tsu der Geshikhte fun der Idisher Zhurnalistik in Argentine/*
צו דער געשיכטע פֿון דער אידישער זשורנאַליסטיק אין אַרגענטינע (Notes on the history of Jewish journalism in Argentina), which the journalist Pinie
Katz—founder of the newspaper *Di Prese*—published in 1929 through
the Idisher Literatn un Zhurnalistn-Fareyn in Argentine (Society of
Jewish Writers and Journalists in Argentina).

"This is your great-grandfather," Toker told me, placing his finger on
the photograph.

If that character reproduced on the paper had felt the idea of making
a newspaper shoot through him like lightning, I felt the same bolt pass
through me when I finally saw his stern face, with a steady gaze and a
twirled mustache, and his suit with a flower on the lapel. (In that photo
Mijl was no longer the man of twenty he'd been when he published
Der Viderkol, but on the same day when Eliahu Toker showed me the
portrait, I was able to force the issue using Photoshop, and I took the
image, removed his mustache, and gave him more hair. And then he
emerged: he was, at last, the young Grodner who'd dreamed of being an
Argentine journalist.)

Toker loaned me Katz's book as well as a long article by Jacob
Botoshansky transliterated in the original as, "Dos gedrukte idische

wort in Argentine"/ דאָס געדרוקטע אידישע וואָרט אין אַרגענטינע (The Jewish printed word in Argentina), published in an old phone book–sized tome that was presented by the newspaper *Di Prese* to celebrate fifty years of Jewish life in the country, in 1938. There was also a book by Shmuel Rollansky, *Dos idishe gedrukte vort un teater in Argentine*/ דאָס אידישע געדרוקטע וואָרט און טעאַטער אין אַרגענטינע (Jewish journalism, letters, and theater in Argentina), from 1941, and one more article, "Historia del periodismo judío en la Argentina" (History of Jewish journalism in Argentina), by Lázaro Schallman—the only one in Spanish!

In each of these texts, Mijl Hacohen Sinay appears as the pioneer of Jewish journalism in Argentina; it says the same thing on the single plaque that adorns his grave in La Tablada cemetery, initialed by the ICUF (the Idisher Cultur Farband, or Federation of Jewish Cultural Entities). With his humble *Der Viderkol*, Mijl was the first one to put Jewish culture on display for everyone in those streets that converged on Plaza Lavalle.

The desire to address the world was impetuous, but a need to speak out did exist as well: *Der Viderkol* was a critical weapon against the Jewish Colonization Association. The first issue was the harshest. It spoke not only in terms of enslavement but even a new inquisition. Of course, the 1897 revolt, spearheaded by the publisher's father, was the foundation. Buenos Aires was looking toward the colonies as the conflict was shifting: Moisés Ville had already been pacified by force; Buenos Aires, on the other hand, was becoming a hotbed of intrigue where Mijl was not alone: the man who ended up doing the paper's accounts was another expelled colonist, a small and haggard Podolier who had cut Mijl off on his way to the lithography studio.

"Mister Joel Rosenblit! You were living in Moisés Ville . . . What are you doing here?" Mijl greeted him, in Yiddish.

"What am I doing here . . ." said the other. "What? You didn't hear what happened in Moisés Ville? Even *La Nación* and *La Prensa* wrote about the conflict . . . Administrator Cohan, may his name be erased! He expelled me from the colony . . . and that's why I had to come to Buenos Aires."

"He evicted you, on your own?"

"No. He evicted me along with eleven others. Eviction, he evicted all of them. But he didn't force everyone to leave, only four: me, Meir Schapiro, Nete Grober, and Tzvi Zainschtejer, an elderly man, whom they put the screws to in a torture block at the San Cristóbal police station. The rest remained living in the colony," said Rosenblit, and lowered his gaze, overwhelmed. "Come with me, you can see where I live and how I spend my time now. Let's go, my wife will be pleased! It's right nearby, in a tenement."

They walked half a block, no more, to number 1200 on Calle Cuyo (today Sarmiento). There, past an entry hall, the hive appeared in all its dismal splendor: a house with two upper stories that could be accessed by a narrow stairway, where the air they breathed was unclean and the languages of mothers and children all jumbled together on a patio criss-crossed by lines of hanging laundry.

Upstairs, Rosenblit's room was damp and dirty. A crate and four kerosene tins served as table and chairs. The rest lay strewn about: cushions, blankets, dirty clothes, rags, and kitchenware. "That scene of poverty was terrible," my great-grandfather wrote in his memoirs. Mashe, Rosenblit's wife, who had once been beautiful, now seemed like one more casualty of poverty: she appeared hunched and drawn.

"It's no wonder," said Rosenblit, having noticed Mijl's impression. "Two days after we found out my wife was pregnant, that evil Cohan sent the police to evict us from the farm, and the brutes took no account of her weak state . . . They forced us out, screaming all the way, and as there was a storm outside, the bad weather did her even more harm. But if God wills it, she is going to recover."

Rosenblit's words flowed in a verbal downpour, and his eyes filled with tears as he spoke while his wife, at his side, dried her own.

"You don't know the pogrom I went through," he continued. "Every object we had in the home was destroyed. Do you want more? There was a basket with a hen and her chicks inside. What did those murderers do? They didn't spare them: they hurled the basket to the ground, with enough impact to kill the hen, and then crushed the chicks under their feet! It costs me my health to tell you everything that happened, but we can make it short. After I was forced off the farm, Administrator Cohan sent an ordinance expelling me from the colony. I was able to sell what little livestock was my property, and with that I had enough to bring us here."

Mashe served yerba mate and the men sat on the kerosene tins. When Rosenblit finished recounting everything he dried the sweat from his brow.

"Yes, yes, yes . . . That's the way it was," he said in resignation, as though wishing to convince himself. "But there are people who don't want to believe and think it's all an invented story . . ."

"And what are you going to do?" Mijl wanted to know.

"What can I do? The truth is, I don't even know what I can do. I'm so alone here, so poor . . . I feel as weary and defeated as if a vicious storm had passed me overhead. I made the rounds for several days, trying to find some work, but everywhere I went they treated me like nobody. My God!" Rosenblit took care that his wife, who'd gone out to change the yerba mate, was not listening. He didn't want to cause her more sorrows.

As he looked at her, Mijl had the thought that Rosenblit could take charge of seeking out subscribers for the newspaper that was being born, and he told him so. They could split the money down the middle.

"Ah!" the other said in excitement. "You want to put out a newspaper! Yes, yes, it will be a fine business! But where will you print it, if there is no Yiddish printing house here?"

And so Mijl told him about the lithography and the etchings, but that didn't matter to Rosenblit now. For him it was enough that a solution existed.

"It will be a grand business!" he insisted, smiling. "But what is it going to be called?"

"A name?" And at that moment my great-grandfather realized that he hadn't even considered that part. But then, almost without thinking, an unexpected voice let slip from his mouth: "The paper will be called *Der Viderkol*, The Echo."

"*Der Viderkol*? I like that name, Vi-der-kol . . ."

"I was on my way to the lithographer to negotiate a price, and after that I'm going to start writing it, by hand."

"I'll go with you!" Rosenblit said, with a smile. "I'd like to see what a lithograph is. But wait a minute, I'll tell my Mashe the news . . . this is going to make her happy!"

And they set out, not knowing that this history would end up, more than a century later, engulfed in a dense enigma.

10

The Enigma of *Der Viderkol*

If *Der Viderkol* was keeping an eye on the colonies, what did it say about the murders? Did those accounts exist within its pages? It's true that it was published while the blood was being shed, but I can't be sure: I have never seen a single copy of *Der Viderkol*.

Der Viderkol is a mystery.

It is, as well, one of the items that flew through the air in the AMIA attack. And although it was rescued, it was lost once again in the chaos that followed the collapse.

I have searched for it at the AMIA, the IWO in Buenos Aires, the ICUF, the Marshall T. Meyer Latin American Rabbinical Seminary, the Buenos Aires Jewish Museum, the National Library, the Center for the Documentation and Investigation of Leftist Culture in Argentina (CeDInCI), the Ibero-American Institute and the Jewish Museum in Berlin, the United States Library of Congress, YIVO in New York, the Harvard University library, the National Library of Israel, and the head office of the Alliance Israélite Universelle in Paris. Without success.

The book detective, Ricardo Zavadivker, couldn't track it down either. At another meeting at La Ópera café, he told me that he'd managed to acquire some other things through a private collector. He showed me a booklet that very precisely reproduced Mijl Hacohen Sinay's article "The First Jewish Victims in Moisés Ville" (an edition I was unfamiliar with, retitled as "The First Jews Fallen in Moisés Ville, Argentina" and published as a pamphlet by the Judeo-Argentine Association for Historical Studies in 1985). I was interested and kept it, but I lamented the newspaper's absence. Across from him, I drank my coffee as if it were whiskey, trying to forget my sorrows.

One day, in desperation, I searched through every corner of my grandmother Mañe's house. I had already found, hidden in a second row in the library, two dusty and valuable books: the same one by Pinie Katz that Eliahu Toker had lent me and *Argentiner IWO Shriftn* III, which contained the biographical article "Harab Reuben Hacohen Sinay." They had doubtless belonged to Mijl and later to his son Moisés, my grandfather Moishe. Mired among the books of that little room on the fifteenth floor of an old tower in Almagro, with the blinds half closed and the city's gray horizon silhouetted against the infinite, my desperation grew. I couldn't accept a failure that seemed impossible to overturn, and as I searched through shelves and boxes of books, I asked my grandmother about *Der Viderkol*. She had already given up hope.

"But, Abuela, Mijl never talked about the newspaper?"

"No, it was already common knowledge, because that was his title: he was the pioneer!" she answered from the living room table. "I never saw that newspaper . . . Who could have it?"

What a question.

In that little room, books by Gabriel García Márquez, Homero Alsina Thevenet, Somerset Maugham, and many others passed before my eyes, as well as a few copies of the magazine *Todo Es Historia*. A phone book from the 1960s and a Moulinex cookbook paraded by. The volumes of the collection Biblioteca Salvat de Grandes Temas, a pair of ten-cent dramas, and children's books for learning Hebrew all reared their heads. And then at last, bingo! The second drawer of the ancient writing desk, likewise overloaded with newspapers and magazines, one of its broken feet supported by an old scale for weighing babies, opened to give me what I sought. Or nearly. In reality, a photocopy.

"Der Viderkol," I read, at long last. It was half a page, no more. Someone had copied it (my great-grandfather? one of his children?), and it had rested in this drawer, folded, for decades. It corresponded to the first

page of *Der Viderkol*'s third issue—the last to be published. There, in the first column, was an advertisement in Yiddish for Dr. Nathan Blitz:

ATTENTION!
Doctor Nathan Blitz
(Dentist),
1097 Calle Callao
We announce to the Jewish public as well as the general public: all manner of dental procedures performed at half price. Teeth pulled for one peso.

A few lines of a dramatic final editorial, again in Yiddish and written by Mijl, appear as well:

> I sit hunched over my worktable, not releasing the pen from my hand for even a minute, even half a second, not even to breathe or go outside, into the open air, where there is sun and light, where there is the smell of perfume and the delight of life . . . For man cannot only live by his work. Two issues of *Der Viderkol* have already appeared and now the third is here. Three large sheets, four pages per sheet, twelve in all . . . and all written by hand! You must sympathize and understand the difficulty of this effort. And all of this great task I have done alone, without the help of any other. I can say as well that much still lies ahead: doing the accounts, writing the addresses, transcribing the articles arriving from abroad, assessing and correcting some, making annotations, and in certain cases, rewriting them. In fact, it is a slave's labor, a task like that done by prisoners in Siberia. From such work, it is no surprise that my head often begins to spin . . . my eyes to cloud over . . . And very deep within my heart begins an echo, *a Viderkol* . . .

As I write these lines, I have nothing more than that. Even so, it is enough to appreciate the meticulous strokes, perfect as if from a machine, of my great-grandfather's hand.

. . .

On the other hand, everything I know about this periodical is what has been told by Mijl Hacohen Sinay himself and the narrators of history. And what do I know?

That there were only ever three issues.

That it seemed to lack a clear editorial line: it was cordial toward socialism, initially contentious and later sympathetic toward Zionism, and more or less obnoxious when it came to the JCA.

That the first issue, published on Tuesday, March 8, 1898, referred to the acquisition of Palestine with irony, criticizing the Zionists in an article under the name of one Bilam Ben Coraj, a pseudonym of the already controversial Abraham Vermont. That it also reserved space for a poem by the editor entitled "The Eternal Flame." And that it called, too, for the remains of Julius Popper ("*a idisher Colombus*," a Jewish Columbus who'd gone exploring Tierra del Fuego in search of gold nuggets) to be transferred from La Recoleta Cemetery to a Jewish one.

That the second issue, released on Friday, March 25, 1898, featured an article by Rabbi Mordejai Reuben Hacohen Sinay in which he called for a degree of peace in a community shot through with disputes. It also contained two poems by a so-called L. Sh. J., who was none other than Jacob Liachovitzky, seeming to have yielded in the face of the resonance of this first Jewish periodical (in fact, one of these cantos is even an ode to the periodical and says: "Here among us there is talk of a *Viderkol* and the truth to come / Talk among us that no longer will lies churn . . . / Unending friendships greet *Der Viderkol* / All wish it their regards and I, too, wish it never knows a lie").

That the third issue, from Tuesday, April 5, 1898, begins with the above editorial in which Mijl displays his exhaustion and anticipates the end.

That a fourth issue had been announced to follow Passover, one written in a smaller format but with larger text, though ultimately it was never lithographed; and even a fifth issue, promised for May 15, which was never even written, as Mijl fell ill and was no longer able to continue.

I have seen a facsimile of *Der Viderkol*'s first issue in one of the books that tell this history. Yes, I'm able to say that it had five columns on the lower half of the first page and a long editorial ("An di liebe lezer!" or "To the dear readers!") on the upper half, beneath an ornate geometric pattern emblazoned with the name of the publication. And I can add that there, next to "N° 1," ran the name "Sr. J. Rosenblit" and the address of the dingy room that acted as the editorial office: Calle Corrientes N° 1257, Buenos Ayres.

Moisés Sinay, Mijl's favorite grandson, the doctor who emigrated to the United States at a very young age, tells me by email that in 1955 he walked the elderly Mijl down that very street when his father, the pharmacist Marcos, purchased the pharmacy La República at 1100 Corrientes: "My father told me to go find my zeide and show him the pharmacy. After we got off the tram at Libertad, we walked toward the Obelisco, and when we reached what was then the Broadway movie theater, my zeide stopped at a door to the right and told me that there, on the second floor, he had published his newspaper. It's a small world: fifty years later his son owned a pharmacy just a few doors down."

Der Viderkol was as brief as a bolt of lightning, but its emergence left spirits in excitement: when the exhausted Mijl threw in the towel, everybody wanted to pick it up. For a community accustomed to living among holy texts, journalism was like a new religion. And after the jolt of *Der Viderkol*, every Jew in Buenos Aires who had the soul of a reporter came out of their stupor. In August 1898, three months later, two new periodicals were published: *Der Idisher Fonograf* (דער אידישער פֿאנאגראף/The Yiddish phonograph) and *Die Volks Stimme* (דיא פֿאלקס שטיממע/The people's voice, whose transliteration appeared in that form on its own pages).

The first of these was financed by Soli Borok, the richest Jew in the city, who lived at 200 Calle del Buen Orden (today Bernardo de Irigoyen), in a home adorned with tapestries, bronze sculptures, paintings, rugs, silk cushions, and mirrors that rose to the ceiling. Mijl was invited there for tea several times in the days of *Der Viderkol*. After its first issue, in April, Borok had paid the hefty sum of six hundred pesos for a set of block letters so that my great-grandfather's periodical could be liberated from lithography. But those letters, forged based on a pattern that Mijl himself designed, would ultimately make up the texts of the two new papers—and lead to a fight between the two new publishers: whoever had the letters would have the words.

The avalanche of periodicals would run on in earnest for some eighty years. Editions followed one after the other, rushed out, almost always in Yiddish but sometimes Spanish and Hebrew as well, with tones of anarchism, socialism, Zionism, socialist Zionism, social democracy, and nationalism, or else addressed toward colonization. Naturally, all of these pages were populated with bloody debates. The conservative newspaper *Di Ydische Zaitung* and its progressive offshoot, *Di Prese*, battled for several decades. Today, the National Library's periodicals archive holds 535 publications from 39 communities. From the Italian community, which occupies first place, there are 107; from the Jewish community, standing at second place, there are 70.

The reign of Yiddish culture continues there, on the library shelves, at once representing a great opportunity and a great difficulty for understanding that world, so prideful in itself and so tangled in its labyrinths. Mijl's generation, that of the pioneers, would multiply into hundreds, thousands of journalists. For that reason, I read Carlos Ulanovsky—my first teacher, and one I'm still learning from—with great attention when, in a paper from the 1980s, he confesses to a path that I believe I know firsthand: "I felt myself to be a journalist first and, quite some time later, a Jew. Although I could say the same about my status as a person, which I debuted not long ago." And later on, several questions about the Jewishness of Jewish journalists: "Jewish journalist? Which one? The melancholy, Chagallian old man from the *Ydische Zaitung*? The admirable Herman Schiller? That fat brawler from *Di Prese*? Or else: does your name have to be Eliahu Toker for you to feel like a Jewish journalist?"

I do not speak Yiddish, yet I can't stop identifying with the figure of Mijl Hacohen Sinay given that, with a hundred years and more now passed, I still find some of his mundane problems so familiar: they are the same problems we've always had as journalists.

As with families who pass on their trades from generation to generation, we, who form a small but consistent family, pass the pen from one to
the next. Five generations ago, Mordejai Reuben, my great-great-grandfather, wrote several pages for Russian and Argentine periodicals. Then
came Mijl, a journalist who had a long trajectory before passing the
baton to his son Rubén, one of my grandfather's brothers. A fervent
communist, translator, playwright, and poet, Rubén left his mark with
the ICUF cultural association and several publications in Yiddish and
Spanish. When I called his daughter on the phone—I had never met
her, and my father, her cousin, hadn't seen her in several years—I told
her about my investigation, and she invited me to her home.

Ana Luz was living in the suburb of Moreno, where she worked as
a doctor in a hospital, and she told me she had many books that once
belonged to Rubén. The Jewish institutions still had yet to give me any
real clues about *Der Viderkol*, and the writer Eliahu Toker's advice, to
comb through my own family, was a serious alternative. Her house was
a long trip away. Afterward, over yerba mate, coffee, and pastries, Ana
Luz told me about her four children and her father, who had traveled
through the Middle East and Russia, and who had written tirelessly for
fifty years to support, explain, and defend the Soviet Union.

"For all his faults, my old man was an idealist of the kind that doesn't
exist today," she told me.

Rubén Sinay had been the fiercest of Mijl's sons: the Peronist movement had not excused his Marxist activism and had sent him away to
the Devoto and Neuquén prisons, and from then on he'd learned how
to preserve his safety. He'd learned, in that way, to never give out his
address or carry it with him in his documents. He'd understood that his
daughter Ana Luz and her sister Paula, two young girls, must memorize
a line that could one day save their home: "We live with our grandparents, we haven't seen our parents in a long time." And even Mijl himself,
their father, had to learn: in the apartment on Calle Cangallo where he
lived for several years, he kept, in a clearly conspicuous place, a portrait
of a military school cadet. It showed a handsome young man in a Prus-
sian helmet; his name was Alejandro Sinay, and he was Mijl's nephew.
The portrait would win over the police, who sometimes came inquiring
about Rubén, his communist son.

In Moreno, Ana Luz was waiting for me with a surprise: an article in Spanish entitled "I Salute My Father," published in 1947 by the newspaper *Der Veg* (The way), in which Rubén Sinay revives Mijl's pioneering work in honor of his seventieth birthday:

> Not long ago I held a copy of *Der Viderkol* in my hands for the first time. (In your carefree generosity, that of an idealist who offers up everything out of a simple need to give, you—as though unaware of its value and significance—did not save even a single copy of that primeval periodical for yourself).
>
> And through its yellowed, timeworn pages—where others may only have seen a dilettante and imperfect style—I came into contact with the first steps of our community in its will to put down roots in these new inviting lands.

Rubén passed on the pen to his nephew Sergio, my uncle, who was raised in Santiago del Estero. When he came to Buenos Aires for his studies, Sergio never hesitated to spend any money his parents sent him on magazines like *Leoplan*, *Primera Plana*, and *El Gráfico*, until he began to earn his own pesos in 1967: the journalist Bernardo Neustadt had accepted two of his film reviews for the magazine *Extra*. Julio Portas, at *Gente*, and Enrique Raab, at *Análisis*, were other mentors in a long career. Even today, my uncle Sergio treasures his first typewriter, a portable Underwood model. His father gave it to him; it had once belonged to his grandfather, Mijl.

"The journalism virus came inside that typewriter," my uncle Sergio claims one day, in the little room full of knickknacks at my grandmother's house (the same room where, at a different point, I found the photocopied page of *Der Viderkol*).

In the background, Mañe is caught up in the rush of her ninetieth birthday and cake is disappearing among the party guests. The two of us are talking under the cold light of a tiny old bulb, and my uncle tells me that, although he never saw too much of his grandfather Mijl, he remembers him all the same, glued to his typewriter, typing and typing away, maybe grumbling about the noise around him as he was caught up in polemics with someone or other.

"Maybe he wasn't like that, but that's how I remember him," he says.
And then he describes his uncle Rubén, able to go without food just
to keep writing.

"I admired those two, nothing could stop them. And I admired the
lovely way those texts sounded in my dad's voice when he read them to
me."

I ask him, then, what he believes is the reason there are so many
journalists in the family—and I think how his answer might help me
understand more about my own path, as I set out on my way knowing
nothing of the experience of those elders. My uncle, who left journalism
and devoted his time to the study of human connections, considers it for
a moment and then begins to speak:

"I believe that as human beings we have two kinds of DNA. One is
genetic; the other, spiritual. And just as there is a collective unconscious
in humanity, I believe there is a collective unconscious in the family as
well." Someone appears in the doorway and leaves, almost apologetically. He continues: "There are abilities, knowledge, and vocations that
are imparted to the new members, yet not with words, but through some
intangible thing that falls upon one keeper in each generation, whoever
is the most absorptive and will take it on. A vocation is a calling: there's
something that calls to you from your past and from your heritage,
something heard not with the ears but with the heart. What calls you to
be a journalist? You can't explain it, but you can say you always enjoyed
it, that even from a young age you wanted to be one. To me, it doesn't
seem like anyone is a missing link, but all of us are links within a chain.
And when I think like that, I feel the peace of being part of something
bigger than myself, because amid the vastness and the mystery of life, we
are held up in a fabric, an invisible web. On the other hand, my way was
not to be in engineering, or pharmaceuticals, or business, which were the
other paths my family offered me."

My own way does not seem to have been psychology either, nor
sociology, accounting, architecture, or medicine. And I had a sustained
avalanche of newspapers, magazines, and books to channel my original
curiosity. But for all that, I still envy Mijl, who never forgot his newspaper boy on the tram. I, on the other hand, still wonder when it was that
I chose my destiny.

News of a Murder in *Die Volks Stimme*

His image was that of a beggar who spat when he spoke, who stared out through mournful eyes and fed himself on two cups of coffee, who slept in a dismal little room and covered himself with newspapers as he had no sheets. As for his past, only the bare minimum was known: he'd come from Romania and, raised by a well-off Jewish family in the Balkans (in a Catholic boys school, some said in spite), had set forth into the world, making stops in Israel, Turkey, Germany, Austria, Italy, Spain, and England before ending up in Buenos Aires. He was a polyglot who could speak several languages yet chose Yiddish for his writing, and he could resort to tricks and lies while still remaining a man with solidarity in his heart who would help the poor. But above all else he was a legendary journalist—a bohemian and a reporter—who left a permanent mark on the beginnings of the local Jewish press, writing articles in which he struck out uncompromisingly at the JCA or set his sights on the cruel business of human trafficking, and stories that included full names were set in a Buenos Aires he referred to as "Sodom."

Of this man, Shmuel Rollansky wrote that he was "the first journalist to create a sensationalist periodical in Argentina" and that "an instinctive sense for the needs of the people and the young community, an ability to fit in with the difficult atmosphere, and a sensationalist style were the secrets why his own periodical saw greater success than others in that early era." It was no accident that his publication lasted for sixteen years and only disappeared with the birth of the ambitious project *Di Ydische Zaitung*, by which time the age of the major newspapers had come.

The fellow's name was Abraham Vermont. And now he becomes a new character in this history.

"Vermont wrote about everything, and there was always the tacit question: did he say what he knew or know what he said? Was it the truth or was it fantasy?" Rollansky added. Vermont's Yiddish periodical hit the streets for the first time on August 11, 1898, three months after *Der Viderkol*. Its name was *Die Volks Stimme* (The people's voice), and it became a stage for polemics great and small, accusations and retractions, rankings of local enemies and global generosities, uncovered stories about the treatment of women, and kaleidoscopic accounts of Buenos Aires life (in a section titled Babel/בבל). And all of it endowed with an unmistakable urban heartbeat, spirited and vibrant.

His enemies would say that he used his paper to blackmail them. "He was a kind of small-time crook; to call him a 'blackmailer' would be going too far," added Pinie Katz, later terming him a "savage journalist" and a "journalist of chaos." His adversaries went further: they referred to *Die Volks Stimme* as *Folks Shmate* (People's rag) and even put on a play ridiculing him, *Vermont oif der catre*, at a theater on the corner of Pueyrredón and Cangallo.

Perhaps because of all that, Vermont was never able to do away with the suspicion that he was actually an ally of those pimps who subjugated women—or, at the very least, that he sold them space to clear their names. It was true that he knew all of them. The brazenness of those characters was striking. And Vermont's newspaper, which made its columns available to anyone who would pay to write, did also serve as an instrument for bribery. The journalist himself would threaten his enemies: "Don't forget that in my newspaper I can paint you black!" he used to warn them in Yiddish. But Mijl Hacohen Sinay, who knew the man well and, as it could never be otherwise, was both his friend and his enemy, ultimately admired him: "If Vermont had not existed, someone would have had to invent him," he wrote in the magazine *Der Shpigl*.

· · ·

However, it was Vermont and none other who delivered the first news of a killing to the Judeo-Argentine public. His commitment to sensationalism demanded it of him, in a mission that was not so much commercial as narrative: to Vermont, the mundane life of one anonymous person mattered just as much as the fate of the famous Captain Dreyfus, and for that reason he could devote—as he indeed did on July 27, 1899—nearly an entire page out of the total four to Rosa Mangel, a Polish woman who had fallen victim to a trafficker.

(Vermont investigated the story and photographed the woman. Later, when other stories about trafficking compelled him, he would repeat the task several times: in a piece on the reflection of World War I in Buenos Aires's community periodicals, the magazine *Caras y Caretas* reported in its February 27, 1915, edition that Vermont "a short time ago took decisive action in a vociferous campaign against the trafficking of white women, achieving fine results.")

In the same way, the "journalist of chaos" fulfilled his commitment to sensationalism and, on the front cover his periodical's nineteenth issue from December 18, 1898, featured the homicide of Jaim Reitich, which had occurred in Moisés Ville two weeks before, on December 2. The title of the piece was "Korbn 22"/22 קרבן (Victim 22), and it didn't skimp on drama:

> One more victim is added to the Moisés Ville cemetery. The grave is for a victim of murder, one more sacrifice to the curse of colonization. A victim of our own flesh and blood, Jaim Raiter, a forty-five-year-old family man, was assaulted in the night by a *shpanyer*, who murdered him.

For Vermont, any pretext for attacking the JCA was fine. And the fact that this latest victim had some loyalty toward the administrator Michel Cohan was, certainly, a good pretext: "We have no cause to sing this man's praises, as by his actions he has not earned them," Vermont wrote. And he accused this Raiter—actually the man's surname was Reitich—of being one of those who assisted the administrator "in oppressing the poor, lonely colonists":

We cannot weep for him, for the punished colonists were bathed in wretched tears yet he took delight as some unfortunate families, who had earned their homes by sweat and a share of poverty, were thrown into the street. He was there at the time, watching the bloody scene with satisfaction.

As writers of a paper it is our responsibility to respect a dead man, but what dead man? He did not die a natural death or from an illness but was attacked by the hand of a murderer. Even so, we must not punish the gaucho alone, but also the gang of administrators and agents from the JCA, who bear the guilt as well. Was there no injustice shed by families who bathed in Jewish blood, who drowned in hot tears and went about dressed in the skins of innocent souls?

I encounter the piece in an old tome treasured at the IWO, a volume of exaggerated dimensions that contains the first year of issues from the periodical *Die Volks Stimme*, the only one of the many years in which it was published to be preserved. Sheathed in latex gloves to prevent the oil of my skin from making contact with the century-old paper, I turn through the newspaper with extreme caution and irrepressible excitement. It isn't *Der Viderkol*, yet its brittle and yellowing pages reflect life in 1898 with an unexpected intensity. The first page of the first issue bore two large portraits of Bartolomé Mitre and Julio A. Roca. "Illustrious Argentines," Vermont noted in Spanish, and then, in Yiddish: "Argentine stars. As both Argentines and publishers of the first Jewish periodical since Argentina was discovered, we honor the republic we live in freely and happily under the command of the sacred Constitution, and we here display the portraits of two of Argentina's great men, well known to all." I find it amusing. It's an irony typical of a huckster like him, who might seek out a far-fetched connection to power.

But I also imagine that Vermont, tired of publishing news about pimps en route to the Polish shtetls to bring more women, might have been waiting for a new murder in the colonies. And that he might, upon discovering that the man killed was Jaime Reitich, have rubbed his hands together, plotting the attack he would aim at the JCA: in his newspaper, everything was worthy fodder for an attack on the JCA. But what led him to act in such a cavalier way? Why did he choose to become one of the association's worst enemies in Buenos Aires? Was it his principles, was it the interests of a secret patron, or was it pure sensationalism? None of the historians of the Judeo-Argentine press have ventured to hazard anything beyond that last option. On the other hand, the only figures who might have had an interest in the JCA's failure were the Zionists, who sought to divert the migratory flow (and the economic apparatus sustaining it) toward Israel; and, although Vermont would send dispatches to the Zionist newspaper *Ha-Melitz*, he had also attacked them, even them, in the first issue of *Der Viderkol*, parodying a hypothetical purchase of Palestine. As such, the "journalist of chaos" left several unanswered questions behind him.

Beyond the cruel caricature drawn by Vermont, Jaim Reitich was in reality the father of a large family, having arrived in Argentina along with his wife, Gitl Brener (who here came to be known as Catalina), and ten children (five male and five female) before seeing the births of two more daughters here—the last, just a month before his own death. In Kishinev (or Chișinău, the present-day capital of Moldova) he had left behind six others, all lost soon after birth. Among the children who did make it to the Pampas, his own and others' mingled together: the youngest, Joseph—later known as José—was one year old and could play with Jaim Reitich's little granddaughter, the child of his eldest daughter, Mariase, aged twenty-eight.

Apart from the young ones, Reitich was also accompanied by his sister Clara and his sister-in-law, Heidi Brener. Each of them looked after one of the children, as they'd heard that in Argentina any child who took ill would be separated from its mother—a distorted account, which, perhaps, had its basis in the 1889 epidemic that had cost the lives of sixty-one Podolier children in the Palacios railway sheds.

Alongside this numerous company, Jaim Reitich set sail from Odessa aboard the steamship *Río Negro* on June 10, 1893, and reached Argentina after a six-month journey, in the course of which there had been an epidemic on board and a quarantine in the French port of Le Havre. Although he had been bound for the Buenos Aires colony of Mauricio, he ultimately ended up in Moisés Ville, having been sent to a larger farm perhaps due to the number of children and relatives he'd arrived with. There, Reitich transformed into a bald and bearded farmer, sturdy as a hardwood tree and tall as a giant, who worked his farm day and night planting alfalfa, flax, and wheat, and learned how to quickly read the signs of the earth so as to yield a successful harvest (often with the help of hired laborers, something that was not within all of the colonists' means) and how to pay the JCA's fees incrementally so that, in five years, he was already in a position to acquire his land outright—it's just that Reitich was killed on December 2, 1898, five years to the day after the December 2, 1893, when he stepped ashore.

His dedication in this work was such that, several decades later, a few of his descendants lamented: "If he'd lived longer, we would have been rich." The reality turned out much more wretched than the colonist could ever have imagined: it was a dagger or a farmer's pitchfork in the back that would bring his end. "In Yiddish, they said he'd been killed by a *pundik*, a laborer," a few of the people who had him as an ancestor say, as well. "It seems that the pundik was waiting for him behind a grapevine and stabbed him through with the knife to rob him."

When Reitich's blood was spilled, the situation in the Pampas had changed little with regard to robberies and homicides. The Moisés Ville police station had been created on May 18, 1898 by decree of the provincial governor. Seven months later, in December—the month of Reitich's tragedy—the provincial governor enacted a law that, in felony and theft cases, prevented provisional release pending trial. But neither vigilance nor the law was any use. David Goldman, the son of Moisés Ville's rabbi, had been living in the town when the crime occurred and recalls it soberly in his book *Di iuden in Argentine*: "Jaim Retech, the father of a family and a big, muscular man, was murdered by one of his laborers over twenty centavos, either because he couldn't pay or refused to overpay for his work during the harvest."

Goldman doesn't go for Vermont's edgy animosity, preferring to conceal the degree of confidence between the victim and the administration, and so the one who speaks is Jaim Reitich himself:

"I was able to take my family away from Kishinev and bring them here. I know these JCA people may not be the best sort, but no matter: it has served me well to join them."

He does so through Graciela Rosentgberg, his great-granddaughter, who attempts to put herself in his place and take up his words.

"I put myself inside my great-grandfather's skin, not knowing if he really thought that way, but he did carry a lot of people on his shoulders and they all lived at his expense," she says in her melodic voice.

Graciela is seventy-five years old, lives in Rosario, and is the daughter of a Reitich woman. But even as she defends her great-grandfather ("he was a great man, an honest and hardworking sort who loved and cared for his family like a lion, and he passed down an honorable name that all of us, now reaching six generations here in Argentina, are proud of"), she understands the bitterness toward the JCA: her grandmother on the other side had detested the administrators.

"I'm in the middle and can understand both positions, and I think Jaim Reitich must have had his enemies, just like anyone who was successful within that group," she considers, rejecting the stain that Vermont left on her great-grandfather's memory.

Other members of the family are similarly surprised when the article, which I've brought them, begins to pass from hand to hand and from email to email. Rebeca, another of his great-granddaughters, writes to me from Chile: "That description immediately made Jaim appear as a living being to me, real and interesting. Like a character out of a novel, who must have been someone very special, daring and adventurous, a personality some of his children inherited, like those of us on the Chilean branch." And in a café at the edge of Avenida Rivadavia, Susana, a retired psychologist, doesn't lose her composure in the face of Vermont's article.

"Fascinating!" she says, instead, with some enthusiasm. I'm amazed by her mettle, but she smiles: "Because I know who my father was. Leiva Reitich was his name; he was Jaim's grandson and worked for many years at an *obraje*, surrounded by Quechuas, and he treated them with great respect. If that's how he was, his grandfather must have been that way too."

For the giant Jaim Reitich, the real issue, far beyond the goodness of the JCA, was to depart as soon as possible from Kishinev, a city that had a Jewish population of 43 percent—a large share displaced from Poland and Russia—and was seeing a rise in antisemitism. In 1903, Reitich's children could confirm that their father hadn't been mistaken in his calculations, for in April of that year a bloody pogrom broke out, incited by the government and the only official newspaper, Бессарабецъ (*Bessarabets*), which left the streets littered with some fifty dead, six hundred wounded, and seven hundred houses plundered. In the face of this violence, the whole world echoed: Theodore Roosevelt, president of the United States at the time, sent a petition to the czar, and Hayim Bialik—future national poet of Israel—wrote a poem entitled "Ba-ir ha-harigah"/בעיר ההרגה ("In the City of Slaughter").

However, the *alter heym* was not forgotten among the Reitichs.

"I have an obsession with Kishinev," Graciela tells me. "I want to go there, though I know there's nothing left and it's become a huge city today. My grandfather Samuel, Jaim Reitich's son, was almost twenty when he left, and he used to tell me the streets looked like the ones in Moisés Ville because the sidewalks were elevated, with little stairways at the corners, for when it flooded, and the houses had large archways for entering the patio with your horses. He always remembered that, from 'Bessarabia': 'It means . . . *el Beso de Arabia*, the kiss of Arabia!' he used to say. I once asked him if he ever wanted to go back, and he said no, there was nothing left now because everything had been destroyed and burned down. As for me, I'd still like to see it all the same."

Graciela thought about Kishinev so much that even as a girl, when she lived in the scrubland of Santiago del Estero, she would dream of Moldavian snowfalls. In the months of European winter, the Reitichs used to set aside provisions and watch as the snow reached up to the windows. Several decades later, Jaim Reitich's great-granddaughter was living with her parents at the sawmill of the well-known Israel Weisburd, an adventurous businessman who'd been friends with Mordejai Reuben Hacohen Sinay before marrying one of Reitich's daughters and setting out for El Impenetrable forest in search of riches. Weisburd, like Reitich, was another tireless immigrant, obsessed with his work, who in the course of his long life built up an empire of hardwood and tannins and became president of the AMIA in 1934. It was to this lost hamlet in the mountains, today known as "Weisburd," that a great writer used to go on retreat: Alberto Gerchunoff, who had family ties to the founder and had also known misfortune in Moisés Ville, would spend his days there writing without pause. Graciela recalls how her mother used to make knishes for Gerchunoff. And how, at eight in the evening, the man would ask for silence and tune in to hear the news on a cathedral radio. It wouldn't be long before she, still a girl, would start secondary school in Buenos Aires and, during a trip with her father, would find out almost by accident that, many years before, her grandfather had been murdered.

"To this very day I wonder why they killed him," Graciela now laments. "And I don't know. It was a matter of that era. Maybe the original people felt the arrival of the gringos was an invasion . . . But I believe my great-grandfather kept to his own, and this was what came to him. Maybe it really is true that he laughed or poked fun at someone, but he didn't deserve to be murdered over that. In short, he was killed by someone who woke up in a bad mood that morning, and maybe he answered in kind. And maybe the other took hold of a pitchfork, out there in the fields, and killed him just like that. And that was it. I think that if Jaim Reitich hadn't been so hardheaded, or if his sons had been closer by, the whole thing might never have happened. If someone told him not to fight over that payment . . . What else would he have been fighting about, if our elders have always told us he was a very good and well-mannered man?"

After the tragedy, the family began to disintegrate. Half of the children departed for Chile, where they founded a fur shop and a chain of cinemas. Two brothers emigrated to Venezuela. The rest shifted around Argentina. And even Catalina Brener herself, Reitich's widow, picked up house one day and left Moisés Ville to live with each of her daughters for a month. At seventy-seven years old, she decided to go to the home of her youngest daughter, Teresa, in Rosario: she wanted to see the famous carnivals they held in Parque Independencia. No sooner said than done. Her great-granddaughter tells the story with a cheerful melancholy. She knows that those parades meant one final joy for her. And that, when she returned to her daughter's house, she lay down and went off into a gentle death, quite different from her husband's unhappy end.

"Ay, God!" sighs Graciela, and shakes away the reaper. "Well, now . . . Now the family is here, and many are gone, but there's still a great deal left ahead. Just right now, even, we're planning a reunion of all of the Reitichs in Rafaela. And we want to go to Moisés Ville and pay our respects to our great-grandfather. There are still a few of us around!"

Vermont is nowhere to be seen.

Some time ago, in the office of the Jewish cemetery in Liniers, a neighborhood of Buenos Aires, an employee discovered the file card for the journalist from *Die Volks Stimme* inside a small filing box. It's one little sheet, no more, listing his name, date of death (December 7, 1916), age at time of death (forty-eight; he never reached old age), and coordinates: plot nineteen, grave five.

One of the undertakers escorts me with that information, but on reaching plot nineteen we discover that time has done its work to erase the last traces of Vermont: the graves here are in hard and weathered stone, the names barely legible. The wind of eternity has been blowing hard in this cemetery, opened more than a hundred years ago, much as it has on the graves in Moisés Ville. Long before the turn of another century, the names on these stones will no longer be legible at all, and then the circle will have closed for these dead: they came from dust and to dust they will have returned. Some epitaphs did not even linger as far as today, and yes, I realize here that time is tangible and undisguised, that its presence is inescapable. I rest my hand on one of these eroded headstones, a pure defeated granite: I am touching nothing more than the passage of time itself.

The grave of old Mordejai Reuben Hacohen Sinay stands in this cemetery as well. It is a small mausoleum, ancient among the other tombs, slightly baroque and still dignified. Its iron door is open and I enter, but there is nothing there. Only four walls of cracking masonry, a cement floor and a strip of earth, where—in the old way—they laid the remains of my great-great-grandfather, dead in 1918. The crudeness of the grave tells me something about his austere personality, and the singularity of his mausoleum says something about his status in the community, which didn't fade after his departure from Moisés Ville but even increased, what with his sermons in the capital, his frequent visits to other colonies, his bellicose columns in the press, and his tireless effort in the formation of an Argentine Zionism to accompany the global movement that Dr. Herzl had been leading since 1897, when Mordejai Reuben himself was failing on his mission to Europe.

As I move among the graves, I leave little piles of rocks on certain ones, as is the way here. All is silent. Outside, the neighborhood of Liniers buzzes with its street vendors and suburban chefs selling loaded hot dogs. Liniers is one enormous market, and Avenida General Paz, dividing two worlds, takes the form of a wall.

In 1910, when this necropolis was opened, Avenida Rivadavia was a dirt road. The Jews in Buenos Aires had been looking for a cemetery of their own for half a century, ever since they had been legally recognized in 1860. Before, they'd lain at rest beside the Protestants and dissidents, until they were given an opportunity to go south, near the properties where the controversial traffickers were buried, in Avellaneda. But many were against it. "I'd rather lie alongside honorable Christians than pimps of our own kind," my great-great-grandfather Mordejai Reuben Hacohen Sinay had said in those days. The prospect that the Jevra Kedusha (or "pious company," a burial society, which later became the Asociación Mutual Israelita Argentina, AMIA) would receive the human traffickers and open a cemetery adjacent to theirs was very close to being cemented but, in the end, they made the decision to go somewhere else.

And so, they arrived at Liniers, the neighborhood/station that today has cleared everything away and surrounds the cemetery in a dense urban experience, a panorama worthy of Abraham Vermont. As we search for the name of the editor of *Die Volks Stimme* among the tombs, the undertaker tells me that they hold few services there. The problem isn't the limited space, but the value: here, one pays a single time and forever.

"This is like La Recoleta Cemetery for the Jews," he says. And when a reference pops up (a number indicating plot and grave, at the base of some headstone), the man marks out an area of some five graves and assures me, with a clinical eye: "It has to be one of these."

And so it is. Time has also done its work on Vermont's grave, but he appears amid the erosion. His name and that of his newspaper (written in Spanish: *La Voz del Pueblo*) are just barely distinguishable. The sculpture of an open book at the foot of a tree stump forms the rest of the decoration. I am finally standing before what's left of Vermont. And all is silent: his force lies in the bound volume of *Die Volks Stimme* that is preserved at the institute. That, more than anything, is what remains of him.

The train takes me away from Liniers and returns me to the city center. As the neighborhoods go by, I think about Vermont and Mijl and consider that it was about writing. About capturing the pulse of history. About honoring the noble and denouncing the villains. About drawing the attention of one's own and others. About taking a stance in the debates of an epoch. About confessing lived experience and living to recount it.

If not, why else would it have been worth the effort to bend your back to the point of falling ill, scratching words onto silken pages that by a chemical process would then mold the blocks to print each page of *Der Viderkol*? Why spend a fortune on a set of letters, kilos upon kilos of lead in the shapes of the Hebrew alphabet, to then arrange them in such a way as to create the words of *Der Idisher Fonograf*? Why survive on two coffees a day, dress in a tattered suit, and sleep under a blanket of newspapers, investing all the money you made to sustain a paper called *Die Volks Stimme* for sixteen years? Why gain enemies, of the kind that follow you to death and further still, through a passionate and uncompromising debate over ideas of the kind that faced *Di Ydische Zaitung* and *Di Prese* for more than half a century?

To create a newspaper in a language of few was also an endeavor of self-legitimization, the pride of raising a voice of one's own: if not us, who? If not now, when? And if not here, where?

And it was an endeavor that would roll and grow like a snowball with the years to come.

12

Cops and Colonists

After Jaim Reitich's death, and for some years, Moisés Ville seemed to forget about the cries of the dead.

Until the calendar marked a new day: July 15, 1906.

Although the Fiesta de la Independencia had already been celebrated, the national flags still festooned the streets in the colony. The political chief of San Cristóbal was coming to visit, and many of the colonists were appearing, riding in sulkies from the outlying cultivated lands—places known as Bialystok, Zadoc-Kahn (in honor of the highly active Chief Rabbi of Paris, known today as "Zadokán"), Veinticuatro Casas, and Doce Casas—and finding themselves with the other residents, those who didn't sow the fields but cherished the same dream: merchants, artisans, and administrative employees from the state and the JCA. Also in attendance was Zalmen Aliksenitzer, a colonist who'd come from Proskuriv, an old organizer from the original journey to Argentina, and a militant in the Zionist ranks. How much had the bearded Aliksenitzer seen in Moisés Ville? Everything: he'd known the terrible days of the first settlement and witnessed the fever-stricken children dropping like flies. He'd endured the bad harvests, the plagues of locusts, and the turmoil brought on by that Litvak, Mordejai Reuben Hacohen Sinay. And he'd watched all of them pass.

Less than ten years after the revolt headed by my great-great-grandfather, Moisés Ville's appearance had been absolutely transformed: the hectares had multiplied with alfalfa, wheat, and flax, and they were being cultivated by 345 colonists—nearly four times the number who'd planted them in that turbulent year of 1897, and nearly a quarter of the total number of JCA agriculturists in Argentina at the turn of the century. The small farms that were given to new arrivals—the majority of them brought from Grodno in groups organized by Noe Cociovich, with others coming from Białystok, Bessarabia, and Volhynia—were larger by this stage, up to 150 hectares.

And even Michel Cohan himself had left his post.

This rejuvenated Moisés Ville colony was holding a dance that Sunday, July 15, to honor the political chief of the San Cristóbal Department, a caudillo named Ramón Vázquez who wanted to inform himself as to the work of the JCA.

The town already possessed a police station, a magistrate, a post office, a railway station, a development committee, and a second temple, the Brener synagogue. If the colonists wanted books, they could get them at the Hatjia library—where it's possible that one could have found the *Manual of Spanish–Yiddish Conversation*, newly published in Buenos Aires by David Hurvitz or Horovitz (brother of the energetic Abraham Itzjak and Noaj, murdered in 1893)—and, if they felt the call of Zionism, they could gather at the Zvi Israel center. What's more, it would not be long before the implementation of public streetlights and the foundation of the agricultural cooperative La Mutua Agrícola.

The colonist Zalmen Aliksenitzer had dreamed of all this ever since the day he first set foot among the scrubland of what would later become Moisés Ville. Many of the farmers who had landed later did not even speak Spanish, yet here they were all the same, celebrating the presence of the political chief, who spoke to them of the significance of July 9 and the glory of the Argentine country. The Russians knew nothing of all that, but they did know about its gauchos, whom they feared and admired in equal measure. They nodded mutely and from time to time would garble a few honorable words of Spanish, which was as much a struggle for them as Yiddish is for me.

But Zalmen, on the other hand, knew. His children were Argentines now: Salomón Alexenicer, born in 1888, had been the first, and though they'd tried to flatten his foreign surname for the Pampas, it still remained more gringo than anything else. Another of his children, Miriam Aliksenitzer, was now "María Alexenicer." She, having arrived in the country while still a girl, had grown up in her father's shadow, but now at age nineteen, the point in time that matters here, was possessed of a beauty that excited the young men, intimidated the devout, and reawakened the criollos. One such man was Golpe Ramos, representative of a hard-to-conjure law, an old gaucho soldier turned national sergeant, a *policiano* fond of hunting American rogues across the country. At the end of the day, he was one more among the criollos stirred by the dulcet beauty, such black hair and pale skin, of that young woman with the angular name; commissioner Ramos was courting her, surely enough, like a large share of the bachelors in the colony, and on that cold and patriotic Sunday he set his sights on her. Forever.

He searched for her all night, and as the hands of the clock spun on and the wine jugs were being uncorked, his friend Ramón Vázquez, the political chief of San Cristóbal, offered him a toast and urged him, with a heavy breath, to look for her, ambush her, take her. Golpe Ramos went headfirst for old man Aliksenitzer once, twice, ten times. Behind the old colonist, the young woman was watching, her almond eyes shining with something between apprehension and curiosity; never willing. After midnight, her father told her it was time to leave. It turned out that the old man, both pious and shrewd, knew the commissioner as if he'd brought him there from Podolia himself: he knew full well that Golpe Ramos could bite like the Cossacks, with sharpened teeth.

And then time passed.

The years forgot the banquet in honor of the political chief. The history that prevailed, instead, was an alternate version that reached back through the century to take María Alexenicer away from the national July 9 celebration (and the prowling of her suitor) and place her in the middle of a surprise raid.

In this new version, the fury of the Mocoví falls upon the colony like a clap of thunder. The Mocoví on horseback become a thousand angry wasps, the spears they wield more like venomous stingers. Only the leaders go on foot, running and brandishing sabers, at full cry, hoisting red banners and the image of a saint. Amid the chaos of the attack all is confusion. The colonists run to arm themselves with pitchforks, and two or three policeman barricade themselves inside the police station, take up their Remingtons, and let fire from the windows.

The volley of the guns is mixed together with screams:

"Raid!"

"Pogrom!"

But all in vain. Dozens of Russians fall, pieced through by spears, catching glimpses of White Russia or Bessarabia before they die, their faces to the sun.

Others, to save themselves, run off toward the pastures, beyond the town, and throw themselves to the ground like weasels, or they make for the telegraph, desperate, to call for aid from the army. While one group of the invading warriors goes after the cattle on the farms, rounding them up in an instant, another takes the provisions. The most audacious ones want the young women: they take them captive, loading them onto horses, to the sound of their desperate cries in Yiddish. If the women resist, the Mocoví strike them with their machetes until they fall unconscious. Some, the most unyielding, they kill.

Amid the dust, María Alexenicer evades her pursuer and runs inside one of the brick houses. The temple, or perhaps the JCA headquarters, no matter. The certain thing is that the walls won't fall. But her pursuer, seeing her enter, begins kicking at the door. Others join and batter away until it crashes down. So María launches herself out through the window and falls rolling to the ground, glimpsing the fields in the distance, fertile, silent, indifferent to the raid. To make it there will be her salvation, and she runs. But no. Halfway there a sharp blow catches her on the back, knocking her off balance.

When she picks herself up, she notices a spike protruding from below her right breast. An arrow. The wounded woman despairs, yet she is not bleeding or in pain. María runs, holding tight to this barb as her footsteps turn more shaky, more entangled. And she falls, not realizing that they have already surrounded her and are laying their hands upon her. All blends together, all becomes a fog. Death is here.

When the dust clears, the undone bodies appear. Houses, spattered with the blood of their inhabitants, appear as burned-out caves. The silence weighs heavy. There are Mocoví people sprawling there as well: some have fallen, pierced by bullets from the Lefaucheux and Remington guns the colonists fired. It was no surprise, for the warriors, to leave a few of their own along the way: their Tata Dios figures had warned as much when proclaiming that America was Indian and not gringo.

In another time, Alberto Sarfson's weary green eyes watch me from beneath a cap that covers his graying hair. This man, with his shirt buttoned all the way to the top, his look of a reserved farmhand, seems straight out of the North American Midwest but is actually the miller in Moisés Ville. Or the mill technician, in his words. It's Friday afternoon and another Kabbalat Shabbat ceremony—my second one in town—is about to begin at the Baron Hirsch synagogue.

Sarfson, with whom I will share a bench during the service, asks me about my work. He's a discreet sort, but once set to talking about history, he—the grandson of a man who arrived in the colony around a century before—seems to be in his element.

"Some don't know anything these days," he laments, "but in my house it was the custom to talk, and the elders used to tell us their stories."

The miller knows the history of the Waisman family and can recall two other victims who come into his mind as if far in the distance: one man who died in front of his home in times immemorial ("a shopkeeper who sold a bit of everything, and someone came early in the morning and killed him for a few pesos": Kantor?); and one with nice boots ("my father said that when he was little, one man killed another out in the fields because he saw he had a nice pair of boots and wanted to take them"). Then, faced with all this spilled blood, Sarfson falls silent.

"Why were there so many killings?" I ask, trying to bring him back.

"And that was it, you know, because they were savages. People back then were brave and went around armed . . ."

"Was there an element of antisemitism as well"?

"But no, if they didn't know anything about that! I remember one man around here, he was a pundik who could speak Yiddish. Many of them learned to speak perfect Yiddish, they knew how to pray and everything. They lived together with the people in the fields, they worked with them and they learned, you know. I even met a goy woman who made her meat *kúsher*," and he says "*kúsher*" and not "kosher," with that echo from deep in the East. "I remember how my grandmother made it, which was the same way because she made everything *kúsher . . .*"

It was this same grandmother who, before 1900, saw one of the indigenous people. There were more canvas tents than houses in the colony back then.

"She peeked out from inside her tent, and when the guy saw her, he left," says Sarfson. "You had to be careful with the Indians. They killed the conqueror Garay, did you know? And they ate him."

Around the 1940s, when a young Sarfson was hanging around on the streets of Moisés Ville, the only indigenous person still left was an incredibly tall Mocoví man, old and coppery, named Filomeno, a famous character who lived under an ombú tree and who almost never spoke, and to whom a monument was dedicated in 1992, at the five-hundredth anniversary of Columbus's arrival in America.

"He lived in the fields, wandering and staying in empty houses," recalls the miller. "Sometimes he came into the town to beg, with several of these bundles that he'd shift and pile up every ten meters as he went along, asking for food. But he didn't talk much because he was half wild, you know."

Ultimately, the passage of indigenous people through Moisés Ville was faint: the lands where the colony stands had been seized from them in 1869 and had never been a considerable exchange. "In the Capivara region, to the north, there's a lake where they were settled, but they rarely came around here, although a scout might have come," Eva Guelbert de Rosenthal, the museum director, had told me while going through my great-grandfather's text in her office.

In any case, the specter of a raid was well known among the colonists. For the ones who'd settled in the north of the province, it was a genuine threat. The roughest of them would nostalgically recall the bloody night of June 8, 1879, when four German men from Grütly—to the southeast of Moisés Ville—caught an indigenous group making away with eighty mares. Immediately they took up arms and went after their property, seeking vengeance. When the men intercepted them, they killed ten.

Although the frontier was already quite far from Moisés Ville's land even before the founding of the colony, the miller Sarfson isn't the only one today with memories of indigenous people passing through (Toba? Mocoví? Abipón? Mepene?). A voice over a long-distance phone connection confirms as much when I call one of the descendants of the Alexenicer family, who lives in Misiones Province (a man who brags of having returned to the countryside, like his ancestors):

"According to the oral tradition I heard, María Alexenicer was killed in an Indian raid. They said she was killed by an arrow, something like that . . . I don't remember well because my grandfather, the nephew of the woman who was killed, told me about it when I was very little."

The rest of the conversation loses course, disjointing into a vague collection of anecdotes, drawn up from oblivion.

So it was that time passed and the years forgot the banquet in honor of the political chief of San Cristóbal. The story that endured was the account that extracted María Alexenicer from the July 9 national celebration and inserted her into the middle of a raid.

But at a certain point, this fiction breaks down; the reality of the case emerges in the worst way possible.

Because María Alexenicer never died in a raid.

On the contrary, her body was found on Monday, July 16, 1906, the day after the festival to honor the political chief in Moisés Ville. Her fine locks of jet-black hair now appeared matted in dried blood. Her white skin, paler still; her forehead caving in with a bullet hole.

This is the only one among all the murders at Moisés Ville to appear in the Courts Archive of the Santa Fe Province Judiciary. A few months after my visit to the director's office, an envelope covered with stamps arrives at my home. It's the answer to my request for information. Evidently, my note, which had seemed like a piece of paper with little real chance of success, did not have such a bad course. In dense legal language, the letter informs me that a ledger book beginning on January 2, 1905, from the criminal investigations court of the First Court

District of Santa Fe, contains a record of the case among its pages, as does another ledger book, from the criminal investigations court of the Second Court District, beginning on June 2, 1905.

But the letter continues with bad news:

> The record states that the information transcribed corresponds to the annotations completed by the respective Courts in their Table Ledger Books at the time of the filing of the suit, reaffirming that in the criminal documents collection contained in the informational base of this department, there is NO record of a suit related to María Alexenicer being filed to this Body.

Stamps and signatures, stamps and signatures. What remains, even if there are a few lines in two worn-out books, is a tiny sample of the uncertain route that case would follow, marked by the involvement of a commissioner and a political chief. And so, if one had to conclusively point to a day on which the Argentine State arrived in the colony of Moisés Ville—and brought it together with several other towns around the province that had routinely complained about the abuse of authority—it would be this one.

Two days after the national celebration in Moisés Ville, the crime caused a commotion in the Buenos Aires press: "Murder of a Young Woman. Mystery Surrounding It—Public Dismay," ran the headline in *La Nación*.

> SAN CRISTÓBAL, 16. A brutal crime has taken place in Moisés Ville. The girl María Alexinisir [sic], aged 19, attended a dance given by residents of that colony for the political chief, retiring at 1 in the morning in the company of her parents. The parents went to bed without sensing anything out of the ordinary during the night; but upon rising this morning the father noticed the daughter's absence and sent a person to look for her.
>
> One hour later, a passing neighbor saw a corpse three meters off the public road in a fallow field. He gave his account to the police, confirming it to be that of the unfortunate young

woman, who exhibited a wound from a revolver bullet in her right temple.

It is at once a treacherous and mysterious crime; the unfortunate young woman must have been preparing for bed, as her body was covered only by a nightgown. She had been taken lifeless in that state away from her parental home, a brutal act having been committed on the murder victim, and to misguide the course of justice the corpse was carried twelve blocks toward the population center, opposite the station, where she was found.

This crime has dismayed the residents of Moisés Ville, as the deceased was highly regarded. The political chief will bring a summary trial.

Some are attributing the event to jealousy; others to vengeance.

The news excited the journalists, who stirred up the telegraphs. *La Prensa*, the newspaper from Buenos Aires, followed the case for two months—lifting material from *La Opinión* in Santa Fe—and even in its first dispatch (from Thursday, March 19) was running an article entitled "Police Involvement," informing its readers that "brutal acts" had been committed on María Alexenicer.

Meanwhile, the outrage in the colony was growing, and colonists were accusing the authorities. The political chief of San Cristóbal, that caudillo Ramón Vázquez, heard the summary trial after an investigating judge named Passeggi had decided to delegate it to him rather than relocate to the colony himself. But the fact that the political chief was the commissioner Golpe Ramos's immediate superior and personal friend, and even that he himself had been present at the dance prior to the murder, did not escape anyone's notice.

However, a week after the crime, the higher authorities of the province pressured the political chief of San Cristóbal to investigate the event, described on the twenty-sixth by the newspaper *La Prensa* as "the most brutal of the crimes to occur" in a province beset with unpunished homicides ("cattle rustling, gambling, and bloody crime prevails in much of the expansive countryside, fostered by certain authorities, who are being charged by the residents as direct accomplices in these vandalistic acts," read the lines). And so the commissioner Golpe Ramos discovered that he wasn't untouchable and got to know the prison of the provincial capital, where they sent him. His boss and friend Ramón Vázquez's favor seemed to be running thin then, but all was not said and done.

On Saturday the twenty-eighth, two accused men, captured in San Cristóbal, arrived in the Santa Fe capital. Of course, these were two innocents sent by the political chief, and it did not take long for them to be set free. On Monday the thirtieth, *La Prensa* announced: "To date, the inquiries conducted by the political chief, Señor Ramón Vázquez, have turned out to be entirely unfruitful . . . It is public belief that the crime is liable to remain unsolved and unpunished."

Yet the case sprang into motion when Zalmen Aliksenitzer, aged a hundred years by the tragedy, hired an Argentine attorney of high lineage, Dr. Severo A. Gómez, who would rise to become acting dean of the Universidad Nacional del Litoral in 1923 but was, at the dawn of the twentieth century, an attorney in search of fame and important cases, one who didn't hesitate to take charge of representing of a poor Russian family (who were drawing the attention of the press). Dr. Severo A. Gómez moved heaven and earth for this new client until he managed to get the investigating judge, the public prosecutor, an employee from the police, and a journalist from the newspaper *La Opinión* to travel to Moisés Ville for two days in order to familiarize themselves with the site of the event and invigorate the investigation.

The party arrived on Thursday, August 9—while the stalls in Buenos Aires were selling an issue of *Caras y Caretas* magazine that bore a portrait of the victim with a caption reading: "Señorita María Alexuitzer [*sic*], murdered in Moisés Ville"—and discovered a village at war with locusts and beset by an icy drought already three months in and that was tormenting the minds of the farmers. Those important men ceased to feel themselves as such in a colony where they were greeted with suspicion, as though they were part of the gang that included the commissioner and the political chief. And so, on the advice of Dr. Severo A. Gómez (who in turn had spoken with Aliksenitzer), they appealed to the only one who could help them: Rabbi Aharon Halevi Goldman, now an old man, who held the respect of all the settlers. He was the one they asked to make those people with evasive eyes and closed mouths talk.

La Prensa picked up the case on Friday, August 10, with a telegram from their correspondent, who did not lack a certain impudence. The headline ran, "Jews and Crime in Moisés Ville":

> The investigating judge has stationed himself in Moisés Ville, seeking an explanation as to the murder of the young woman I have reported on. Today he set up in the Synagogue, where the Rabbi is administering oaths to Russians and Jews. The case is the first to have occurred in the province, and there is faith that the statements delivered in this way will shed some light, as the Jews do not believe themselves obliged to speak the truth under any other form of oath.

The party returned to the city of Santa Fe just in time to avoid a storm that covered all of Moisés Ville in darkness. They brought a new detainee with them, but they still hadn't pinned it on the commissioner Golpe Ramos, who did a stint behind bars during which "he is not treated in the same way as others who find themselves in a similar case," as the correspondent from *La Prensa* noted. Then, on Wednesday, August 22, the province's Superior Court of Justice received the lawyers and heard their pleas.

The defense attorney followed the typical steps and warned that, in light of the deficiencies of the investigation, the crime would go unpunished. Opposite him, the plaintiff Severo A. Gómez elaborated on the evidence and the circumstances, finally demonstrating that the law would not be able to elucidate the crimes without the cooperation of the people. "And that is the case primarily because the inhabitants of the country," he said, "far from seeing the authorities as a guarantee, a defense, see only an enemy and possible persecutor. That may well become the subject of an investigation by government men or those charged with safeguarding the enforcement of the law. Surely the secret behind the lack of punishment for the many crimes that take place in our countryside is to be found there."

Faced with the growth of attention the matter was earning, the attorney suggested to Aliksenitzer that he counterattack with all of his force, and on Friday, September 7, a committee of colonists from Moisés Ville was received in the capital by Governor Echagüe. The Russians—Zalmen among them—called for the resignation of the political chief of San Cristóbal. The governor made promises.

A track imprinted on the soil—a wide path among the reeds—leads toward the boundaries of Moisés Ville, beyond the houses and the wire fences, toward where a large, white house with a tin roof can be discerned far ahead. From a distance, a TV antenna is visible. Up close, a step ladder, a bicycle leaning against the wall, and a chainsaw among the grass take shape as well. Three dogs (one black, one brown, one white) come out to investigate, but they don't show their teeth.

In reality, the large, white house is what remains of Moisés Ville's oldest station—not that of Palacios, where the pioneers of 1889 settled, but one that does resemble it. In former times, the train would stop here before continuing on toward the cities. But years have passed since any train has blown its whistle: I suspect the tracks are still there to be found beneath the dense undergrowth, but I'm not certain. The vegetation rises so high that I can't see what it hides, and the only thing poking out is a punctured ball.

Was it on this ground that the murderer abandoned María Alexenicer's body? That was how it ran in the newspapers. Today nothing remains. No one remembers.

I advance toward the old platform with curiosity. It has turned into a kind of fallow ground, where I see a moped and a few odd pieces of junk. I make a sound with my palms, but no one answers. Where is the family that inhabits the station?

Yes, it is a suitable setting to abandon a body.

Or at least to conceal a memory.

A line of hanging shirts, set out to dry between one of the columns on the platform's porch and a tree, cuts across the space that saw the powerful motion of the train in former times. Today, this path is useless: now not even the station sign is left.

• • •

If the Jewish periodicals of Buenos Aires were competing, even starting with *Der Viderkol* and *Die Volks Stimme*, to design the narrative of an epoch (and thereby to mark out the field of stories to be told: the question of *what*), the next problem was that of the form, the way to fit a dissonant piece into a story already being written with the music of another genre: the question of *how*.

Between the secret and the revelation comes the terror of death, sailing through the days of the century and forcing those left alive to accept the troubling news that horror exists even in the promised land of Argentina. What arguments, then, will justify the business of traversing the world, of traveling from Kamenetz-Podolsk to Santa Fe, seeking a time of peace?

The account of the killing that my great-grandfather gives in "The First Jewish Victims in Moisés Ville" falls from a pen that lets itself be carried away by the devil. The question of *how* seeks to please no one with its answer there. But Mijl is mistaken when he places the Alexenicer killing in February of 1897 (once again, bad memory on his own or others' part threatens the accuracy of the text). Beyond that, the blood flows free. In a room at the IWO Institute, over coffee and cookies, Jana, the translator, reads nervously, a knot in her stomach:

> The colonist Zalmen Aliksenitzer, from the first Podolier families, had a position in the administration of Moisés Ville and had two sons of seventeen, more or less, and one daughter, possessed of an exceptional beauty, whose name was Miriam. One morning the girl's mother realized that she wasn't there, and the news that she was missing spread throughout the whole colony. The father came running back from the administration, trembling, and all of the neighbors gathered and ran out in search of Miriam until they found her, already dead, in the back garden of her own home. She was lying in a pool of dried blood, almost naked, wearing only her nightgown. And she was

cut in pieces. Her breasts were strewn beside her body, which was slashed from the base of the stomach up to the throat. Her entrails, pulled out. Her throat, slashed across. And her eyes, removed from their sockets. Only a murderer truly more savage and bloodthirsty than a beast could have acted in such a way.

"How horrid!" says Jana. Naturally, many others have approached her seeking translations of family letters or community documents. No one, until now, had come with so terrible a text. We fall silent.

But who was this brutal murderer? Because, clearly, a bullet in the girl's temple was all the commissioner Golpe Ramos needed to commit his crime. Reading between the lines of all the news pieces, the idea emerges that he abused María Alexenicer: the nightgown mentioned a thousand times if once, and all that about "most brutal of the crimes to occur" and the fact of "brutal acts" being committed on the young woman before her death. But none of the news stories written in the heat of the events mentions the use of a sharp weapon—not to mention the mutilation—or the location of the back garden at her own house. What brutal murderer was my great-grandfather thinking of when he wrote all of that?

I'm still wondering this, slightly bewildered, when I hear the voice of another descendant of the Alexenicer family over the telephone. This time it's Oscar, a neurosurgeon from Rosario who knows something about the real history:

"I remember my father, Isaac, telling me that María had been killed by a commissioner from Moisés Ville, that he was courting her and she didn't reciprocate, and he took her away into the bush, where she turned up dead. But they never found out if he killed her himself or ordered her killed."

That history made its way to him in a haphazard and singular way, dodging between silences, when one day he asked his father about the siblings of his grandfather Salomón, Zalmen's first son—the same one who'd had his last name altered from "Aliksenitzer" to the simpler version of "Alexenicer" once naturalized. And just as it had come, the history was gone. By contrast, Oscar is more familiar with the fates of

Zalmen and Salomón, two major names in Santa Fe Judaism, enthusi-
astic promoters of colonization, Zionists from the first era, and generous
organizers of the aid campaigns for Jewish victims of the wars in Europe.

No other members of the Alexenicer family in the twenty-first century seem to know about the family's gruesome chapter involving María;
many show surprise when I call them on the phone or write over email,
so that a hesitant pity prevents me from blurting out everything I know.

Aunt María's murder was not spoken of. Or it was spoken of very
little and in quiet tones.

It's understandable. The problem, in effect, was that of the form: how
to tell the children and the young that their aunt had been assaulted
and murdered by the chief of police? What yield would it have for their
life in this new country? An immigrant, whether Jewish or otherwise,
is used to turning the other cheek. To taking it over and over again. To
moving forward without complaint, always looking toward the future.
And so, the unfortunate Zalmen Aliksenitzer was left with no choice
but to carry on ahead; he had nowhere to return to now. He buried his
daughter under a stone that is still legible today:

פנ

הבתולה מרת

מרים בת ר זלמן

אליקסעניצער

הנהרגה בידי

אכזרים ליל יום

ב כג לחדש תמוז

התרסו ת'נ'צ'ב'ה'

This sorrowful notice in Hebrew reads as follows: "Here lies / the
young maiden / Miriam daughter of Zalmen / Aliksenitzer / who was
killed at the hands of / monstrous people on the eve of / the 23rd day of
the month of Tammuz / in the year 5666. May her soul be bound up in
the chain of life."

And he decided for himself, and for his children, that Miriam's tragedy would follow him the rest of his days as a sorrow from which there
could be no refuge, but it would not last beyond him.

That was the reason why some of his descendants would have received that alternate version, with the raid and the arrow, while others would not even be aware of the crime.

At the end of the day, the death in the raid was a worthy one, typical of the wild America that might have been glimpsed from Russia. As something to appeal to, it could have been much more common than one would suppose today, as the same thing had happened with Michel Jérémie Magnin, the Swiss man who took vengeance after the Lefebre family's massacre: his death—a desperate suicide while facing the troops who pursued him—was told around the Swiss municipality of Charrat in the form of an imaginary ambush by ferocious Indians.

But María Alexenicer's murder was not the only one onto which a castle of myth was built: naturally Alberto Gerchunoff, one of the greatest writers of Jewish Argentina, would have given metaphorical form to the blow with which a gaucho darkened his own fate as well.

13

Alternative Histories

Holding the number six, Giovanna Graffione made her two walks down the runway before a panel composed of five people. For the first one she wore casual garments; for the second, a black dress that fit as though it had been crafted specially for her but was, in fact, the official dress given by the Moisés Ville Commune's Culture Committee to all of the girls who were vying for the crown of Queen of Cultural Integration. Giovanna, a sixteen-year-old student who spends the afternoons doing her homework while working the counter at a convenience store, did not let her smile falter as she crossed the floor of the Club Tiro Federal y Deportivo with calculated steps. She'd been in the running the year before and was chosen as Miss Elegance. Now she knew that, if she wanted to be Queen, she'd have to display herself as serene and cheerful, pretending that those ten eyes studying her did not exist.

That night the whole town took to the streets as in the festivals of old: apart from the selection of a Queen of Cultural Integration, a quinceañera was being celebrated only a short way along. It was Saturday, March 17, 2012, and Moisés Ville—Moisesvishe—was remarkably alive.

It turns out that at certain times this Moisesvishe awakens and shakes off its drowsiness.

Giovanna Graffione's grandfather is always telling stories that she can't quite understand because he relates them over the phone, in a garbled Italian that another relative there in Italy confirms on the other end of the line. What Giovanna does know is that her family arrived in these Pampas long ago, when there were no such queens or committees, and settled in Humberto Primo, a neighboring town where her grandfather's own grandfather founded the Italian Mutual Aid Society. There the Graffiones stayed; there they multiplied. Until one young descendant moved with his wife, a daughter of Moisés Ville, to that nearby town of the Jews, who were growing ever fewer. There had never been any in Giovanna's family, and maybe that very reason was why the crown of Cultural Integration would suit her well: her Italian ancestry also speaks to the coexistence in this corner of the gringo Pampas.

Every girl in Moisés Ville dreams of being a queen, thinks Giovanna, and all of them should have their chance.

She, participant number six, received the highest score that night; the dream of any Moisesvillian girl came true for her. Behind her came two names that spoke of the much-touted integration: First Princess, Sheila Jarovsky, and Second Princess, Caren Vila. Amid the applause, Gisela Isabel Espinosa, the previous Queen, rose onto the stage to present Giovanna with the red cape, crown, and scepter, and the community president handed the Queen her sash. The fairytale continued with a presentation of gifts: a voucher for a trip to the Iguazú Falls for two, a check for eight hundred pesos, insurance to cover the entire year of her reign, a makeup set, a pair of earrings, and several kinds of perfume.

Giovanna will, indeed, come to know the responsibility of representing her town with a smile in every corner of Santa Fe: she'll be walking in pursuit of another crown at the Provincial Sorghum and Dairy Industry Festival in Suardi, the Bagna Cauda Festival in Humberto Primo, and the Provincial Locro and Empanadas Festival, in Constanza, where, once again, she will go on to be crowned queen. With her two titles, Giovanna, who speaks with a shy wisp of a voice and gazes more with the ingenuousness of a girl than the intensity of a femme fatale, will tell anyone who asks that, between her two victories, she prefers that of Cultural Integration over Locro and Empanadas.

"Because this is my land, and its history always lovely to hear," she'll say.

. . .

But the fact that integration should be a title that this Moisés Ville—
Moisesvishe—bestows on its much-loved daughters is also owed to a
myth constructed in large part by one old resident, a boy from Russia
who in the Pampas would receive the name Alberto and who later, in
Buenos Aires, would publish a book of short stories entitled *The Jewish
Gauchos*.

His father, Gershom Gerchunoff—a man as learned as he was hope-
less in economics—had recognized some time before that he wouldn't be
able to pick himself up again in Russia, after a series of bad decisions by
which he'd squandered the fortune inherited from his grandfather, who
had also left him a posting house and a Claim to Perpetuation similar
to the titles of noblemen, which was handy for avoiding abuses but not
for eating.

Even so, all was not lost. The ruined Gershom would grow excited
when the word "America" was uttered at the social discussions held at
their home and would forget about his bad luck. For "America" meant
a new beginning, and going away to strike it big in America was something being spoken of—without too much certainty—throughout the
length of Russia. And so, the decision to emigrate did not fall far behind.

The farewell brought on two turbulent days of joy and sorrow, celebrations and goodbyes; and then, in the blink of an eye, Gershom Gerchunoff crossed the border with his family on a journey to the port.
There, he pointed to show his son the last Russian watchman as he was
left behind them, farther and farther away, in that sordid and sorrowful
city that they were now leaving forever.

"Take a good look at him," he said. "You'll see no Cossacks in Argentina, for that, my boy, is a free country, where all men are equal."

That boy—a little thing with a round face and pronounced
near-sightedness, who would have an impact of considerable force on
Argentine culture—never forgot him.

The Gerchunoff family crossed the ocean and arrived in Moisés
Ville at a point, now erased, between 1889 and 1891. (Some believe its
members to have been "Pampistas," as they called the immigrants who

arrived aboard the steamship *Pampa*, a mythic boat outfitted with a group of travelers who'd been detained in Constantinople while waiting to make it to Jerusalem and finally received help from Baron de Hirsch in 1891. No Gerchunoff appears on the roster of travelers from that ship, but "Gerschin" does show up, and it could possibly be them. Perhaps the need to place the Gerchunoffs on that boat is owed to the fame the steamship acquired through the brilliance of its passengers, with future emblems of Judeo-Argentine culture both among them and their children: the politician Enrique Dickmann, the journalist Jacob Liachovitzky, the writer Israel David Fingermann, the father of playwright Samuel Eichelbaum, the father of biologist and writer José Liebermann, and the father of economist Benedicto Caplán.)

Several years later, the characters in *The Jewish Gauchos*—the collection of short stories that Alberto Gerchunoff published in Buenos Aires in 1910—reflected the dream of working the land and returning to a biblical way of life, far from the trade and profiteering their ancestors had been corralled into. Gerchunoff's Jewish characters were very different from the Barón de Mackser, who appeared in the novel *La bolsa* by Julián Martel, or a few other caricaturized Jews created by contemporaries of his such as Lucio Vicente López, José María Ramos Mejía, and even his mentor Roberto Payró. His Jews, by contrast, were humble and hardworking, strong and sincere, ecstatic and energetic. For them—as for their author—it was not worth it to live in Israel over some other place where they might live in peace. For example, Santa Fe or Entre Ríos.

Even despite the singular crimes.

It so happens that the vignettes in *The Jewish Gauchos* have a dose of knife play as well: a horse comes galloping back without its rider, the saddle stained with blood; an old gaucho, able to "forgive all sins but cowardice," stabs his own son after he backs down in a duel; and—in "The Death of Rabbi Abraham"—another gaucho throws himself upon his boss when given a bad command, a story that certainly reads best when taking into account that Gerchunoff's own father fell victim to a gaucho and inscribed his name among those fallen in Moisés Ville.

The writer made poetry out of his tragedy. It is, once again, the question of the form. How should a murder be told? As in the case of the Alexenicer family—with their murder rebranded as a raid—Alberto Gerchunoff delved into the description of horror and created a different plot with the same pain.

In 1892, when Ana Korenfeld watched her husband, Gershom Gerchunoff, die with a dagger buried in his chest, she determined to leave Moisés Ville behind and move to the colony of Rajil, a short way from Villaguay in Entre Ríos. She had tried to stay, yes, but fear had pursued her in Santa Fe: she simply couldn't bear life in a canvas tent at the edge of a half-sown field. She and her children lived in Entre Ríos for three years, during which the locusts gave them no peace, but it was long enough for Alberto, on the threshold of puberty, to put down moorings there: he wore bombachas, a wide-brimmed hat, and ringing spurs; he plowed the fields, guided the harvester, looked after the cattle, mastered the lasso and bolas, listened to criollo legends, and learned to ride from a herdsman who'd fought at Urquiza's side and now strummed a guitar with melancholy, reciting country poems.

There, Gerchunoff became a gaucho; that is, a Jewish gaucho.

The first edition of *The Jewish Gauchos* was published with a prologue by Martiniano Leguizamón by Talleres Gráficos Joaquín Sesé, of La Plata, on May 10, 1910. It was an immediate success.

The book took these new men—the strangest exponents of the racial melting pot—and spread them far and wide; and it would follow its author forever, even though he went on to publish another sixteen titles. In 1910, when the famous writer Leopoldo Lugones invited Gerchunoff to present his work at the celebrations for the centennial, two years had already passed since the first of his vignettes had seen the light of day in the Sunday supplement of *La Nación*, a newspaper Gerchunoff made it into by the hand of his patron, Roberto Payró.

The two had met at a socialist library; at the time, the Tulchin-born writer was just a boy newly arrived in Buenos Aires in 1895 (when his mother, Ana Korenfeld, decided to desert the colony in Entre Ríos). He was living in a tenement on Calle San Juan, working by day—kneading dough, brushing bronzes, rolling cigarettes, dying silks, or hawking goods as a cuentenik on the streets—and studying by night, on his own, reading from a borrowed *Don Quixote*, picking through books at the National Library, or, finally, as a student at a national high school.

When 1910 arrived and the book was published, Gerchunoff was now a young man with a round face and circular eyeglasses who'd lost his naivety hobnobbing with some of the protagonists of his generation in *tertulias* and editorial offices: Payró and Lugones, Horacio Quiroga, Manuel Gálvez, José Ingenieros, and the Nicaraguan poet Rubén Darío.

The Jewish community was no longer naive either: among the immigrants it probably came in third, after the Italians and Spanish; differing calculations (made at the time and later) estimate the Jewish population to have been between seventy thousand and two hundred thousand people. Many of these Jews were not interested in colonization: they had arrived with the urban migratory wave of 1905, which had brought Russian socialists escaping from czarist repressions and the war with Japan. On the other hand, the immigrants registered in the 1914 census made up 49 percent of the population in the city of Buenos Aires. Between 1910 and 1930, the country absorbed more Europeans than any other nation.

This loss of naivety also came with some xenophobic rumblings but, more than anything, new murders—and some with a decidedly antisemitic tone, like that of the Arcushin family. It had happened in Basavilbaso, Entre Ríos, in the autumn of 1909: a man named Severo Castellanos who was known as "Alpargata" had set his sights on the Russians, thinking that they would be keeping money. "I'm going to do away with those Jews," he told someone in the tavern, who would end up being the primary witness in the trial, and then went on his way, resolved to commit a massacre. Alpargata held back no horror: he raided, set fire to the house, and killed the ten occupants. Eight were from the Arcushin family, and there were another two girls whose last name was Matzkin; their mother was cooking for a large community event and couldn't look after them on that accursed day. Only a baby survived. At ten that night, Alpargata returned to the tavern: "I didn't leave a single seed to grow!" he bragged to the other.

However, his easy living didn't last long: Alpargata ended up in jail, and the whole country, horrified by the case, found out about him. "The prisoner reveals himself to possess an instinctive shrewdness for evading the judge's questions and is, furthermore, a perversely shameless man," the magazine *Caras y Caretas* reported on July 3, 1909. Meanwhile, the colonists of Basavilbaso, amid sobbing and dismay, buried the Arcushin family in a single enormous grave, larger even than the one occupied by the Waisman family in the Moisés Ville cemetery.

One Sunday afternoon, a little more than a century later, Jana (the Yiddish translator I'm working with, who now says I inspired her to go on a tour around the Entre Ríos colonies with her friends) surprises me with a text message on my phone: "took you a picture from the multiple murder in Basavilbaso xo."

The Argentine Jews' loss of naivety was confirmed with the first local pogrom, which occurred on May 14, 1910, a few short days after the celebration of the centennial. That night, a nationalist youth group led by the politician Carlos Carlés (brother of Manuel, the founder of the Argentine Patriotic League) went out hunting for socialists and immigrants on the streets of Buenos Aires. After seizing control of Balvanera—a neighborhood where Jews were already beginning to settle—they took the Russian Library, which held the largest collection of books in Russian and Yiddish, and everything they found they brought outside to set a great bonfire. A state of siege began its reign that very day and would only be lifted in September, after the passage of the Social Defense Law, which extended the 1902 Residence Law and prohibited anarchists and foreign rebels from entering the country.

That fact the Jews would be the target of these attacks corresponded to a latent antisemitism, one reinforced on November 14, 1909, by the actions of Simón Radowitzky. Despite his age of seventeen, the young man already knew that bourgeois exploitation was worldwide and must be combatted in all nations, and so he felt no fear as he lit the fuse of the bomb he launched through the air at Colonel Ramón Falcón, chief of the Capital Police and perpetrator of many repressions.

But the centennial would prove, in the end, to be a sumptuous affair. Against that backdrop, *The Jewish Gauchos*, with all its concerns over ethnic conflicts, assimilation, and tradition, appeared as a bid for multiculturalism.

And even though Gerchunoff didn't write his stories in Yiddish, one exercise in my Yiddish class comes with one of his tales rendered as: דער דאָקטער אין דער קאָלאָניע, "The Doctor in the Colony," which tells the story of Dr. Iarcho, the same one who lends his name to a street in Moisés Ville and enjoyed the position of a famous doctor, well loved around the colonies of Entre Ríos.

The tale relates how Iarcho rode in his sulky to a remote house out in the country, to visit a sick man, and how on his way back, now quite late, he was intercepted by a bandit, who showed up with a blunderbuss in hand and screaming bloody murder. And the doctor, calmly:

—און וואָס מאַכסטו, קואַן, אויף דער האַנט, זי האָט זיך דיר שוין אינגאַנצן אויסגעהיילט?

We're already weary from reading. We reach the end of the line as if we'd just run a race. But we still manage a smile when the professor, Débora, explains the meaning of Iarcho's words: "And how's that hand of yours, Juan? Is it all healed now?"

Somehow, the Jewish gaucho became fashionable with Alberto Gerchunoff's book. But did Jewish gauchos exist in Moisés Ville? Maybe. I, as of now, have never seen one.

But Eva Guelbert de Rosenthal, the museum director, has.

"The gauchos knew very well how to a ride horse and would keep one trained as a rule; on top of that, they knew how to run a ranch," she told me in the museum. "The Jews learned all that from the gauchos, and they traded in their heavy European clothing, which wasn't suited to their rural labors. Hence the famous figure of the Jewish gaucho. A lot of the time people come, especially from abroad, and want to take photos of the Jewish gauchos. There are some Jewish gauchos around here . . . but they're out working in the fields! And yes, they do wear bombachas and slouch hats, because it turns out that's more comfortable for them."

Ingue Kanzepolsky, on the other hand, showed himself to be more skeptical.

"The most we can say is that Jews have adopted the local criollo ways, but saying 'Jewish gaucho' is like saying 'Jewish Bedouin': there's no such thing. The gauchos had their qualities, positive and negative, and they didn't resemble those of the colonists coming from Russia and Lithuania. What happened was that, over time, the Jews started to grow closer in appearance, once they learned to ride and throw a lasso and started wearing the bombachas and espadrilles."

Ingue had been thinking that way for some time when he decided to cross-check his musings against paper. He read through José Hernández and Esteban Echeverría, and then he found a heavy anthology on gauchos at the Baron Hirsch Library. "Lucky me!" he thought. And he read the whole thing through, but he didn't find anything resembling what he'd seen in his father and uncle, full-blooded Jewish farmers who respected the traditions.

"All that about the Jewish gaucho is something Gerchunoff invented, and the people like it, so it stuck," he considered, one day, as we were walking around the block.

In the synagogue before the Shabbat ceremony, the miller Alberto Sarfson had explained to me for his part that the gauchos became tamed with the Jews there, just as the latter learned the rules of the country.

"My grandfather was a colonist in Carlos Casares, but all he knew how to do was study . . . They taught him how to do the milking, but first, to mess around with him . . . they gave him a bull instead of a cow!" he laughed. And he could remember good friends from among the heirs of the gauchos: "When a criollo is your friend, he's a very good friend. Sometimes better than your paisano, even. The thing is, a criollo will start a fight if you do something to him. If you don't do anything, he won't. But it's true they can be quick to take offense and might think you're saying something to provoke them. I used to do some things with this one illiterate man, a really hard worker, and one time someone took him to buy bread. When they were almost there, the guy told him to get out at a particular shop. 'How do you know that shop is a bakery?' he asked, angrily. The thing is, he didn't know how to read and believed they were trying to trick him. But when a criollo is a friend, he's a good friend: faithful, like your paisano."

In 1916, the conservative theater company of Elías Alippi—a Sephardic producer of shows who would go on to work with the famous tango singer Carlos Gardel—premiered a play by Carlos Schaefer Gallo, *The Jewish Gaucho*, at the Teatro Marconi. The Jewish gaucho in question, named Esaú, who was as blonde as he was skilled with a knife, had killed a famous bandit and gotten himself in trouble over the love of a girl as well. Esaú—more a gaucho or a Jew?—had been formed from two different kinds of clay that were difficult to meld in such a perfect mixture. "So to you, Christian gaucho, Esaú, a blond gaucho, comes from wretched stock? So my hair and face tell that the heart I carry in me is lifeless as a campfire choked in the frost?" said Schaefer Gallo's Jewish gaucho. "So you'll never give your daughter's hand but to a criollo who carries blood like yours? And didn't God make us from the same clay? You, a Christian, insult God!"

Leaving the Jewish gauchos behind him, Alberto Gerchunoff went after more. In 1914, he was sent as a government delegate to disseminate Argentine culture in Spain, Germany, and France, and while there he met Miguel de Unamuno and Marcel Proust. In Europe, on the threshold of World War I, he wrote his autobiography. He was barely thirty years old. And though he still had much to live through yet (during the years of fascism he would be a freedom fighter; later on, a fervent propogandist for the state of Israel), he already believed it was time to commit his life to paper.

But he never did publish that autobiography, which only appeared in 1952 thanks to his son-in-law and biographer Manuel Kantor. After his death, the latter discovered among his papers those twenty-seven pages, scribbled in cramped letters of violet ink, which tell of Proskuriv and Entre Ríos, of Tulchin and Buenos Aires, of joys and tragedies, and bring out, too, the killing of Gershom Gerchunoff—which his son once more articulates in an artistic piece.

In the text, Gerchunoff noted that, near the canvas tents where the colonists of Moisés Ville lived, a tavern had been founded that was run by a man from Galitzia. Cut off from the center of the colony and instead closer to Palacios, the Russians mowed the pastures, drew water from the wells, and pulled the plow, and they—who didn't even have a rifle for hunting partridges—looked askance at that lair, a place of frequent scandal. The first incident came with "a countryman of a shifty look, covered in scars, dusky, with restless eyes, who carried a long, curved knife," according to Gerchunoff's record. That man had taken a horse from the colony and, when the owner complained to the sergeant, was forced to return it. "That countryman turned out to be an idler from the outskirts, averse to work, a troublemaker and drinker," Gerchunoff continued in his autobiography. "After giving back the horse, he became fonder still of the tavern, where he would spend his afternoons, quarreling with other gauchos."

One day, not long before Easter 1892, the man was seen completely up to his neck in alcohol. He'd spent a good while at the tavern and at sundown managed to bring himself to leave. Through his alcoholic fog he glimpsed a family of Russians drinking tea outside their tent. Among them was a chubby boy, some nine years old: the young Alberto Gerchunoff. Could his father have been the horse's owner? They'd have to settle the score. If not, it could serve as a warning.

> Suddenly the gaucho appeared with his knife bared, twirling it through the air. It was one instant, a terrible and dreadful instant. Cries of horror cut through the air. A minute of indescribable confusion passed, and then I could understand the full immensity of our misfortune. I do not know how, but we found ourselves in the Administration house, opposite our tent. Sprawled on the ground lay my father, drenched in blood, and in the next room, on two cots, neighbor women were tending to my gravely wounded mother and my older brother, wounded too; the whole of the colony, dismayed, was in the patio, where the murderer had been beaten to his end: his face was mutilated, his body broken.

Mónica Szurmuk, who holds a doctorate in comparative literature from the University of California and is a researcher for CONICET (the National Council for Scientific and Technical Research, which promotes the development of science and technology), knows that text well. She read and reread it, taking notes for an intellectual biography of Gerchunoff that she's been putting together for several months, which led her to Paris and Ukraine in pursuit of his trail but also to the IWO Institute where she could learn Yiddish and pry into his world of origin. It was there that we met, at a long table where, alongside Iván Cherjovsky and Andrés Kilstein, we attempted to master the Hebrew alphabet—though she had an advantage as her grandmother had taught her to write up letters in Yiddish when she was a girl.

"Writing an autobiography at age thirty is an act of a certain arrogance, but Gerchunoff's path is an astonishing trajectory, one that was unthinkable in Europe and the United States," she tells me one day as we're having coffee after class. "It's wild to think that this immigrant boy, who'd arrived without knowing a word of Spanish and witnessed his father's death, would go to Europe before his thirtieth birthday as an emissary for the Argentine government and be received by Proust and Unamuno. And that's what he wants give an account of."

Something about that, too, was what led Mónica to think of the intellectual biography genre rather than literary criticism: Gerchunoff's intersections, his polyvalent figure that carried forward his late father's dreams of freedom.

Regarding the murder, Mónica points out the singular aspect of its textual form:

"Gerchunoff refers to himself as an eyewitness to his father's murder, but he doesn't describe the emotions it caused him and gives no account of how the family's life changed. It's a text that avoids speaking of pain and vulnerability. I think all that was so shocking that Gerchunoff couldn't contextualize the horror of the death and instead transformed it into text, making it an anomaly for what the Argentine countryside was. He always wrote that his father wanted to come to Argentina, a promised land where his children would be free. But he'd paid with his life. And so, around all that, he had to construct a narrative that would re-idealize the country, transform it back into an idyllic place."

. . .

In the Moisés Ville of today, the dog poisoner wasn't lynched like that "troublemaker and drinker" of a countryman, but he did have a reciprocal fate: today, the man from the plaza who was arrested under those allegations is a pariah.

The commune fired him. No one wants him around. No one will give him work. No one will greet him. And he, not understanding how it came to this, considers the whole thing to be an injustice. He thinks the guilt is the sole property of its mastermind, the woman who paid him.

The poisoner lives in an ancient, peeling house, with exposed brick, on Calle Doctor Iarcho. The windows have broken panes and shutters unopened for decades, and, at the back, it is possible to make out a patio covered with weeds. The house looks like a ruin, but it's the only place in the world where the man would have wanted to be in that moment while the San Cristóbal police were conducting their blunt interrogation. When he returned to town, the man from the plaza related to the few who'd still listen that one of the guards had gotten behind him and another in front, both carrying bludgeons, and sooner or later—putting the rules aside—they'd made him spit out the name of the person who paid him to do the poisoning.

But how can a man put out poisoned bait fifty times, sixty-seven times, eighty-three times, or however many it was, and even after seeing his handiwork in the animals' purple snouts, even after being unmasked, still continue to believe that everyone has conspired against him? What is his morality? What is his law?

The poisoner's house has no doorbell and I try clapping my hands for quite a while; five dogs surround me in the meantime, dogs that belong to the man from the plaza himself. There's a greyhound, a sheepdog puppy, and three skinny mutts: any of them could have died at the stroke of a pen in the era of the organophosphate pesticide attacks. When the door opens, several barefoot children dressed in worn-out clothing sprout up from the dark interior. One has a remote control in his hand.

They tell me their father isn't there, so I ask for his wife.

"Mami, someone's looking for you . . ." calls one of the boys, not taking his eyes off me.

"Who," she says, from farther in. Her voice sounds cracked and distant.

"A . . . A man."

"Tell him I'm coming."

"Chichi, shut up!" one of the girls yells at the sheepdog puppy, which is barking nonstop.

I wait.

Not certain what to expect.

Then a head of messy graying curls pokes out from the shadows. Two deep-blue eyes stare at me, slightly crossed: measuring me openly. Leaning on the doorframe, the woman listens and then tells me what I already know, that her husband isn't there.

"When could I come back?" I ask.

"I'm not sure. But he isn't here right now."

"I need to talk to him . . ."

"And why do you want to talk?"

"I want to ask about the poisoned dogs."

"Who sent you here? How do you know he lives here?"

"In town everybody knows where he lives. But I'm just here to listen, that's all, I can't judge."

"He isn't here. And don't come back. What happened here, the whole thing was a . . . a . . . how can I say it, they pinned it on him without proof. He isn't to blame for what happened."

"That's why I'd like to listen to him, ma'am."

"Tell whoever sent you here to send you someplace else because there's no one here to talk to. They've done us too wrong."

"Not everyone believes all that about your husband . . ." I try to reassure her. But it's a lie.

"I already know there are good and bad people, but in this town there's more bad than good."

"That's how it goes in the world, as a rule."

"*Nena*, what are you doing!" she tells off one of her daughters. And then she goes back inside.

Her gaze, that untrusting glance, resentful of the world, forever haunted, will pursue me in the days to follow.

. . .

The Gerchunoff murder is not overly developed in the recollections of another family member, the well-respected historian Tulio Halperin Donghi, either. In his book *Son memorias*, Halperin Donghi, the grandson of Sofía—Alberto's older sister, wounded during the incident—and great-grandson of Gershom, reviews that autobiography written in 1914 and notes:

> The only part I didn't need those writings to teach me was that my great grandfather died in front of the tent where his family still was living, stabbed to death by a drunk countryman, who also managed to injure his wife and my grandmother Sofía before being beaten to death by the colonists who'd flocked toward the commotion.

It turns out that his grandmother, her arm split through with a scar that would remind her of the tragedy forever, spoke rather little about the colonies.

Later, Halperin Donghi responds to me over email:

> With my highest regards: Thanks very much for your message. Although I have no issue at all talking to you about the episode, the problem is that I have nothing to add to what you read in *Son memorias*, and part of the reason is that, as I explain there, the whole subject of Jewishness was taboo. But from what I remember of the occasional conversations involving the period in Santa Fe and Entre Ríos, which I could listen to but not take part in, my impression is that they didn't remember it as a saga they'd like to reminisce on; they spoke a good deal more about the first few years in Buenos Aires, the dampness of the house in San Fernando, things in that vein. The result—as you will have noticed—is that to fill in that gap I had no resort but to turn to the writing of A. Gerchunoff, who is really my only source. Possibly my cousin Dr. Isabel Kurlat, Rosa Gerchunoff's

granddaughter, who's interested enough in the topic to have visited the colonies last year, can tell you a bit more about all that. I'm truly very sorry not to be of more assistance to you. Very sincerely, Tulio Halperin.

Isabel Kurlat—the historian's cousin—is excited about our meeting and arrives in the bar lugging a computer that has the photos from her trip around the colonies. She's a doctor on the verge of retirement, yet she still seems young and cheerful. She knows that she's descended from several distinguished last names (not just the Gerchunoffs but the Kurlats, who came to country in 1883, and the Liebeschützes, who were involved in the construction of the first temple on Calle Libertad) and that each generation is a bridge between the one before and the one to follow.

"My husband's grandfather had been a railway man in Entre Ríos, and my mother-in-law was born there as well. So, when we had a week off, we decided to go out to the colonies," she tells me.

Isabel has the same passion for genealogy that I saw before in Gabriel Braunstein, the descendant of the Waisman family, and Graciela Rosentgberg, the great-granddaughter of Jaim Reitich. That was why she decided to travel to Entre Ríos and Santa Fe as if she had some unfinished business there, and she was also inspired by the preface from *The Jewish Gauchos*, a few lines in a pure Argentine strain: "Wandering Jews, tortured and torn, redeemed captives, let us bend the knee beneath the unfurled banner [of the Argentine flag]; in unison beside choirs bejeweled by light, let us intone the song of songs that begins thus: 'Hear Oh ye mortals . . .'" Isabel has always been moved by that preface. The figure of Alberto Gerchunoff had been a guiding force in her family, and his anecdotes were present all the time. She, who had been reading that introduction for years and continues to today, thought each time she did so about the frigid anguish of the shtetls and the spirit that had fueled the boilers of the steamships to bear the Russians in their pursuit of freedom.

And so, she began her own trip, illuminated by those words, setting out from Buenos Aires toward Entre Ríos and Santa Fe, and she couldn't contain her emotion when she saw a school named "Alberto Gerchunoff" in Villa Domínguez, right in the place where, not far from Colonia Clara, Jewish colonization had first begun in the lands of Entre Ríos. A large part of that history is told in Villa Domínguez's museum: in one of its rooms, Isabel opened an old copy of *The Jewish Gauchos*; she was reading that magical preface and realized that it wasn't her own inner voice carrying those words but the very real and solid voice of Osvaldo Quiroga, the director of the museum, who was reciting them from memory. Now, as the photos go by on her computer, she intones them once again.

Her journey continued in the areas surrounding Villa Domínguez and Basavilbaso, where the colonists had left behind a cemetery, a synagogue, and several other traces. Then Isabel and her husband set their prow toward Moisés Ville and, arriving there, saw for themselves the still-living efforts of a community that maintains its traditions. Isabel was amazed by the Kadima theater and managed to visit the cemetery, which was opened for her with some clemency even though it was Sukkot, the Feast of Tabernacles, in remembrance of the Jewish people's wanderings through the desert after their enslavement in Egypt. There, in section 5, Isabel could stand before her great-grandfather's tomb.

She was familiar with multiple accounts of the crime, which had never been concealed from her; on the other hand, it wasn't until 1963 that she was exposed to the scope of another crime, the monumental crime of the Holocaust, when her parents took her traveling through Europe. They visited the house in Amsterdam where Anne Frank had lived, a girl who'd been the same age, at the time she wrote her diary, that this Argentine girl named Isabel Kurlat was then, visiting their hiding place and shuddering to the bone. And now the woman who once was that girl asserts that it was that very day, as she came down from Anne Frank's hideaway with a copy of her *Diary* in English, that her adolescence began, and she became conscious of what it meant to be Jewish. Kurlat had read about her great-grandfather's murder in Gerchunoff's autobiography and *The Jewish Gauchos*, and she could remember the version her mother used to tell, which agreed with the others as far as the gaucho's drunken state but added that the criollo hadn't come to the colonists' tent on a whim but to ask for the hand of Sofía (the eldest daughter, future grandmother of the historian Tulio Halperin Donghi). Gershom, who couldn't understand the man's words, had offered him bread. The gaucho set himself on edge, brandished his blade, and ran him through.

Several elements of this account overlap with that of the first killing, of David Lander: how much confusion and how much truth is contained in each?

In Moisés Ville, the headstone of the grave appeared restored, and there, on a metallic plaque, Isabel read:

> HERE LIE THE REMAINS OF RABBI GERSHOM
> GERCHUNOFF, BELOVED FOR HIS WISDOM AND
> VENERATED FOR HIS GREAT PRUDENCE, A JUST
> AND CHOSEN MAN.
> HOMAGE BY THE MOISÉS VILLE FOUNDATION.
> OCTOBER 1995.

And she stood silent.

"It was there I finally understood my family's history," she says now. "This crime marked my family so, so much, that the children and grandchildren of Ana Korenfeld, Gerschom's wife, spent many years of their lives preoccupied with her."

Isabel discovered that Moisés Ville's soil (like that of Entre Ríos) had the appearance of a base where her ancestors, having felt stateless on the other side of the ocean, could at last put down roots. In the 1970s, when Isabel's grandmother traveled to Israel to see her son, she refused to leave Argentina with a Russian passport. "I will not travel as a Russian," she told her granddaughter. "Because when it came time for your father to enter elementary school, I took him to the door, handed him over to the teacher, and no one asked me if he was Jewish or not. And now I will not travel as a Russian: I am Argentine." So it was that, at age eighty, her grandmother got an Argentine passport. Isabel feels moved once again:

"That's why I have a feeling that my roots lie there as well, in that grave in Moisés Ville."

• • •

Of course, the versions of Gershom Gerchunoff's death don't end with the poetic and family accounts. In "The First Jewish Victims in Moisés Ville," my great-grandfather has something to say on the subject as well:

> The next death is that of a middle-aged Podolier, Gershom Gerchunoff, the father of a family, who left the colony one morning with a pair of bulls and a plow to work his land. A while later, the bulls returned with the plow, alone. He was not there. One day went by, two days, a full week passed before at last he was found, dead, in the high grass of another colonist's land. His body had been chewed and eaten away by the birds of prey and the animals of the field, such that only his bones could be buried. None can imagine the terrible wails that murders like this one brought forth among the colonists of Moisés Ville.

And in *Di iuden in Argentine*, David Goldman writes:

> The first victim in Moisés Ville was Moshe Gerchunoff, father of the journalist Alberto Gerchunoff, who not long ago was sent to the International Literary Conference in Leipzig as a representative of the Argentine government. Moshe Gerchunoff and his family ran a small business, where bottles of *bronfen* [alcohol] made up half of the merchandise. A drunken *schpanier* who wanted more to drink but did not receive his cup straight away, and so he leapt upon the man with his sharp knife, driving it into his chest and through to the other side. Then he went for the woman and the three children, who in time were healed of their wounds.

These do not seem, in the final analysis, to be the most accurate of accounts.

On the other hand, when did the crime actually occur? The date on the grave is February 12, 1891, while Mijl Hacohen Sinay places it "at the end of 1891" and Pinjas Glasberg's book (that improvised first civil register of Moisés Ville) gives March 1, 1892.

"The matter of all those versions is fascinating," Mónica Szurmuk says one day, when I tell her I'm getting tired of hearing different stories.

But she has yet one more to offer me: during her research, she heard the story, from the mouth of another of Gerchunoff's descendants, that Gershom was inside the tent with a lit lantern, and the gaucho aimed for the light and threw a stab that pierced his heart through the canvas, without ever seeing his face.

"The number of different versions doesn't limit the history," suggests Mónica. "On the contrary, it complicates it."

At long last, I discover the closest version in *La Unión*, the newspaper from the Esperanza colony. Back before the years and bronzes had done their work on Alberto Gerchunoff's public figure, the real circumstances of his father's killing and even the name of the killer—which the literature never chose to record—appeared without as much suspicion. The news piece, "Crime in the Palacios Colony," which comes from its March 3, 1892, issue, reports that the incident occurred on February 27, 1892, meaning that neither of the dates given by Pinjas Glasberg and Mijl Hacohen Sinay, and not even the one on the grave, is correct. It was indeed, as Gerchunoff tells us, at seven thirty in the evening, when a gaucho from Córdoba by the name of José María Ríos, an old soldier for a magistrate—that "countryman of a shifty look, covered in scars, dusky, with restless eyes, who carried a long, curved knife," according to Alberto Gerchunoff's recollection—wanted to court the beautiful Sofía and saw her father as getting in his way. Ana Korenfeld, fearing that something would happen to her daughter or husband, ran to stop Gershom. The father, who had no idea how to fight but knew he must do so now more than ever, was caught up in a tangle with his wife that prevented, from landing the first blow, and he may have realized, in terror, what was going to happen.

Which is what the journalist from *La Unión* tells us:

> Taking advantage of that opportunity, the wretched murderer drew his knife and buried it to the hilt in the belly of the poor defenseless father. The murderer's weapon penetrated into the man's intestines, severing the major arteries.

The death took place a few minutes later. With the father out of combat, the murderer fell upon the mother, inflicting a wound to the side of her stomach, peircing [*sic*] her thigh and causing a horrible injury that may have mortal consequences.

The scent of human blood had so blinded the ferocious murderer that, not content with having killed the father and gravely injured the mother, he then threw himself upon the young woman mentioned above, aiming a thrust of his knife toward her heart, but by a lucky movement of the young woman's arm he only managed to slash her arm, grazing her ribs. At the victims' cries, the neighbors came to their aid, seizing and disarming the murderer.

Immediately news of this treacherous crime spread through the population in the town of Moisesvile [*sic*] and the Palacios colony, bringing the majority of the inhabitants together to take justice for themselves and lynch the wretched man.

The magistrate arrived at 7 or 8 the following morning, accompanied by the police medic from the Sunchales colony, to mount the summary trial pertaining to the case. The murderer's corpse was loaded on a cart and thrown into a lagoon next to the cemetery, by order of the magistrate, as the population protested against his admission into the cemetery. The behavior of the police medic drew much attention from those present, as he spent the majority of his time examining the body of the criminal while largely ignoring the body of the unfortunate victim.

This event has left the population of those colonies dismayed and the unhappy orphans completely forsaken!

In this way, Gershom Gerchunoff's murder has several of the elements that my great-grandfather would relate for the killing of David Lander, that first murder in which gaucho and Jewish blood came together in communion. Myth and reality are combined once more.

Later, a brief reference would appear in *El Economista Argentino*, a Buenos Aires periodical, when it published a piece in its seventeenth issue, from March 26, 1892, by one of the major figures of Rosario (a superintendent, minister, lawmaker, assemblyman, pedagogue, historian, and geographer), Gabriel Carrasco: "The First Lynching: Consequences of Poor Legislation and Worse Enforcement." The article, a long study on criminality in Santa Fe Province, records an average of seventy-one murders per year and describes the Gerchunoff case:

> Some thirty-odd inhabitants, agriculturists from one of the most remote colonies of Santa Fe Province (Moisesville), have taken a well-known outlaw who was notorious in that area, being the terror of the countryside, and, catching him in flagrante at his latest crime, they have lynched him!
>
> This is the first case in a new variety of popular justice, with no precedent, yet, in the Argentine Republic.
>
> The colonists, all of them, have been apprehended and find themselves prisoners in the stated province.
>
> That is the incident.
>
> Now, then: in the face of such an event, what should the honest press say? What should the national authorities do?

What follows is a long dissertation that Alberto Gerchunoff might well have been interested to read.

And so the accounts of the Alexenicer and Gerchunoff murders have been built and rebuilt from the clay of myth, and only at certain times has the truth seeped in through the cracks of their legends.

But the thing that sparks my attention more intensely is what my great-grandfather has done: with those two cases in particular, he has also performed an operation by constructing the question as to the how. What's all that about how María Alexenicer had her eyes removed from their sockets? What's that about how nothing was left to be seen of Gershom Gerchunoff's body when they found him but the bones? Mijl Hacohen Sinay chose a stance in his histories as well: no one is innocent.

And I can demonstrate that on the next page.

14

Final Versions of an
Incomplete History

The sign of the transgression is an asterisk: an ink star leading me to understand that, in the act of relating history, innocence does not exist.

On a wide table at the IWO Institute are scattered the files on Noé Cociovich, that leader of colonization who founded several institutions in Moisés Ville and allied himself with the administrator Michel Cohan in his fight against my great-great-grandfather, Mordejai Reuben Hacohen Sinay. Various papers, written by hand or printed in Yiddish, Russian, and Spanish, well worn by the passage of the century, tell the history of the colony and the Baron de Hirsch organization through Cociovich's routines. A photo peeks out from among the documents, showing Cociovich himself as a modern and urbane man, dressed in a suit and tie with a thirties fedora.

However, it is a handwritten asterisk on one of the printed texts authored by the man himself that draws my attention more than anything else. At the foot of the page, I find a note, written in a familiar hand. Even though the letters are Hebrew and the message runs in Yiddish, I discover the initials מ. ה. ס. / M. H. S., Mijl Hacohen Sinay.

There below, also in handwritten Yiddish, it reads:

The journey [by Mordejai Reuben Hacohen Sinay and the other delegates] to the JCA headquarters in Paris did not come about because of crossbred cattle, as Cociovich tells it, but for other reasons about which there is much to say. What's more, one of the travelers, Braunstein, had nothing to regret when they returned in failure, because, as the reality proved, he was already one of Administrator Cohan's men even before the journey. And Cociovich had personally been the intermediary who brought them together . . . M.H.S.

Cociovich was dead, but it didn't matter. The debate must go on: you had to set down your own version of history, whatever it might be.

Evidently, my great-grandfather, who worked in his last fifteen years as an archivist at this institute, took the liberty of intervening with absolute impertinence on a printed text (a conserved and registered source) to clash against the account given by its author, Noé Cociovich.

No one is innocent in the act of telling history, and I discover through this and other signs that Mijl Hacohen Sinay continued fighting until the end of his days to impose his own version of what had occurred in Moisés Ville; in fact, the matter was one of his favorite topics when it came to polemics. It was as if he could never do enough to refute the official history, dignified by the administrator Michel Cohan even in spite of his abuses against the colonists and the violence he'd deployed in the colony to put an end to the revolt of 1897.

Mijl's eagerness to give his point of view was substantial, and it was that same will that had led him at the age of twenty to create a periodical of denunciation like *Der Viderkol*. And though he waged a half-century battle, he would never return to Moisés Ville: the wound the JCA had inflicted on his father—Rabbi Mordejai Reuben, my great-great-grandfather—could never scar over completely.

"A handwritten asterisk in a printed text? Don't be surprised. All that was done with the greatest respect. Some other texts are underlined and crossed out in red, cropped short or overlaid with other paragraphs pasted on top of the original," says Silvia Hansman, the current director of the library and archives at the institute, when she sees me bent over the article. My expression of surprise gives everything away. "The corrections they would make to one another had to do with their visions of the world. On the one hand there's the will to make a document part of the heritage, to archive it at the institute, but on the other hand there's the archivist's impulse to intervene and leave their own trace on the material. We still do that as archivists now, only outside the document, in the way we describe and organize the material, providing it with a framework by which we somehow say what we think. At least now the material's own voice is allowed. In the past, one idea would get covered up with another. It would've been better to have a separate manuscript with the corrections, so as to respect the original . . . but it would be less exciting."

If my ancestor's battle on the subject of Moisés Ville continued until his death, only I, able at long last to set foot in the town, could reconstruct the relationship between that territory and this family. Albeit with uncertain results.

Then again, when my father sent that email telling me about Mijl Hacohen Sinay's article, I likely knew much less about my family than I would, in reality, have believed. At some point I'd heard the word "Grodno." But I would have failed in any attempt to locate the city on a map. The name *Der Viderkol*, on the other hand, was unknown to me. Nor did I know about the battle with the Jewish Colonization Association; I had no idea what the JCA even was. I know now: the crimes of Moisés Ville hold within them, like a Pandora's box, the secrets to my own history and Jewish identity. Though descended from a rabbi, in my life I've known nothing of Jewish liturgy except by vague approximations. It's not unusual. At the end of the day, I am the perfect heir to four generations who've been shedding off religiosity as if it were the old clothing brought from Russia. A sign of the times: one hundred years of progressive secularization. Who will be able to judge those four generations and then my own? My own great-grandson?

The text of "The First Jewish Victims in Moisés Ville" was written and published in 1947, when Mijl Hacohen Sinay, now old, was spending his days at the IWO. He worked there as head of the archive from 1944 to 1958. A draft of that article appears among the dozens of my great-grandfather's papers that I received through my uncle Sergio's hands. Like the majority of Mijl's documents, it is handwritten in tiny, meticulous blue letters. The article was published in the fourth volume of the IWO yearbooks alongside "Jews in the Tragic Week," written by Pinie Wald, "The First Synagogues in Latin America" by Arturo Bab, and "German Jews in Argentina" by Moshe Katz, among others. It's a shame that reading it, in Yiddish, should be a privilege for only few today, one that even I can only access with enormous limitation after completing my reading course in the language.

With the book open, reading and rereading, I wonder what it was that led my great-grandfather to write this short criminal history, and what led him to write it at that particular moment. The key to several other questions concerning Moisés Ville's myths, the accuracy of the details, and the repeated sensationalizing of the events may lie in the answer.

For Mijl Hacohen Sinay, 1947 wasn't just another year. It was, on the contrary, the year in which the IWO and the Union of Jewish Residents from Grodno and Its Surroundings in Argentina (the landsmanshaft society whose magazine *Grodner Opklangen* he himself would edit from 1948 onward) paid homage to him on the occasion of his seventieth birthday. In the IWO archive where some of my great-grandfather's papers, articles, and letters are preserved, I also discover the invitation to his tribute, written in Yiddish. The event was held on December 13, 1947, ten days after his birthday, at the Union of Residents from Grodno's assembly hall at 3243 Valentín Gómez.

It was not a large room, but there was space that night: the convocation hadn't been ideal. Mijl occupied an uncertain territory, very near oblivion, despite the fact that nearly fifty years before, with the publication of *Der Viderkol*, he had marked the initiation of the Jewish written word in the country. In 1898, while a pioneer at twenty years of age, he had known the happiest days of his life. In the decades that followed, he had contributed to fifty-seven national and international publications (among them Vilnius's *Ha Zman* and New York's *Ha Toran* and *Di Zukunft*) in Yiddish, Hebrew, and Spanish. But he had never risen to be, like his first friend Jacob Liachovitzky, a protagonist of his era; or like Pinie Katz, founder of the newspaper *Di Prese*, the creator of an empire of paper and ink.

Fifty years after *Der Viderkol*, the general public no longer remembered him. But the intellectuals did, and several attended the event for a chance to speak. The president of the Union of Residents from Grodno and some of his peers alluded to Mijl's work. A representative from the ICUF (the Idisher Cultur Farband, or Federation of Jewish Cultural Entities, which Mijl's son Rubén Sinay was active in) described the guest of honor's life, asserted that he'd always remained close to their people, cited his articles, and proposed to have his name inscribed in the golden book of Zionist aid fund Keren Kayemeth LeIsrael. And another of Mijl's fellow countrymen referenced his Grodner character and called for the Union of Residents to publish his complete works once and for all, also requesting the ICUF's help in doing so. The suggestion led to general applause. Mijl Hacohen Sinay, now old, was touched. His own colleagues were wishing for his recognition much more than anyone had for the last half century. It was as if they'd remembered, at long last, that he was still there.

The writer Simja Sneh, newly arrived that same year from London (having been discharged from the British Army's Jewish Brigade, which he'd fought in for much of World War II), spoke on behalf of the newspaper *Di Prese* and wished Mijl many more years in which to continue bolstering the Judeo-Argentine cultural edifice with his pen.

The night progressed as in a dream: Mijl Hacohen Sinay wished it would never end.

Shmuel Rollansky, who had spent two decades of his forty-four years of life in Argentina and was by now an intellectual guiding light, took the floor on behalf of the IWO. Rollansky hadn't experienced those days of 1898, but he knew *Der Viderkol*'s value and in some way felt ashamed of its mysterious fate (a fate already elusive even in 1947): "Unfortunately scarcely any traces of that periodical have remained, which is proof of the poor connection we have with the pioneers in general," he wrote later. That same year, Rollansky had published a biographical pamphlet on Mijl in Yiddish with the seal of the IWO: "Miguel Hacohen Sinay: Forefather of Yiddish Journalism in Argentina" (the title being the only line of Spanish anywhere in the work). In it, he analyzed the man's work and classified his texts into various categories: "On the Written Word and Its Pioneers," "On the Emergence of the Community," "On Judaic Education," "On Antisemitism."

That night, at the Union of Residents, Mijl was the last to take up the microphone. Life had granted him an unexpected gift: for a short while, he could once more feel the same emotion he'd known in March 1898, when a thousand well-wishing letters had inundated the little room at 1257 Corrientes that had served as *Der Viderkol*'s editorial office. His voice cracking with feeling, he thanked Rollansky and the IWO committee that had staged the tribute, and he recalled the old city of Buenos Aires that had been the backdrop for the birth of the Jewish press. Finally, the meager audience gave him an ovation that sounded like the applause of many more.

A short time later, as Mijl walked through the crowded neighborhood of Once (already empty by that hour) with his sons and daughters-in-law, he wore a different face. It had gone slack. The joy had been as intense as it was fleeting. Perhaps there, in the darkness and silence of Calle Valentín Gómez, Mijl felt a sense that he was seventy years old, and the young man Sinay, the daring creator of *Der Viderkol*, was now one piece filed away beneath several layers of memories: one more entry in the archive he himself directed at the IWO. My grandmother, who by then was two years into her marriage with Moisés—Mijl's middle child and my future grandfather Moishe—was with the group that night. She was walking beside her husband, sharing his smiles over the praise the old man had just received from his colleagues, when one comment troubled her. After the event, that melancholy father-in-law of hers said to them (or to himself): "I don't know why everyone is so happy, why they're celebrating so much, if I'm not so pleased to be seventy years old now myself . . ."

With the experience of *Der Viderkol* behind him, Mijl contributed to Abraham Vermont's *Die Volks Stimme* for a short time, until Vermont launched one of his typical campaigns of pure polemics against Mijl's father and their relationship cooled. In October, still in that same year of 1898, Mijl worked for *Der Kolonist*, a weekly paper edited by a young man named Paul Raphaël Grinblat who'd come there from Paris and became a short-lived friend before joining the ranks of the human traffickers; in the long run, Grinblat would end up in the Tierra del Fuego prison. Mijl went on writing as new publications emerged, but the money didn't go far enough. In early 1900s Buenos Aires he worked as a cuentenik—going door to door selling all manner of items on credit—and also found work at a real estate agency. However, and just as it had been in Moisés Ville, the profession he would later adopt as his own was that of teaching—though he never abandoned letters entirely.

And so, for several decades, Mijl led a nomadic life as a teacher and school inspector for the Central Council on Jewish Education in the Argentine Republic, the Vaad Hajinuj. He left Buenos Aires before the centennial, heading to Rosario. While there, he created a new periodical, *Der Veker* (The alarm clock), in 1910, and another, *Dos Peysekh-blat* (The passover page), in 1911. Along those banks of the Paraná River he worked as a teacher, and, in 1914, he set out for Bernasconi (to the Narcisse Leven colony in La Pampa), where he would dedicate himself to writing several short stories and a novella in the years to follow. His stories were published in 1919 under the title *Gam zu letovah* (This, too, is for the good) in the thirteenth edition of the collection *Bijlaj far yeden* (Little books for everyone). His novella, *Baleydikt a mes . . .* (A corpse is wronged . . .), saw the light of day in 1920 for the twenty-second edition of the same collection.

In both of those volumes, my great-grandfather's characters are poor immigrants, achingly humble, dragging their way through the city after crusts of bread without understanding the social injustice they are victims of. I can tell that Mijl wasn't inventing his stories, or at least not entirely, but knew immigrants just as afflicted as his characters. And I suspect he may have lived some of his own days with the same desperation, that of an outsider not knowing where his next meal will come from.

But it's also certain that, when he wrote these stories, in Rosario and Bernasconi, he lived without such hardships. In that little La Pampa town he saw the passage of the 1920s and, along with his second wife, Lea Raginsky, raised my grandfather and his two younger brothers, Marcos and Rubén. There had also been a fourth son, Levi Isaac, the eldest, who I suspect was born in Rosario, to a mother Mijl divorced under now mysterious circumstances. Mijl's grandson Moisés, who lives in the United States today, tells me in an email: "I could never understand why my zeide got divorced and then remarried to a woman who was very big and completely deaf, who couldn't hear you even if you yelled at the top of your lungs." One account says that Mijl was too much of a ladies' man, and that his first wife, Sara Fistel, wouldn't excuse him for it: she was an attractive modern woman, who had character. His father, Rabbi Mordejai Reuben, would have been the one who found his second wife and married him off to her by way of straightening him out.

Mijl Hacohen Sinay also spent time around Corrientes, Coronel Suárez, San Miguel de Tucumán (where his son Moisés would meet a young pharmaceutical student who already had the nickname "Mañe": my future grandmother), and Villa Alba, in La Pampa. He knew cities, towns, and colonies. And every time, in each of these places, even the most remote, he would found publications and take on the role of correspondent for the major newspapers of Buenos Aires. "He built a bridge between the city and the country: it was a real contribution, especially in the early years, when they seemed like two different worlds," noted the writer Moisés Senderey in *Di Prese*, in an article to celebrate Hacohen Sinay's eightieth year.

When outsiders turn up in Moisés Ville with investigative aims, their chances of having dinner with Ingue Kanzepolsky are high. Ingue is not only a sensitive and generous conversationalist—whom I find to have been shaped by his university career as an accountant but much more so by his tireless and autodidactic reading—but also distinguishes himself with his simple and savory cooking. He has invited me, for example, to come for dinner almost every night. The conversations stretch on over a main course, soup, dessert, and tea or coffee. It comforts me to think that, very near the house where Ingue lives with its lofty ceilings and spacious rooms, maybe even facing it, the school where my great-grandfather and great-great-grandfather taught their first classes in Argentina once stood. But, faced with the asphalt street of today, the modern houses, and the majestic Baron Hirsch Synagogue, it's impossible to imagine the dirt road at the end of the nineteenth century that accommodated the makeshift brick structures and sheds that once consolidated community life in the colony.

"It's hard to tell the history today," Ingue once told me, between plates, one night when he'd invited me over for chicken stew. The night before it had been cannelloni; the final course of squash soup, on the other hand, was the usual. "My father knew much more than I do, but I don't know if he experienced history with the same intensity as people investigating it today do. Instead, for him, everything that happened here was the most natural sort of thing."

As my host was shredding chicken legs and nestling in some boiled carrots, I pulled him out of the past and asked him about the future. It was an issue that distressed many people around here, who saw the Jews growing ever fewer in this Jerusalem of South America. Ingue, on the other hand, was taking it with serenity. Like almost everything else.

"For the past thirty or forty years, Moisés Ville has kept itself going with older people who no longer have so much enthusiasm, and no longer have the drive that made it great," he asserted. "When the town's last Jewish person dies, the history will keep going with other people and other concerns, but there's still plenty to be done as long as someone is around to tell what happened here, while the buildings still stand. And clearly they aren't just going to collapse, because people are always coming here to visit or to live. Many of these people are young: three new young residents have moved in on my block over the past few years. I'm not so interested in why they're coming, but they are coming, and they'll end up being assimilated."

"But we may well be talking about the end of the Jewish community in Moisés Ville. And you don't look too sad about it to me, Ingue . . ."

"Ah, no. Not at all. Because I came to a conclusion: we never did anything to stop fate from going that way. Don't forget that the Kadima Society was created in 1908 with the aim of having an assembly hall, a library, and a university. And the university never came to be. We did everything backward: we created a teachers' seminary so the children can go out into the world, but we never made any sources of employment so the children could stay here. Now we have some vacant spaces where we could set up a school of higher education. I proposed that we should do it. And? The idea went by like Sputnik; no one wanted to hear anything. Now I won't harp on. I have to adapt and seek out an interesting life, at least for myself . . . that's why I like to make friends with everyone who comes."

A few days later, we hug goodbye. "Don't lose your way," he says.

The Jewish Colonization Association is also a memory in Moisesvishe, the Moisés Ville of today. The end of the town's major institutions came as a slow but final wave: the cooperative La Mutua Agrícola, founded in 1908, closed in 1995; the Banco Comercial Israelita became a branch of the bank Bisel in 2000 and later a branch of Macro; the cooperative Socorro Fraternal, a mutual credit society launched in 1912, broke up in 1972; the SanCor factory, opened in 1981, was shut down in 2001, although it would open its doors again in 2007 for production at a smaller scale and under a different brand name.

The JCA's end was the one that left the biggest void: the company withdrew at the end of the 1950s. The arrival of the last family, the Merejens, had come some time before that, and they bought the administration's house when it was vacated.

The withdrawal of the Baron de Hirsch organization from Argentina was slow and silent, quite different from the manner of its arrival. The life of small farmers in the nation had gone through several phases of turbulence over the course of the twentieth century, and industrialization during the 1930s, as well as the control of agricultural prices set by President Juan D. Perón, were not unrelated to the exodus in the colonies run by the JCA, which responded with the action of the cooperatives but also with cultural activities.

While many colonists had already obtained the title deeds to their lands, disputes with the Fraternidad Agraria—which had picked up the torch from the old rebellious colonists—continued. In 1950, the association freed up large expanses of land that it had been saving for the arrival of new colonists, who were now no longer coming, and made them available to the children, about whom there had been so much debate over the course of two generations.

In 1958, the JCA deemed that it was time to cease bringing in new immigrants: Argentina's political and economic fluctuations were not generating confidence in Europe, and Israel was now a reality. On top of that, the blow from World War II had never entirely abated and finances had fallen into disarray. In little more than a decade, half of the population in the colonies had departed for the cities or moved abroad.

Roberto Schopflocher, the last of the administrators alive in Argentina, had told me his in-laws were forced to settle in the city for his mother-in-law's medical treatment. Others simply grew tired of the sacrifices of country life. "It was hard," asserted Schopflocher. "There were beautiful things about that country life as well, but you can't live off poetry, and you can't judge unless you were there."

In 1958, about 95 percent of the 2,045 Jewish farmers already owned their land. In Entre Ríos, that process had accelerated with the emergence of two controversial taxes of an expropriative nature (targeting large estates and absenteeism), which were particularly damaging to the JCA's situation.

Meanwhile, the JCA's personnel kept decreasing until in 1966 there were only three, assembled in an office in Buenos Aires. The association began to pack its bags in 1972: the land it still possessed (around five hundred hectares; that is, less than 0.1% of the six hundred thousand it had owned at its peak) was sold to the cooperatives, auctioned off, or donated to the municipalities, and its thousands of files were sent away to Israel . . . although, in point of fact, they had previously been deposited for years in a basement at the ORT school, where a broken pipe had flooded them. What could be salvaged was later transferred to the Central Archives for the History of the Jewish People, at the Hebrew University of Jerusalem. There, a group of volunteers—the majority of Argentine origins—is still working on a systematic registration of the files. In 1975, the association carried out an official liquidation of what remained.

And it was gone.

"But what imprint is left from the JCA?" I ask Eva Guelbert de Rosenthal at the Moisés Ville Museum.

"The debate is very arduous, and there's a great deal to be said, because the colonizing enterprise has its positive and its negative sides. You have to bear in mind that its gaze was set on rescuing Jews and not making them rich; from that point on, whether each one grew or not would be their own responsibility. Was all of the conflict that occurred here the fault of Baron de Hirsch? I'd say that he had an altruistic idea for the people's productive transformation into working the land. Although the Baron died after a few short years, he won major recognition because, if it hadn't been for him, many would not have been saved from what was to come. Then what was left were the administrators, who had to consult Paris about everything: bureaucracy and stringency brought on clashes with the colonists. But at the same time, in all of the colonies, they created schools, hospitals, and libraries, which were for the residents of the entire region. The mentality was one of progress. And I think that, if we do an objective analysis, the balance is ultimately positive. The rescue of the German people who were brought over right before World War II was very timely, and on the other hand, what would have become of the immigrants brought at the turn of the century if they'd stayed in Europe?"

And the people themselves? Would they also have thought about that? About how close they believed they were to cruelty while facing the administrators in the colonies, but how far, as they could confirm in the end, they really had been. Antisemitism lingered like a bitter poison until the last days of the war, and then beyond as well. I wish I could imagine the mental oppression felt by the Jewish survivors of the Holocaust, but I cannot. And I don't mean only the most concrete survivors—those who continued their lives with a number tattoo—but Jewish people all around the world, even those who had followed the war from the warmth of their homes in Argentina.

But, I repeat, I cannot.

In the Buenos Aires of 1946 and 1947, Argentina's Jews looked like distant survivors of war; an anguish could be glimpsed on their long faces, one made of the private certainty of having avoided death and the painful absence left by the death of one (or many) relatives across the ocean. Little time was left before the United Nations General Assembly would approve the partition of Palestine, by which the state of Israel would emerge and a period of some redemption would begin. Until then, public acts of homage to the victims—endless, repetitive—responded to the need to restore some dignity to their memory.

At some point during the war, my great-grandfather participated in one of those events; inside a school notebook preserved among his writings, I discover what he wrote for the occasion. I'm unaware of the exact circumstances, although I suspect he must have been with a group of young people or at a non-Jewish institution, as over the course of the several pages Mijl dispensed with Yiddish to instead write in Spanish:

Yes! Galitzia and Poland on this day are no more than simple butcheries, which would be well suited by a signpost bearing the same grim inscription that Dante saw carved upon the gates of the Inferno: 'Per me si va nella città dolente, per me si va nell'eterno dolore, per me si va tra la perduta gente.'

Yes, now! When we are here in the twentieth century, in the Modern Era, with the triumph of science, with the omnipotence of technology, with the wireless telegram, with airplanes to lift us like birds into the skies, with submarines that render us equal to the fish in the sea; in short, now, when we are here with all the admirable and truly splendid progress of the human spirit, now, when human heroism has broken through the chains that held the people's thoughts in slavery, now is the time that all these crimes and killings come to pass. Yes, now, even at this very moment!

Oh, what shame! What sorrow!

O twentieth century! What have you made of all your glory? Where are all your sublime appointments—Liberty, Brotherhood, Equality, and Justice? Yes, where are they! In Galitzia and Poland, in those two Sodom lands, there at least they are no more!

And many words in kind.

That was what the people breathed. The heavy air of grief.

Sometime later, faced with the certainty of victory but also the horror of all that had occurred, my great-grandfather composed the text of "The First Jewish Victims in Moisés Ville." The year was now 1947, and rescuing those murders committed fifty years before from oblivion took on a special meaning.

To better understand the forces that inspired the text, it is necessary to interpret the atmosphere enshrouding it.

In those days the motives were perhaps more evident than they are today. And maybe that was why my great-grandfather's journalistic rigor proved less exacting as it ought to have been. A different rigor, the rigor mortis of those killed in the war, was at that time much more real and imposed an urgent tempo on literary production, still down in the trenches.

Maybe that—the urgency of cauterizing open wounds—was why the text is plagued with hard-to-confirm names and imprecise dates.

Maybe that was why Mijl Hacohen Sinay allowed himself to write that Gershom Gerchunoff's body had been missing, that when it was found it already appeared "chewed and eaten away by the birds of prey and the animals of the field, such that only his bones could be buried," when in reality the corpse was never lost from sight.

Maybe that was why text makes room for the spectacle of horror in the killing of María Alexenicer, "cut in pieces," whose breasts "were strewn beside her body, which was slashed from the base of the stomach up to the throat," whose organs seemed to have been "pulled outside," her throat, "slashed across," and her eyes, "removed from their sockets." My great-grandfather wrote: "Only a murderer truly more savage and bloodthirsty than a beast could have acted in such a way."

The real beast was in Europe: in Galitzia and Poland, those "simple butcheries" with a signpost bidding welcome into hell, but also in Auschwitz and Stalingrad, in Treblinka and Kursk, in Berlin and Moscow.

In essence, in that imagery so present in the 1940s: the Jewish body emaciated, dead, crushed.

Mijl Hacohen Sinay wrote "The First Jewish Victims in Moisés Ville" in 1947, half a century after the events had unfolded. After the war, recounting those crimes was also a way of speaking about a present in which an immense crime cast its shadow over everything. My great-grandfather's text seemed to arrive right on cue.

And when I would have wished to share some of my conclusions with Eliahu Toker, the writer who—with that message advising me to seek the truth about Mijl Hacohen Sinay, the crimes of Moisés Ville, and the newspaper *Der Viderkol* within my own family—helped me summon the nerve to begin this investigation, I was surprised, reading the newspaper from November 4, 2011, by news of his death.

Toker had passed away the day before.

He had suffered, as they say, from a long illness. What remains of him now is a body of work dedicated to Yiddish and Jewish culture. He left behind a great deal for others and knew what it was to make the most of his place along the chain of generations. In *Lejaim*, his book of poems, the verses of "Yiddish" run like this: "Yiddish surrounds me, sustains me / unfolds me with the form of flight / I fall in love with each of its voices / and on my lips each leaves / the taste of its most hushed essence."

The Hotel Bristol—where the coffee overflows, the bellhops communicate in shouts, and the Obelisco of Buenos Aires is visible through the window—is, finally, the setting of my long-awaited meeting with a representative of the JCA. I come upon him in an unexpected way: in February 2012, a group of young people from Israel and Argentina visits the towns of Moisés Ville and Basavilbaso as part of the worldwide Jewish Heritage Program, registering what has been and what still is, and they bring along one of the former directors of the JCA as a guest star.

The man's name is Yoki Lothan. Born in 1938 in Germany, he was able to escape in time along with his family, who initially settled in Jerusalem and later in Tel Aviv. At age eighteen, he joined a kibbutz with a group from the newly formed Israeli army. He didn't know it then, but he would dedicate his life to what he calls the "Kibbutzim Movement": later, he would move on to Ruhama and even live for thirty years in Nir Eliyahu along with his wife, Sara, who is also here at the Hotel Bristol.

Lothan doesn't have the charm of a French regent from the Belle Époque. Nor the severity of an administrator willing to humiliate colonists so as to turn them into vassals. Nor the bitterness to speak about agitators. Nor the detachment of a bureaucrat who forces silence and obedience. Lothan possesses none of the signs I had expected to find in an executive from the Jewish Colonization Association. He seems so different from that image that I have trouble recognizing him in the hotel lobby. This JCA man looks like a retiree out on a stroll. And he is a retiree out on a stroll: he has just retired after eighteen years spent steering the reins of the JCA in the small city of Ra'anana, in Israel, the only place in the world where the association remains active.

It turns out that the Baron de Hirsch company, which at one point was the largest philanthropic society in the world, today has only three part-time employees. Its administrative council, seated in London and composed of fifteen members, is made up of volunteers, and the flight and hotel expenses demanded by their annual meetings in Israel are paid from each of their own pockets. Lothan, today an honorary member of the administrative council, tells me that not very much of the baron's money is left. Yet something is left: according to the online index Charities Direct, the outstanding capital stands at forty million dollars.

And that is fascinating. After more than 120 years, two world wars, and no end of economic transformations, the project still survives.

The majority of the baron's money was used to purchase land around the world, the largest portions being in Argentina and Israel. But today, long after the colonists were able to obtain the lands for themselves, the JCA has not a single hectare of its own. As for Hirsch's money, it is well positioned in the New York and London stock exchanges and sometimes operates in that of Israel as well. The market earnings are used in agricultural, educational, and touristic development for Israel's outlying regions of Galilee and the Negev. For Lothan, it's possible to achieve change even without much money. His work until quite recently consisted of seeking out new projects, continuing those that the JCA was funding, and evaluating their success. Today, the "protégés"—as Baron de Hirsch liked to call his beneficiaries—aren't stateless colonists but Israeli inhabitants of kibbutzim and moshavim, whom Lothan, of course, does not call "protégés."

I wanted to confront a representative of the JCA with all of the injustices once committed in Baron de Hirsch's Argentine lands. I'd thought of demanding a historic apology for the cruelties of Moisés Ville's administrator Michel Cohan, who ejected my family from the town. I'd even imagined the very moment in which the JCA representative would feel shame and be left at a loss for words. But with Lothan, nothing of the kind happens.

"In the current JCA we're all familiar with the Argentine experience, but none of the details. And none of us, apart from me, has ever been in Argentina," he tells me. The history of the murders and revolts is completely unknown to him. "Yes, we know that Baron de Hirsch's largest colonizing project was here, that it marked the beginning of the Jewish community in this country, that it operated here for some time, and that, if we observe the results a hundred years later, it's hard to decide whether it was successful or not."

In any case, I want to hear what he has to say about the colonists' revolts. And I tell him about Mordejai Reuben Hacohen Sinay.

"Ah, yes," he continues. "Those kinds of events were also occurring in the Israeli colonies, at the same time that they were happening in Argentina. One of the consequences of all that in Argentina was the emergence of agricultural cooperatives, which were born in the colonies and still exist today. The same thing happened in Israel. For that matter, the first kibbutz, Degania, emerged in 1905 after one very famous revolt when the administrators withdrew and left the colonists on their own."

For Lothan, it's too late now to judge who was right and who was wrong in the conflict that shook Moisés Ville in 1897:

"I think both were wrong. Plenty of people ask me: how could Baron de Hirsch, who was such a major philanthropist, fail to realize that his employees would do something with his money that hadn't been in his head? How can it be that a man could give millions and at the same time wonder about the fate of each of his pennies? From what I understand, the baron thought that if he was going to bestow all that money, the beneficiaries would have to make responsible use of it. But what does it matter, that's all part of history now . . . And it may be that it's also part of our essence as human beings."

As the years passed, Mijl Hacohen Sinay became an elderly man who would stroll around the neighborhood of Once laden with books. "You can find him now walking down Calle Pasteur, at a steady pace, on his way to work," the writer Moisés Senderey said in his piece for *Di Prese* in December 1957, when Mijl turned eighty.

> He does not look like a lion or an eagle but rather a modest ant who's always wanted to be useful in his work, both for others and himself. I remember how he used to say that people want to learn from lions or eagles, but you need to learn from ants. Look at their paths and you'll be more intelligent, he would say.

And, in an article published in the *Grodner Opklangen* in 1956, Shmuel Volpovitch honored him by writing that he'd always been an idealist: "Mijl Hacohen Sinay, the humble, the perfect Jew, the maskil, the *moreh*, the poor (and I'm more than certain he will feel great satisfaction reading that last epithet), plowed along working without personal ambitions or self-aggrandizement."

On the other hand, Mijl is remembered by his grandson Moisés, the doctor who has lived in the United States for several decades, as a great hero. And as a man who always kept his documents on him so as to confirm with a smile—and the same pride as Alberto Gerchunoff—that he, too, was Argentine. His grandson also recalls him as a notable calligrapher both in Yiddish and Spanish, who used a common pen to the last of his days, the same kind used by children in school. Because of that, his fingers were always stained with ink—and tobacco. He describes him, too, as a man who wanted all four of his children to pursue a university education, and who sent Marcos, the only one who did get his degree, a peso every week over the four-year course of his pharmaceutical studies in Tucumán: "They really were poor, but all of them were surrounded by books," he writes in one of his many emails. Moisés remembers his grandfather, also, as a father who carefully saved each of the letters that another of his sons, Rubén, wrote to him from the Neuquén prison, or "Capicúa" in slang, where he was imprisoned for two years due to his communist activities. There, in jail, Rubén had written a play, "Don Quixote in Capicúa," which spoke of freedom and dreams.

"I remember that when my grandfather died we went through all the books and papers," the grandson's message continues.

> Uncle Rubén decided where each book and each piece of writing would go, because he was the most knowledgeable in Yiddish. I read the letters Rubén sent from prison then, and I don't think I've ever cried so much. My grandfather must have read them a ton: they were very well cared for.

In 1944, during another of the stints Rubén spent behind bars—this time at the Devoto penitentiary, once more because of his political activism—Mijl brought his grandson along for a visit and they brought him an enormous cake. "That's one of the things I'm very grateful to him for: to a boy of six like I was then, it was the adventure of a lifetime," Moisés recalls in the message.

In this grandson's life, Mijl also has the unhappy honor of having been the first to die. Moisés, who was a young student in his third year of medicine, watched him pass away in his own arms. Mijl's death was simple: at age eighty he went out to buy cigarettes, and for some reason when he returned, he had to climb up all seven stories by the stairs. His heart couldn't take the effort. "He died in peace," says his grandson.

That was August 8, 1958.

Shmuel Rollansky then dedicated a memory to him in his column "Schtrijen" (Characteristics) for the newspaper *Di Ydische Zaitung*. In an affectionate but critical obituary, the IWO man lamented my great-grandfather's having been "one of the pioneers of Argentina who was not able to play the role he should have played." His self-imposed exile in the country and his distance from the centers of intellectual production had conspired against his opportunities. Rollansky noted that many who had less to say than Mijl had managed to publish their books, while he had never been able to put out more than "a few slim booklets." And he called once more—because his words in 1947 had not been heeded—for his complete works to be published:

> If we leave them for later, the same thing will happen to them as did to the author and they will be forgotten. And so it is necessary to prevent them from going without their due importance and now, in a moment while those texts still remain alive, to turn them into a reality. This is a duty for the IWO. Mijl Hacohen Sinay, the pioneer of 1898, who had his start writing articles, continued as a short story writer, and ended as a chronicler, left behind him many scattered columns that can help this 1958 generation remember how difficult life once was, and how difficult it proves today to believe everything that has grown grew out of that first generation.

But his works were never collected.

On the one-year anniversary of Mijl's death, his friend and colleague Meir Besovic commemorated him with several lines in issue XI of the *Grodner Opklangen*. Besovic had shared his final years, working alongside him at the IWO archive. In his piece, he noted that Mijl held onto many memories and spoke at great length about his father as well as his first friend, Jacob Liachovitzky. "One day, while he was praising Liachovitzky's talent for argumentation and lamenting how the man had been senselessly discredited, I said to him, 'That's all true, but who's going to remember him, and who's going to revive his words?'" wrote Besovic.

> He thought for a while and then, still lost in his reflections, answered: "That's true, who's going to remember his work?" At this moment, one year after his death, I am facing his chair and his table, in the very place where he worked, and it seems to me as if Sinay is sitting right there, looking at me and saying: "Who will remember my work? Who will remember me?"

And then the time comes to leave Moisés Ville behind.

But I can't go without hearing out the pair who've been accused as masterminds behind the mass poisoning of dogs. The man from the plaza who was caught opened his mouth and gave them away. His account earned them a place in the dark history of the town even though they are an ordinary married couple who run a shop selling clothes and gifts. But over and over again the neighbors had warned me about them: "They're odd people," "It won't do you any good talking to them," "He used to wait for dogs to come into his house and then stick them with a pitchfork, and he'd laugh."

I wonder if they'll boast of the things people say about them.

I wonder if my questions will be fair inquiries.

I wonder, too, if there's a pitchfork waiting for me inside.

And without thinking too much about it, I open the door to the shop. There she is behind the counter, watching me with curiosity. A woman of around sixty with short red hair, and she's the one the man from the plaza accused of being the intellectual author of a mass poisoning. On street corners in Moisés Ville there are still comments that she paid the plaza man twenty pesos for every dog killed. It may be nothing but a myth, one more among all those of Moisés Ville, where there are many. I tell the woman, then, who I am. And what I want. And her eyes run bloodshot. It isn't anger, but pain.

Although she agrees to speak and tell me her truth, she asks me to take mercy and forget her name. Because, she explains, it took them a great deal of effort to restore their good name, and her husband—the other one identified—is very ill, so she must recover her strength to care for him.

Inside the shop, the silence is total. When the woman's wisp of a voice fades, there is only the vibration of a fluorescent lightbulb in the ceiling. I can breathe easy: no one has greeted me with a pitchfork.

"I'm not from here," she says. "I was born in Buenos Aires, married in Córdoba, and came to live in Moisés Ville where my kids were studying at the Hebrew School. We never shut our doors to any institution, and we had an excellent relationship with everybody, but . . . do you know what it's like to own a business and have everything fall apart on you? And how do you feel morally while unable to prove it's all slander? That completely disoriented us as people."

The woman says and reaffirms, she swears that she is innocent. That the whole thing is a lie. That nothing ever came of the matter and the truth was never discovered. That for some unknown reason she and her husband were implicated without proof. That someone mentioned their name in spite and threw her to the dogs—the most dangerous kind of dogs. That some dogs had always been poisoned in Moisés Ville. That they were still getting poisoned today. And that, worse still, she was a victim of the poisoner herself: five of her own dogs died from eating the bait.

"The last one was Noren . . . The thing is, we love animals: we have cats, we have dogs . . ." she goes on, with more conviction.

Then she brings in a magnificent collie, beautiful, who appears with a canine grin and stares at me with interest. The dog is four years old and lives inside a little room at the back of the shop; it was a decision the woman's son made when he discovered that a neighbor had shot at him with pellets. "I'm not going to let them take this dog from us too," the boy said. "This dog is going to the shop. And he'll go out only for short times. We're going to take care of him, and he's going to live with us."

"Maybe the dog was bothering them, but why wouldn't they say something about it to me?" she now laments, unconsciously repeating the same words used by the other neighbors who were affected by the poison. "It means that there are aggressive people in town who don't like animals. I don't want any more animals now because of that," she admits, and the Lassie stares at her as though expecting a bone. "The day we lose him I'm not going to want another, because we get too attached to these pets, and I don't want to suffer like that again."

"But why did the police arrest you if you had nothing to do with it?"

"I wasn't arrested, but I spent a few hours at the police station because the cops wanted me to say I was guilty. The whole thing was a set up. They told me I had to come and present myself, but I didn't know what for. And right there they started accusing and accusing and accusing me . . . I didn't lack the claws to defend myself, because however meek a person is injustice still stings. It's very unpleasant being there, blamed for something you have nothing to do with. And not just that. What's just as bad or worse is that afterward everyone accuses you with their eyes, simply because of a rumor . . . That's terrible."

The day after she was apprehended, Moisés Ville was celebrating Father's Day, and everything at her gift shop had been ready for a long time. She, having been at the police station the day before, got up in the morning, bathed, and looked at herself in the mirror. "No one's going to come looking for me at home to take pity on me. I'm going to go to the shop and open it, the same as always," she told herself. "If someone wants to come in and say something to me, no matter what, let them. I won't hide because I didn't have anything to do with it." And that's what she did. Several people stopped by the shop that day. Several bought things. And several asked her, surprised, what had happened. Now the stillness surrounding her—in a shop that she's picked up again and again against all the finger-pointing—seems to weigh on her. As her story progresses, her eyes grow damp.

"One of the people who accused me without proof at that time will now stop by and greet me, but I turn away," she continues, and just the image of it causes her disgust and tears. "It left me with so much, so much hate . . . The taste it left in my mouth is very bitter. Really, really ugly . . . It's never going to leave me . . . Never. Never, never."

I mention that expression about the smaller the town, the bigger the scandal. Her eyes remain steeped in tears.

"For me there's a before and an after: it had only been a year since we'd lost a daughter . . . this girl . . ." she reaches a hand into the back and removes a portrait from the display case. Her daughter was thirty-two years old when she died unexpectedly in Tucumán. The woman's tears fall in despair and the words catch in her throat. But she manages a few to tell me about her son, a fine boy who came back to Moisés Ville to be with his parents during their mourning and then refused to leave them on their own. "We already had too much of a burden to take any more. Too much!"

We stand in silence. The buzzing of the light bulb reappears.

Slightly calmer now, she dries her tears.

"I don't know the reason why they accused me."

I leave Moisés Ville on a bus. And as kilometers of the Pampas slide by through the window, the question about the past remains: where is it?

It's no simple task to approach a series of murders of which all that remains are the oral accounts of the victims' descendants; my great-grandfather's text, dramatically cut through by its time; and scattered, infrequent articles in a few periodicals. There are different paths to reconstructing the past: that of memories is one, and that of documents, another. In the way Mijl Hacohen Sinay's chronicle contrasts with journalistic sources contemporary to the homicides, we can appreciate the overload of horror in pursuit of an idea of his own (was Mijl exaggerating on purpose or not realizing he was doing it?). But in the same way, the major newspapers could have recounted those murders according to their own interests as well. The press is not ingenuous: not even such a periodical as one entitled *Der Viderkol*, created by an exiled boy of twenty to denounce the abuses of the largest philanthropic company in the world, to rouse a wave of admiration and controversy in the great city where he's just arrived. In any case, reaching an impartial account of those events would require legal documents as well. Ones that do not exist today.

Back in Buenos Aires, my grandmother Mañe turns up with a letter from Pepu, her niece and partner in crime: they are only a few years apart and were raised very nearly as twins. Today Pepu lives in Israel, along with one of her grandsons, after having decided to emigrate from La Banda (in Santiago del Estero) at age eighty. She knew nothing of Hebrew when she departed, which is why now, as she's learning it with the speed of necessity, one of her favorite readings is the police report section in the newspaper, an exercise charged with suspense.

There has always been a fluid epistolary exchange between Pepu and Mañe, and now my grandmother takes the latest letter in her hands to read me her niece's words:

> Very admirable, that work Javier is thinking of doing. I think there's an interest around the world right now in rediscovering and reestablishing family history, beginning with the oldest ones who left traces of their past. I read that interview you sent where Javier talks about his book *Sangre joven*. I can't quite manage to connect his sad responses to the image I have of him, of a healthy and carefree little boy, with this new Javier, profoundly trapped in his investigations into sordid criminal events. Obviously, Javier grew up and is now interested in unraveling the motives that lead people to commit crimes. Is it ever possible to

reach clarity for something that arises in a shadowy inner world? And if the psychiatrist has already been dispatched, who has the final say? The explanations are usually frustrating. When I started trying to read the newspaper, straight away I set about unraveling the criminal events using a dictionary. They were bloodcurdling: a mother of French origins is residing in Israel with a young daughter, born after a one-night stand that lasted a couple of hours between her and an Israeli in France. She'd tried to take her away from the father, who was raising her with the grandmother, and had succeeded. She had more children, but as the girl was not intelligent and irritated her, she told her lover: "Take her and do what you want with her." He did as much and threw her into a river.

Mañe interrupts the reading at my expression of surprise: "Yes, yes! She says there are such chilling crimes in Israel!"
She continues:

Another case. A man from an excellent family, a professional, married to a beautiful woman, finds out his wife is going to file for divorce. His three-year-old daughter now lives with her mother in Jerusalem while he is in a moshav in the center of the country. Every fifteen days he has the right to take her for the weekend. One Saturday he takes her, he offers her candy and the girl says: "Mamma told me not to eat anything you give because you might try to poison me." The man tucks her into bed, tells her a story, and when he's sure that she is in a deep sleep, he smothers her with a plastic bag. To make the mother suffer, he later explains. A week ago he took a free-fall in prison and killed himself.

"Just like in any other nation, there are murders there too!" my grand-mother insists.
And she goes on: "One more case. A Jewish immigrant arrived from Russia with his family . . ."

An aside:

"They're afraid of people from Russia because they say they're very tough, like back in the days of the czars."

More from the letter: "He found work at a high-class café in a major city, but the owner of the place told him off for drinking all the whisky and ordered him not to come back. But the man got his wife, who was still working at the café, to make a copy of his former boss's house key, and he went there at night, and when the boss arrived, he stabbed him. The Russians almost always use knives. He did the same thing with the wife and then waited for the son, who also worked at the café, and kill him the same way too. In another room, an eight-month-old baby and a three-year-old girl were sleeping. He killed the girl and, as the baby was crying, gave him the bottle before stabbing him as well."

This time my grandmother falls silent.

Pepu's letter continues: "These crimes, there are at least three per day . . ."

My grandmother and I exchange looks and understand, in the same moment, that it's time at last to let the matter go.

Bibliography

Books and Articles

50 años de colonización judía en la Argentina. Delegación de Asociaciones Israelitas Argentinas (DAIA), Buenos Aires, 1939.

50 años de la prensa judía progresista en la Argentina 1923–1973. Buenos Aires, 1973.

Adler, Elkan Nathan, *Jews from Many Lands*. The Jewish Publication Society of America, Philadelphia, 1905.

Aleijem, Scholem, "El pasajero de Buenos Aires," in *Tercera Clase*. Acervo Cultural, Buenos Aires, 1955.

Alpersohn, Marcos, *Colonia Mauricio. Memorias de un colono judío*, 3 vols. Prometeo, Buenos Aires, 2010.

Alpersohn, Mordejai, *Di kinder fun der "Pampa"* [in Yiddish]. G. Kaplansky, Buenos Aires.

—, *On Argentine Soil* [in Yiddish]. Librería de G. Kaplansky, Buenos Aires, 1931.

Anthology of Jewish Writers in Argentina [in Yiddish]. Sociedad de Escritores Israelitas H. D. Normberg, Buenos Aires, 1962.

Anthology of Yiddish Literature in Argentina [in Yiddish]. Comité de Homenaje al diario *Di Prese*, Buenos Aires, 1944.

Anuario 5714 año hebreo. 1953/1954. Vida comunitaria judía [in Yiddish]. Asociación Mutual Israelita Argentina, Comunidad de Buenos Aires, Buenos Aires, 1953.

Argentina: 50 Years of Jewish Life in the Country. 20th Anniversary of Di Prese [in Yiddish]. Buenos Aires, 1938.

Arredondo, Marcos F., *Croquis bonaerenses*. Fondo Nacional de las Artes, Buenos Aires.

Aslanov, Cyril, *Sociolingüística histórica de las lenguas judías*. Lilmod, Buenos Aires, 2011.

Astro, Alan, "Más allá de la represión: la literatura ídish de América Latina," in Alejandro Meter and Ariana Huberman (comps.), *Memoria y representación: configuraciones culturales y literarias en el imaginario judío latinoamericano*. Beatriz Viterbo Editora, Rosario, 2006.

Astro, Alan (ed.), *Yiddish South of the Border: An Anthology of Latin American Yiddish Writing*. University of New Mexico Press, Albuquerque, 2003.

Avni, Haim, "La agricultura judía en la Argentina, ¿éxito o fracaso?," *Desarrollo Económico*, vol. 22, no. 88, January–March 1983a.

—, *Argentina y la historia de la inmigración judía 1810–1950*. Editorial Universitaria Magnes, Universidad Hebrea de Jerusalén y AMIA, Buenos Aires, 1983b.

—, "El proyecto del Barón de Hirsch: la gran visión y sus resultados," in *Índice para el análisis de nuestro tiempo*. Centro de Estudios Sociales-DAIA, Buenos Aires, 1990.

Bab, Arturo, "The Jews in Argentina before the Colonization of Baron Hirsch [in Yiddish]," in *Argentiner IWO Shriftn (anales del Instituto Científico Judío Argentino), 3*. Instituto Científico Judío-IWO, Buenos Aires, 1945.

Bendersky, Baruj, *In Jewish Lands* [in Yiddish]. Buenos Aires, 1931.

Bianchi, Susana, *Historia de las religiones en la Argentina: Las minorías religiosas*. Sudamericana, Buenos Aires, 2004.

Bizberg, Pinjas, "Following the Traces of the First Jewish Colonists in Argentina," [in Yiddish] in *Argentiner IWO Shrifts (anales del Instituto Científico Judío Argentino), 3*. Instituto Científico Judío-IWO, Buenos Aires, 1945.

—, "Conflicts between Colonists and the Local JCA Administration" [in Yiddish], in *Argentiner IWO Shriftn (anales del Instituto Científico Judío Argentino), 4*. Instituto Científico Judío-IWO, Buenos Aires, 1947.

Bonaudo, Marta, and Sonzogni, Élida, "Cuando disciplinar fue ocupar (Santa Fe, 1850–90)," *Mundo agrario*, vol. 1, no. 1. Universidad Nacional de La Plata, La Plata, 2000.

Botoshansky, Jacob, *Mame Idish* [in Yiddish]. Buenos Aires, 1949.

—, *The Life of a Jewish Journalist* [in Yiddish]. Comité para editar las obras escogidas de J. Botoshansky, Buenos Aires, 1942.

Caimari, Lila, *La ciudad y el crimen. Delito y vida cotidiana en Buenos Aires, 1880–1940*. Sudamericana, Buenos Aires, 2009.

Caplán, Benedicto, *Memorias. Un gaucho judío en la Casa Rosada*. Milá, Buenos Aires, 2001.

Carlino, Carlos, *Gauchos y gringos en la tierra ajena*. Plus Ultra, Buenos Aires, 1976.

Carrasco, Gabriel, "El primer linchamiento. Consecuencias de la mala legislación y de su peor cumplimiento," *El Economista Argentino*, no. 17. Buenos Aires, March 26, 1892.

—, *La colonización agrícola en la Provincia de Santa Fe. Cuadro general*. El Progreso, Santa Fe, 1893.

Cecchini de Dallo, Ana María, "La sociedad santafesina en la segunda mitad del siglo XIX: la violencia entre los grupos pobladores," Noveno Congreso Nacional y Regional de Historia Argentina (Rosario, September 26–28, 1996). Academia Nacional de Historia, Buenos Aires, 1996.

Chasanowich (Jazanovich), Leon, *Der Krizis fun der idisher kolonizatsye in Argentina un der moralisher bankrot fun der IKA-Administratsyon* [in Yiddish]. A. Salat, Lviv, 1910.

Cherjovsky, Iván, "La faz ideológica del conflicto colonos/JCA: el discurso del ideal agrario en las memorias de Colonia Mauricio," in Emanuel Kahan et al. (comps.), *Marginados y consagrados: nuevos estudios sobre la vida judía en Argentina*. Lumiere, Buenos Aires, 2011.

Chumbita, Hugo, *Jinetes rebeldes. Historia del bandolerismo social en la Argentina*. Colihue, Buenos Aires, 2009.

Cociovich, Noé, *Génesis de Moisés Ville*. Milá, Buenos Aires, 1987.

Crónicas judeoargentinas 1. Los pioneros en ídish, 1890–1944. Milá, Buenos Aires, 1987.

Delegación de Asociaciones Israelitas Argentinas (DAIA), *Medio siglo en el surco argentino. Cincuentenario de la Jewish Colonization Association (JCA)*. Buenos Aires, 1942.

Di Biasio, Pascualina, and Montenegro de Arévalo, Liliana, "Fuentes para una historia social de la Justicia." Santa Fe, 2008, mundoarchivistico.com.

Djenderedjian, Julio, *Gringos en las pampas: Inmigrantes y colonos en el campo argentino*. Sudamericana, Buenos Aires, 2008.

Drucaroff, Sansón, *Pioneros (en homenaje al cincuentenario de la Rivera "Barón Hirsch")*. Movimiento de Ex-Colonos Residentes en la Capital, Buenos Aires, 1957.

Dujovne, Miriam S., et al., *Los judíos en la Argentina*. Betenu Ediciones para el Hogar, Buenos Aires, 1986.

Dujovne, Alejandro, "Cartografía de las publicaciones periódicas judías de izquierda en Argentina, 1900–1953," in *RMA, Revista del Museo de Antropología*. Universidad Nacional de Córdoba, 2008.

Dyleiko, Aleksandr A., *Belarus Facts 2010*. Ministry of Foreign Affairs of the Republic of Belarus, 2010.

Feierstein, Ricardo, *Historia de los judíos argentinos*. Planeta, Buenos Aires, 1993.

—, *Comunidad judía de Buenos Aires 1894–1994*. Milá, Buenos Aires, 1995.

—, *Los mejores relatos con gauchos judíos*. Ameghino, Rosario, 1998.

—, *Alberto Gerchunoff, judío y argentino. Viaje temático desde "Los gauchos judíos" (1910) hasta sus últimos textos (1950) y visión crítica*. Milá, Buenos Aires, 2000.

—, *Vida cotidiana de los judíos argentinos. Del gueto al country*. Sudamericana, Buenos Aires, 2007.

Fernández, Miguel Ángel, *Bandidos rurales en la campaña santafesina 1870–1880*. Escuela de Historia, Facultad de Humanidades y Artes, Universidad Nacional de Rosario, Rosario, 1998.

Ferrero, Jorgelina, et al., *Palacios: 100 años de historia*. Palacios, Santa Fe, 1990.

Fischman Slemenson, Marta, *Recreaciones*. VH, Buenos Aires, 2009.

Fistemberg Adler, Felipe, *Moisés Ville. Recuerdos de un pibe pueblerino*. Milá, Buenos Aires.

Freidenberg, Judith Noemí, *The Invention of the Jewish Gaucho*. The University of Texas Press, Austin, 2009.

Gabis, Abraham, "The Depopulation Process of the Agricultural Territories" [in Yiddish], in *Argentiner IWO Shriftn (anales del Instituto Científico Judío Argentino)*, *4*. Instituto Científico Judío-IWO, Buenos Aires, 1947.

—, "Evolution and Present State of the JCA [in Yiddish]," in *Anuario 5714 año hebreo. 1953/1954. Vida comunitaria judía*. Asociación Mutual Israelita Argentina, Comunidad de Buenos Aires, Buenos Aires, 1953.

"Galería de sospechosos." Policía de la Capital, Buenos Aires, 1898.

Gallo, Ezequiel, *La pampa gringa. La colonización agrícola en Santa Fe 1870–1895*. Edhasa, Buenos Aires, 2004.

—, *Colonos en armas. Las revoluciones radicales en la provincia de Santa Fe (1893)*. Siglo XXI Editores, Buenos Aires, 2007.

García de D'Agostino et al. (comp.), *Imagen de Buenos Aires a través de los viajeros 1870–1910*. Colección del IV Centenario de Buenos Aires, Universidad de Buenos Aires, Buenos Aires, 1981.

Garfunkel, Boris, *Narro mi vida*. Self-published, Buenos Aires, 1960.

Gerchunoff, Alberto, *El problema judío*. Ediciones Macabi, Buenos Aires, 1945.

—, *Entre Ríos, mi país*. Editorial Futuro, Buenos Aires, 1950.

—, *Buenos Aires, la metrópoli de mañana*. Cuadernos de Buenos Aires XIII, Municipalidad de la Ciudad de Buenos Aires, Buenos Aires, 1960.

—, *Los gauchos judíos*. Raíces, Milá, Buenos Aires, 1988. [First edition, Talleres Gráficos Joaquín Sesé, La Plata, 1910.]

Ghiraldo, Alberto, *Los salvajes*. Librería Renacimiento, Madrid.

Gilbert, Martin, *Atlas de la historia judía*. Raíces, Milá, Buenos Aires, 1988.

Glombovsky, Moisés I., *Los gringos*. Buenos Aires.

Goldman, David, *Di iuden in Argentine* [in Yiddish]. Krasilovsky, Buenos Aires, 1914.

González Arrili, Bernardo, *Buenos Aires 1900*. Centro Editor de América Latina, Buenos Aires, 1967.

Gori, Gastón, *La pampa sin gaucho. Influencia del inmigrante en la transformación de los usos y costumbres en el campo argentino en el siglo XIX*. Editorial Raigal, Buenos Aires, 1952.

—, *Vagos y mal entretenidos*. Ediciones Colmegna, Santa Fe, 1965.

—, *El indio y la colonia Esperanza*. Museo de la Colonización, Esperanza, Santa Fe, 1981.

Guelbert de Rosenthal, Eva (comp.), *Memoria oral de Moisés Ville. Al rescate de la identidad*. Milá, Buenos Aires, 2008.

Guelbert de Rosenthal, Eva, et al., *Patrimonio urbano arquitectónico de Moisés Ville. Inventario de la primera colonia judía en la Argentina*. Universidad Nacional del Litoral, Santa Fe, 2004.

Gutiérrez, Eduardo, *Juan Moreira*. Arte Gráfico Editorial Argentino, Buenos Aires, 2011.

Gutkowski, Hélène, *Vidas . . . En las colonias. Rescate de la herencia cultural*. Editorial Contexto, Buenos Aires, 1991.

Halperin Donghi, Tulio, *Son memorias*. Siglo XXI Editores, Buenos Aires, 2008.

Hansman, Silvia, et al., *Oysfarkoyft. Localidades agotadas. Sold out. Afiches del teatro ídish en la Argentina*. Del Nuevo Extremo/Fundación IWO, Buenos Aires, 2006.

Hernández, José, *Martín Fierro*. Librería La Facultad, Buenos Aires, 1942.

Herzl, Teodoro, *El estado judío*. Organización Sionista Argentina, Buenos Aires, 2004.

Hirsch, Baron Maurice de, "My Views on Philanthropy," *North American Review*, vol. 153, no. 416, July, 1891.

Hirschbein, Peretz, *Fun vayte lender* [in Yiddish]. New York, 1916.

Hobsbawm, Eric, *Bandidos*. Crítica, Barcelona, 2011.

Hojman, Boruj, "Cooperativism in the Jewish Colonies [in Yiddish]," in *Argentiner IWO Shriftn (anales del Instituto Científico Judío Argentino), 8*. Instituto Científico Judío-IWO, Buenos Aires, 1961.

—, "Materials on the History of Jewish Colonization and Agricultural Cooperativism in Argentina [in Yiddish]," in *Argentiner IWO Shriftn (anales del Instituto Científico Judío Argentino), 9–10*. Instituto Científico Judío-IWO, Buenos Aires, 1964.

Hurvitz, Meier, "Notes on the History of Jewish Colonization in Argentina [in Yiddish]," in *Argentiner IWO Shriftn (anales del Instituto Científico Judío Argentino), 6*. Instituto Científico Judío-IWO, Buenos Aires, 1955.

Hurvitz, S.I., *Lucienville Colony: 37 Years of Jewish Colonization* [in Yiddish]. Buenos Aires, 1932.

Jacobo Simón Liachovitzky: In Memoriam. Krasilvosky, Buenos Aires, 1938.

Jewish Colonization Association, *Report of the Council of Administration for 1894*. Jewish Chronicle Office, London, 1894.

——, *Au conseil d'administration de la Jewish Colonization Association*. Jacobo Peuser, Buenos Aires, 1901.

——, *Atlas des colonies et domaines de la Jewish Colonization Association en République Argentine et au Brésil*, Supplement au rapport annuel pour 1913. Jewish Colonization Association, Paris, 1914.

——, *Su obra en la República Argentina*. Buenos Aires, 1954.

——, *75 años de colonización judía en la Argentina*. Buenos Aires, 1964.

Jurkewich, Aarón, "Jewish Colonization Reflected in Judeo-Argentine Literature [in Yiddish]," in *Argentiner IWO Shriftn (anales del Instituto Científico Judío Argentino)*, 9–10. Instituto Científico Judío-IWO, Buenos Aires, 1964.

Kantor, Manuel, *Alberto Gerchunoff*. Biblioteca Popular Judía, Congreso Judío Latinoamericano, Buenos Aires, 1969.

Kaplan, Isaac, *Recuerdos de un cooperativista agrario 1895–1925*. Círculo de Estudios Cooperativistas de Buenos Aires, Buenos Aires, 1969.

Kapszuk, Elio, *Shalom Buenos Aires. Recorrido judío de la ciudad*. Buenos Aires, 2000.

——, *Shalom Argentina. Huellas de la colonización judía*. Ministerio de Turismo, Cultura y Deporte, Buenos Aires, 2001.

Katz, Pinie, *Notes on the History of Jewish Journalism in Argentina* [in Yiddish]. Sociedad de Escritores y Periodistas Israelitas en la Argentina, Buenos Aires, 1929.

——, *Páginas selectas*. Editorial ICUF, Buenos Aires, 1980.

Klein, Alberto, *Cinco siglos de historia. Una crónica de la vida judía en la Argentina*, Cuadernos de estudios judíos. Oficina Sudamericana del Comité Judío Americano, Buenos Aires, 1976.

Korn, Francis, *Buenos Aires 1895. Una ciudad moderna*. Editorial del Instituto, Buenos Aires, 1981.

Lansky, Aaron, *Outwitting History: The Amazing Adventures of a Man who Rescued a Million Yiddish Books*. Algonquin Books, Chapel Hill, 2005.

Larker, José M., *Criminalidad y control social en una provincia en construcción: Santa Fe, 1856–1895*. Ediciones Prohistoria, Rosario, 2011.

Leibovich, Adolfo, *Apuntes íntimos 1870–1946*. Imprenta López, Buenos Aires, 1947.

Levy, Larry, *La mancha de la Migdal. Historia de la prostitución judía en la Argentina*. Grupo Editorial Norma, Buenos Aires, 2007.

Lewin, Boleslao, "Free Immigration and Religious Tolerance in the Argentine Republic [in Yiddish]," in *Anuario 5714 año hebreo. 1953/1954. Vida comunitaria judía*. Asociación Mutual Israelita Argentina, Comunidad de Buenos Aires, Buenos Aires, 1953.

—, *Cómo fue la inmigración judía en la Argentina*. Plus Ultra, Buenos Aires, 1983.

Lewitan de Eidelsztein, Graciela, *Pu, pu, pu. La dicha del ídish: dichos, refranes y proverbios populares*. Sudamericana, Buenos Aires, 2010.

Liachovitzky, Jacob Sh., "Shpas un ernst. Funm idish-argentinishen ishuv" (series) [in Yiddish], in *Penimer un peninmlej*, 1925.

Liebermann, José, *Tierra soñada*. Ediciones LL-Luis Lasserre y Cía. S.A., Buenos Aires, 1959.

—, *Los judíos en la Argentina*. Editorial Libra, Buenos Aires, 1966.

Literat-Golombek, Lea, *Moisés Ville. Crónica de un shtetl argentino*. La Semana Publicaciones Ltda., Buenos Aires, 1982.

Llamgot, Alberto, "The Centenary of Jewish Colonization in Argentina [in Yiddish]," in *Argentiner IWO Shriftn (anales del Instituto Científico Judío Argentino), 15*. Instituto Científico Judío-IWO, Buenos Aires, 1989.

Marchevsky, Elías A., *El tejedor de oro*. Bastión, Buenos Aires, 1964.

Martel, Julián, *La bolsa*. Editorial Guillermo Kraft, Buenos Aires, 1959.

Micheletti, María Gabriela, "Criminalidad y extranjeros: ¿víctimas o victimarios? Una visión desde las elites santafesinas (1880–1900)." Facultad de Derecho y Ciencias Sociales del Rosario, UCA.

Mirelman, Víctor A., *En búsqueda de una identidad. Los inmigrantes judíos en Buenos Aires 1890–1930*. Milá, Buenos Aires, 1988.

Mocho, Fray, *Un viaje al país de los matreros*. Memoria Argentina, Emecé.

—, *Memorias de un vigilante*. Los libros del mirasol, Buenos Aires, 1961.

Moseley, Christopher (ed.), *Encyclopedia of the World's Endangered Languages*. Routledge, New York, 2007.

Norman, Theodore, *An Outstretched Arm: A History of the Jewish Colonization Association*. Routledge & Kegan Paul, London, 1985.

Oggero de Angeletti, Liliana, et al., *100 años: escuela N° 6054 "Vicente López."* Moisés Ville, Santa Fe, 2010.

Onega, Gladys S., *La inmigración en la literatura argentina, 1880–1910*. Galerna, Buenos Aires, 1969.

Orlian, Natan C., *Moisés Ville. Paraíso perdido*. Buenos Aires.

Oteiza Gruss, Viviane Inés, "Bibliotecas y periódicos de inmigración. Una reflexión basada en el estudio del periodismo francés," at 5° Encuentro de Bibliotecas de Colectividades. Biblioteca Nacional, Buenos Aires, 2010.

Palacios, Alfredo, *Alfredo L. Palacios en nuestros pagos*. Fundación Moisés Ville, Buenos Aires.

Pérez Amuchástegui, A. J., *Mentalidades argentinas (1860–1930)*. Editorial Universitaria de Buenos Aires (Eudeba), Buenos Aires, 1965.

Piazzi, Carolina A., *Justicia criminal y cárceles en Rosario (segunda mitad del siglo XIX)* . Ediciones Prohistoria, Rosario, 2011.

Pomer, León, *Historias de gauchos y gauchisoldados*. Colihue, Buenos Aires, 2007.

Priamo, Luis, "Vistas de la provincia de Santa Fe 1888–1892. Fotografías de Ernesto H. Schlie." *El Litoral* newspaper, Santa Fe, 2000.

Reisen, Zalman, *Leksikon fun der yiddisher literatur, prese un filologie* [in Yiddish], first volume. Vilnius, 1926.

Reynal O'Connor, Arturo, *Paseos por las colonias*. Casa editora N. Tommasi, Buenos Aires, 1908.

Rivanera Carlés, Federico, *Los judíos y la trata de blancas en Argentina*. Self-published, Buenos Aires, 1986.

Rollansky, Samuel, *Miguel Hacohen Sinay: Precursor of Yiddish Journalism in Argentina* [in Yiddish]. Instituto Científico Judío (IWO), Buenos Aires, 1947.

—, *I. L. Peretz y su inquietud por la Argentina*. Instituto Científico Judío (IWO), Buenos Aires, 1966.

—, *Jewish Journalism, Letters, and Theater in Argentina* [in Yiddish]. Buenos Aires, 1941.

—, *Martín Fierro, exiliado en su propia patria. La Biblia de la literatura argentina*. Buenos Aires, 1992.

—, *Sarmiento y los judíos*. Buenos Aires, 1993.

Rollansky, Samuel (ed.), *Anthology: Yiddish Literature in Argentina. Poetry, Prose, Theater, and Criticism/Musterverk*, no. 70 [in Yiddish]. Ateneo Literario en el Instituto Científico Judío, Buenos Aires, 1976.

Rosenfeld, Horacio Guillermo, *Castelli 330 y otros sitios de interés*. Di Prese *en mis recuerdos*. Milá, Buenos Aires, 2011.

Rubel, Iaacov, "Argentina, ¿sí o no? Ecos de la inmigración judía a la Argentina en la prensa hebrea de Rusia entre 1888 y 1890," in *Comunidades judías de Latinoamérica*, Oficina Sudamericana del Comité Judío Americano. Editorial Candelabro, Buenos Aires, 1974.

Ruppin, Arthur, *Los judíos en América del Sur*. Editorial Darom, Buenos Aires, 1938.

Santos, Juan José, *El Tata Dios. Milenarismo y xenofobia en las pampas*. Sudamericana, Buenos Aires, 2008.

Sbarra, Noel H., *Historia del alambrado en la Argentina*. Letemendia, Buenos Aires, 2008.

Schaefer Gallo, Carlos, "El gaucho judío" (drama en tres actos), *La Escena*, theater journal, vol. 3, no. 79. Buenos Aires, January 1, 1920.

Schallman, Lázaro, *Los pioneros de la colonización judía en la Argentina*. Biblioteca Popular Judía, Congreso Judío Latinoamericano, Buenos Aires, 1969a.

—, *Barón Mauricio de Hirsch*. Biblioteca Popular Judía, Congreso Judío Latinoamericano, Buenos Aires, 1969b.

—, "Historia del periodismo judío en la Argentina," in *Comunidades judías de Latinoamérica*, Oficina Sudamericana del Comité Judío Americano. Editorial Candelabro, Buenos Aires, 1970.

—, *Memorias documentadas*. Editorial Moi, Buenos Aires, 1980.

—, *Historia de los "pampistas."* Biblioteca Popular Judía, Congreso Judío Latinoamericano, Buenos Aires, 1989.

Schoijet, Ezequiel, *Páginas para la historia de la colonia Narcis Leven (en adhesión a su cincuentenario)*. Buenos Aires, 1961.

Schussheim, A. L., "En torno del surgimiento de la comunidad judía de Buenos Aires," in *Pinkás. Los comienzos*. Asociación Mutual Israelita de Buenos Aires, Buenos Aires.

—, "Contribution to the History of the Origins of the Argentine Yishuv [in Yiddish]," in *Anuario 5714 año hebreo. 1953/1954, Vida comunitaria judía*. Asociación Mutual Israelita Argentina, Comunidad de Buenos Aires, Buenos Aires, 1953.

Scobie, James R., *Revolución en las pampas. Historia social del trigo argentino, 1860–1910*. Ediciones Solar/Hachette, Buenos Aires, 1968.

Senkman, Leonardo, *La identidad judía en la literatura argentina*. Editorial Pardes, Buenos Aires, 1983.

—, *La colonización judía*. Centro Editor de América Latina, Buenos Aires, 1984.

Shijman, Osías, *Colonización judía en la Argentina*. Self-published, Buenos Aires, 1980.

Sigwald Carioli, Susana B., "Historia de barbas y caftanes." Publicación del Centro Cultural José Ingenieros y del Archivo Histórico Antonio Maya, Carlos Casares, Buenos Aires.

Sinay, Mijl Hacohen, *Baleidigt a mes . . .* [in Yiddish], Bijlaj Far Yeden, no. 22. Buenos Aires, March 1, 1920.

—, "Der oifkum fun higen ídishn ishuv [in Yiddish]," in *Argentiner IWO Shriftn (anales del Instituto Científico Judío Argentino), 5*. Instituto Científico Judío-IWO, Buenos Aires, 1952.

—, *Gam zu letovah* [in Yiddish], Bijlaj Far Yeden, no. 13. Buenos Aires, November 10, 1919.

—, *Los primeros judíos caídos en Moisés Ville Argentina*. Asociación Judeo-Argentina de Estudios Históricos, Buenos Aires, 1985.

—, "Rabbi Rubén Hacohen Sinay [in Yiddish]," in *Argentiner IWO Shriftn (anales del Instituto Científico Judío Argentino), 3*. Instituto Científico Judío-IWO, Buenos Aires, 1945.

—, "The First Jewish Victims in Moisés Ville [in Yiddish]," in *Argentiner IWO Shriftn (anales del Instituto Científico Judío Argentino), 4*. Instituto Científico Judío-IWO, Buenos Aires, 1947.

—, "The First Local Jewish Writers [in Yiddish]," in *Anuario 5714 año hebreo. 1953/1954. Vida comunitaria judía*. Asociación Mutual Israelita Argentina, Comunidad de Buenos Aires, Buenos Aires, 1953.

Sneh, Perla, "Situaciones judeo-argentinas: entre el guión y la fremdshpraj," in Alejandro Meter and Ariana Huberman (comps.), *Memoria y representación: configuraciones culturales y literarias en el imaginario judío latinoamericano*. Beatriz Viterbo Editora, Rosario, 2006.

—, "Alberto Gerchunoff, entre el nombre y el pronombre," in Alberto Gerchunoff, *Los gauchos judíos. El hombre que habló en la Sorbona*. Colihue/ Biblioteca Nacional, Buenos Aires, 2007.

—, "Ídish al sur: una rama en sombras," in Haim Avni et al. (coord.), *Pertenencia y alteridad. Judíos en/de América Latina: cuarenta años de cambios*. Bonilla Artigas Editores, 2011.

Sneh, Perla (comp.), *Buenos Aires ídish*. Gobierno de la Ciudad de Buenos Aires, Buenos Aires, 2006.

Sneh, Simja, *Breve historia del ídish*. Biblioteca Popular Judía, Congreso Judío Latinoamericano, Buenos Aires, 1976.

Stämpfli, Guillermo, "Hechos históricos y textos dramáticos: el campo santafesino y el drama rural entre 1904 y 1920," in *Memoria Americana*, 15, 2007.

Szurmuk, Mónica, "Home in the Pampas: Alberto Gerchunoff's Jewish Gauchos," in Simon Bronner (coord.), *Jewish Cultural Studies II: Jews at Home*. Littman, Oxford, 2010.

Tiempo, César, "Gerchunoff, mano de obra," in *Protagonistas*. Editorial Guillermo Kraft, Buenos Aires, 1954.

Toker, Eliahu, *Lejaim*. Ediciones de la Flor, Buenos Aires, 1974.

—, "Alberto Gerchunoff, entre gauchos y judíos," in Eliahu Toker (comp.), *Alberto Gerchunoff, entre gauchos y judíos*. Secretaría de Cultura de la Nación/Editorial Biblos, Buenos Aires, 1994.

—, *El ídish es también Latinoamérica*. Ediciones del Instituto Movilizador de Fondos Cooperativos, Buenos Aires, 2003.

Toker, Eliahu, and Weinstein, Ana E., *La letra ídish en tierra argentina. Bio-bibliografía de sus autores literarios*. Milá, Buenos Aires, 2004.

—, *Sitios de la Memoria. Los cementerios judíos de Liniers y Tablada*. Milá, Buenos Aires, 2005.

—, *En el espejo de la lengua ídish. Selección de textos argentinos*. Ministerio de Cultura, Gobierno de la Ciudad Autónoma de Buenos Aires, Buenos Aires, 2006.

Tron, Rubén, *El cielo de Jeremías*. Editorial Municipal de Rosario, Rosario, 2004.

Tur, Carlos M., *Colonias y colonizadores*. Centro Editor de América Latina, Buenos Aires, 1972.

Vogel, Mario (dir.), *Moisés Ville. 1889–1989*. Moisés Ville, 1989.

Wald, Pinie, *Nightmares: Account of the Tragic Week* [in Yiddish]. Buenos Aires, 1929.

—, "Notes on the History of the Cultural Movement among the Jews in Argentina (1895–1920) [in Yiddish]," in *Argentiner IWO Shriftn (anales del Instituto Científico Judío Argentino), 6*. Instituto Científico Judío-IWO, Buenos Aires, 1955.

Watson, Ricardo, et al., *Buenos Aires de fiesta. Luces y sombras del Centenario*. Aguilar, Buenos Aires, 2010.

Wolff, Martha, *Pioneros de la Argentina. Los inmigrantes judíos*. Manrique Zago, Buenos Aires, 1982.

—, *Judíos & argentinos. Judíos argentinos*. Manrique Zago, Buenos Aires, 1988.

Zablotsky, Edgardo, "El proyecto del Barón de Hirsch, ¿éxito o fracaso?," Universidad del CEMA, Buenos Aires, 2005.

Zak, Fany, "Society of Jewish Residents from Grodno [in Yiddish]," in *Argentiner IWO Shriftn (anales del Instituto Científico Judío Argentino), 14*. Instituto Científico Judío-IWO, Buenos Aires, 1988.

Zelkovicz, Hirsh, *El proceso Dreyfus*. Biblioteca Popular Judía, Congreso Judío Latinoamericano, Buenos Aires, 1972.

Periodicals

Amanecer: issues from April and December 1957.

Argentiner Lebn [in Yiddish]: April 25, 1957.

Cadena3.com, Córdoba: April 22, 2011.

Caras y Caretas: issues from 1898, 1899, 1900, 1901, 1902, 1903, 1904, 1905, 1906, 1907, 1908, 1909, 1910.

Clarín, Buenos Aires: issues from April 1999, June 2011, August 1997.

Crítica: issues from August 1941.

Der Argentiner Magazin [in Yiddish]: no. 67, no. 87.

Der Shpigl [in Yiddish]: no. 345, no. 346, no. 347, no. 395 (May 1944), no. 396 (July 1944), no. 397–398 (August 1944), no. 399–400 (September 1944), no. 401 (October 1944), no. 402 (November 1944), no. 403 (December 1944), no. 404 (January 1945), no. 405 (February 1945), no. 408–409, May 1945), no. 410 (June 1945), no. 411 (July 1945), no. 412–413 (September 1945), no. 414 (October 1945), no. 415 (November 1945), no. 416 (December 1945), no. 417 (January 1946), no. 418–419 (February–March 1946), no. 420 (April 1946), no. 421 (May 1946), no. 424 (September 1946), no. 431 (April 1947), no. 432 (May 1947), no. 433 (June 1947), no. 555 (December 1957), no. 563–564 (August–September 1958).

Der Tog [in Yiddish]: issues from January and July 1914.

Der Veg [in Yiddish]: issues from 1946, 1947, 1948.

Der Weker [in Yiddish]: February 1, 1924.

Di Prese [in Yiddish]: August 18, 1939.

Die Volks Stimme [in Yiddish]: from no. 1, August 11, 1898, through no. 49, July 20, 1899.

Di Ydische Zaitung [in Yiddish]: issues from 1916, 1929, 1930, 1936, 1941, 1947, 1948, 1954, 1958.

El Municipio, Rosario: issues from November 1897.

Generacionesmv.com

El Alba, vol. 18, no. 904, Edición extraordinaria en homenaje al cincuentenario de Moisés Ville, October 15, 1939, Moisés Ville.

El Litoral, Santa Fe: May 18, 1932; October 25 and 26, 1971; September 13, 2008.

Fraie Schtime [in Yiddish]: October 1969.

Grodner Opklangen (published by the Union of Residents from Grodno and Its Surroundings) [in Yiddish], issues 3–4 (September 1950), 5–6 (1951), 8–9 (November 1955), 10 (December 1956), 11 (September 1959).

Ha-Melitz [in Hebrew]: issues from July 1889, May 1890, August 1893.

Ha-Tzfira [in Hebrew]: issues from July 1893, November and December 1894, December 1896.

ICA-is.org.il

Iungt-Avangard [in Yiddish]: May–June 1945.

JewishEncyclopedia.com

Judaica: no. 3 (September 1933), no. 15 (September 1934), no. 18 (December 1934), no. 25 (July 1935), no. 26 (August 1935), no. 35 (May 1936), no. 45 (March 1937), no. 46 (April 1937), no. 50 (August 1937), no. 54 (December 1937), no. 55 (January 1938), no. 57 (March 1938), no. 58 (April 1938), no. 59–61 (May–July 1938).

La Capital, Rosario, issues from June and July 2011.

La Nación, Buenos Aires: issues from 1881, 1889, 1891, 1893, 1896, 1897, 1898, 1906, 1908, 1909, 1914, 1995, 2009, 2001, 2012.

La Opinión, Rafaela: issues from June and November 2009.

La Prensa, Buenos Aires: issues from 1889, 1897, 1898, 1906.

La Unión, Esperanza, Santa Fe: 1892, 1893.

Morgnzaitung [in Yiddish]: issues from august 1938 and January 1939.

Mundo Israelita: issues from August 1960, November 1942, October 1989.

Noticias Gráficas: August 5, 1941.

Nueva Época, Santa Fe: July 19, 1906.

Ñ: June 11, 2011.

Rosarier Lebn [in Yiddish]: issues from 1931, 1932, 1934, 1937, 1943, 1944, 1945, 1948, 1952, 1953, 1955.

Todo Es Historia, Buenos Aires: issues from 1976, 1977, 1982, 1988, 2000.

Toldot: no. 1 (1996), no. 35 (April–May 2009).

Undzer Zait [in Yiddish]: January 30, 1942.

Uno, Santa Fe: July 19, 2008.

Vida Nueva/Nei Lebn, Buenos Aires: May–June 1947.

Documents

Interview with Frida Kaller de Gutman, at Archivo de la Palabra, Centro Marc Turkow, AMIA.

Interview with Máximo Yagupsky, at Archivo de la Palabra, Centro Marc Turkow, AMIA.

GENERAL ARCHIVE OF SANTA FE PROVINCE

—Caso Lefebre. Expedientes Criminales, no. 30, 1871.

—Encargado del registro civil de Moisés Ville, dpto. San Cristóbal, presenta como fiador a Miguel Cohan. Ministerio de Hacienda/Sección Justicia, Expd. 31, Sec. 1. 1899.

—Instalación de una oficina de registro civil en Moisés Ville. Ministerio de Hacienda/Sección Justicia, Expd. 62, Sec. 1. 1900.

—José Nagubonin y Levi. Sunchales, s. abuso del comisario. Ministerio de Gobierno/Sección Gobierno, Expd. 2, Sec. 1. 1897.

—Moisés Ville, vecinos de la col. en queja contra la cía. de la Jewish Colonization. Ministerio de Gobierno/Sección Agricultura, Expd. 28, Sec. 1. 1903.

—Persecución de matreros. Ministerio de Gobierno/Sección Gobierno, Expd. 94, Sec. 1. 1899.

—Sumario instruido a Ramón Vázquez, jefe político de San Cristóbal. Ministerio de Gobierno/Sección Gobierno, Expd. 19, Sec. 1. 1906.

—Sumario instruido con motivo de la muerte del asesino Teodoro Fernández. Ministerio de Gobierno/Sección Gobierno, Expd. 30, Sec. 1. 1899.

—Sunchales, denuncia y sumario contra el comisario general. Ministerio de Gobierno/Sección Gobierno, Expd. 7, Sec. 1. 1894.

—Vecinos de la col. Moisés Ville agradecen la intervención de la inspección general. Ministerio de Gobierno/Sección Gobierno, Expd. 3, Sec. 1. 1898.

—Vecinos de Monigotes, Dpto. San Cristóbal, solicitan la libertad del comisario. Ministerio de Gobierno/Sección Gobierno, Expd. 7, Sec. 1. 1896.

Archive of the Jewish Colonization Association at the IWO.

Archive of Mordejai Alpersohn at the IWO.

Archive of Noé Cociovich at the IWO.

Archive of Jacob Sh. Liachovitzky at the IWO.

Archive of Mijl Hacohen Sinay at the IWO.

Letters to Mijl Hacohen Sinay.

Manuscripts of Mijl Hacohen Sinay.

Manuscripts of Mordejai Reuben Hacohen Sinay.

ON THE HOMICIDE OF THE LEFEBRE FAMILY

Barriera, Darío G. (dir.), "Deudas impostergables," in *Archivo del Crimen*, Segunda Serie, no. 6, *La Capital* newspaper, Rosario, February 12, 2010.

Green, Aldo Gastón, "El escuadrón de lanceros del Sauce. Una aproximación a las transformaciones operadas en una sociedad india durante la 19° centuria," at Congreso Argentino de Inmigración, IV Congreso de Historia de los Pueblos de la Provincia de Santa Fe, Esperanza, Santa Fe, 2005.

Gschwind, Juan Jorge, *Historia de San Carlos*. Universidad Nacional del Litoral, Rosario, 1958.

La Patria, Rosario, October 26, 1869.

Larker, José Miguel, "Manifestaciones del bandolerismo rural y de la acción estatal en la Provincia de Santa Fe. Un caso particular: la trayectoria delictiva de los hermanos Alarcón (1865–1871)," *Historia Regional*, no. 23, 2005.

Maffucci Moore, Javier Leandro, "Indios, inmigrantes y criollos en el nordeste santafesino (1860–1890). Un caso de violencia en una sociedad de frontera," *Andes* magazine, no. 18, Universidad Nacional de Salta, 2007.

Films

Un amor en Moisés Ville, by Daniel Barone.

Legado (documentary in Yiddish and Spanish), by Vivián Imar and Marcelo Trotta.

Sources

In Chapter 1, I was able to reconstruct the itinerary of the Podoliers from the *Weser* thanks to books by Haim Avni (*Argentina y la historia de la inmigración judía, 1810–1950*), Víctor Mirelman (*En búsqueda de una identidad: Los inmigrantes judíos en Buenos Aires 1890–1930*), Noé Cociovich (*Génesis de Moisés Ville*), and Lázaro Schallman (*Los pioneros de la colonización judía en la Argentina*), as well as DAIA's 1939 anthology, *50 años de colonización judía en la Argentina*, where articles by José Mendelson and Alberto Gerchunoff stand out in particular. And for their first days in Santa Fe, I used Adolfo Leibovich's memoirs (*Apuntes íntimos 1870–1946*) and an anthology by Leonardo Senkman (*La colonización judía*).

The killing of David Lander is based on Mijl Hacohen Sinay's account in "The First Jewish Victims in Moisés Ville," published in Yiddish in the *Argentiner IWO Shriftn* (annals of the Instituto Científico Judío Argentino), no. 4.

The details about the *Weser* and its replica were related to me, in a direct interview, by the naval model expert Héctor Camilleri.

In Chapter 2, to reconstruct the action with Baron de Hirsch in Russia and the founding of the JCA, my visits to the Museum of Communal History and Jewish Colonization in Moisés Ville and the IWO Institute were valuable, as were books by Haim Avni (*Argentina y la historia de la inmigración judía 1810–1950*), Víctor Mirelman (*En búsqueda de una identidad: Los inmigrantes judíos en Buenos Aires 1890–1930*), Lázaro

Schallman (*Barón Mauricio de Hirsch* and *Los pioneros de la colonización judía en la Argentina*), Ricardo Feierstein (*Historia de los judíos argentinos*), José Liebermann (*Tierra soñada* and *Los judíos en la Argentina*), David Goldman (*Di iuden in Argentine*), Boleslao Lewin (*Cómo fue la inmigración judía en la Argentina*), and DAIA's anthology *50 años de colonización judía en la Argentina*. Also articles published in issue 18 of the magazine *Judaica* (from December 1934) and some by Haim Avni ("El proyecto del Barón de Hirsch: la gran visión y sus resultados" and "La agricultura judía en la Argentina, ¿éxito o fracaso?") and Edgardo Zablotsky ("El proyecto del Barón de Hirsch, ¿éxito o fracaso?").

There are at least a dozen books that recall Moisés Ville from other places: *Memoria oral de Moisés Ville*, compiled by Eva Guelbert de Rosenthal; *Moisés Ville: Recuerdos de un pibe pueblerino*, by Felipe Fistemberg Adler; *Moisés Ville: Paraíso perdido*, by Natán C. Orlan; *Moisés Ville: Crónica de un shtetl argentino*, by Lea Literat-Golombek; *Los gringos*, by Moisés I. Glombovsky; *Génesis de Moisés Ville*, by Noé Cociovitch; *Moisés Ville: 1889–1989; Alfredo L. Palacios en nuestros pagos*, a pamphlet that collects certain lines by the socialist lawmaker; *Patrimonio urbano arquitectónico de Moisés Ville*, a technical study by Adriana Collado, María Elena del Barco, and Eva Guelbert de Rosenthal; *Losers and Keepers in Argentina*, a novel in English by Nina Barragan; *Shalom Argentina*, by Elio Kapszuk; and *Aromas y sabores de las bobes de Moisés Ville*, a cookbook by Lili González de Trumper. To these must be added the many and often lengthy chapters that refer to Moisés Ville among the shelves on agricultural colonization in Argentina and, of course, the films *Un amor en Moisés Ville*, by Daniel Barone, and *Legado*, a documentary in Yiddish and Spanish, by Vivián Imar and Marcelo Trotta.

In Chapter 3, I based my observations about Yiddish on interviews with Silvia Hansman, Abraham Lichtenbaum, and Ester Szwarc (all from the IWO), with Perla Sneh, Ricardo Feierstein, and Ana Weinstein (from the Marc Turkow Center at the AMIA), as well as with the actor Max Berliner. Also the books *Sociolingüística histórica de las lenguas judías* (an essential work written by Cyril Aslanov), *Breve historia del ídish* (by Simja Sneh), *Buenos Aires ídish* (by Perla Sneh), *En el espejo de la lengua ídish: selección de textos argentinos* and *La letra ídish en tierra argentina: Bio-bibliografía de sus autores literarios* (both by Eliahu Toker and Ana Weinstein), and *El ídish es también Latinoamérica* (by Eliahu Toker).

Several articles about Yiddish appeared in issues of the magazine *Judaica*, as indicated in the bibliography. Perla Sneh's article "Ídish al sur: una rama en sombras" is also important (see bibliography).

Liebermann (*Los judíos en la Argentina*) and Lewin (*Cómo fue la inmigración judía en la Argentina*) both wrote about the IWO.

In Chapter 4, I wrote about the robbery at the Banco Comercial Israelita on the basis of articles that appeared in the newspaper *El Litoral* (from Santa Fe) on the days of October 26 and 27, 1971, and the note dedicated to it in the magazine-book *Moisés Ville: 1889–1989*. Also the memories of Abraham "Ingue" Kanzepolsky, Osvaldo Angeletti, and Alberto Lind.

In Chapter 5, the details about the Moisés Ville cemetery were derived from the book *Shalom Argentina*, by Kapszuk, and from *Patrimonio urbano arquitectónico de Moisés Ville*, by Collado, del Barco, and Guelbert de Rosenthal. The director of the Museum of Communal History and Jewish Colonization in Moisés Ville contributed a significant share of the information.

In Chapter 6, I reconstructed the Grodners' arrival in Moisés Ville in December 1894 thanks to Noé Cociovich's book and the articles by Mijl Hacohen Sinay that are listed at the end of Chapter 5.

The administrator Michel Cohan has been depicted, mainly, by Cociovich, Hacohen Sinay, and David Goldman. On Grodno, Hacohen Sinay wrote "Nuestros pequeños pueblos destruidos en la Gobernación de Grodno" and "La antigua Grodno" (both in the magazine *Grodner Opklangen*), and the Embassy of Belarus in Buenos Aires provided me with Belarus Facts 2010 (by Aleksandr Dyleiko). Additionally, the consul Sergei Lukashevich told me about historical and modern Grodno.

The mentions of the JCA were gained through the Archive of the Jewish Colonization Association at the IWO.

The letter from the residents of Monigotes is at the General Archive of Santa Fe Province: Vecinos de Monigotes, Dpto. San Cristóbal, solicitan la libertad del comisario. Ministerio de Gobierno/Sección Gobierno, Expd. 7, Sec 1. 1896.

The articles "La política inmigratoria de la JCA del año 1894," by Tchaicovsky (in the yearbook *IWO Shriftn V*), "Argentina, ¿sí o no?" (by Yaacov Rubel) and "50 años de vida judía argentina en la Biblioteca de la Universidad de Harvard" (by A. A. Roback, which appeared in the special tenth anniversary issue of the magazine *Judaica*), and the books *La pampa gringa* and *Colonos en armas* (both by Ezequiel Gallo), the extremely important *Criminalidad y control social en una provincia en construcción: Santa Fe, 1856–1895* (by José Larker); and *Crónicas judeoargentinas 1: Los pioneros del ídish, 1890–1944* (compiled by Ricardo Feierstein) also served to provide contrasting accounts.

For this and other chapters, I employed information found at the General Archive of Santa Fe Province: Instalación de una oficina de registro civil en Moisés Ville. Ministerio de Hacienda/Sección Justicia, Expd. 62, Sec. 1. 1900; Persecución de matreros. Ministerio de Gobierno/Sección Gobierno, Expd. 94, Sec. 1. 1899; José Nagubonin y Levi. Sunchales, s. abuso del comisario. Ministerio de Gobierno/Sección Gobierno, Expd. 2, Sec. 1. 1897; Vecinos de la col. Moisés Ville agradecen la intervención de la inspección general. Ministerio de Gobierno/Sección Gobierno, Expd. 3, Sec. 1. 1898; Sumario instruido con motivo de la muerte del asesino Teodoro Fernández. Ministerio de Gobierno/Sección Gobierno, Expd. 30, Sec. 1. 1899; Sunchales, denuncia y sumario contra el comisario general. Ministerio de Gobierno/Sección Gobierno, Expd. 7, Sec. 1. 1894; Encargado del registro civil de Moisés Ville, dpto. San Cristóbal, presenta como fiador a Miguel Cohan. Ministerio de Hacienda/Sección Justicia, Expd. 31, Sec. 1. 1899; Moisés Ville, vecinos de la col. en queja contra la cía. de la Jewish Colonization. Ministerio de Gobierno/Sección Agricultura, Expd. 28, Sec. 1. 1903.

The final dialogue between Cociovich and Mijl Hacohen Sinay is reproduced from the latter's autobiographical series, published sporadically in the magazine *Der Shpigl* (The mirror) between May 1944 (no. 395) and June 1947 (no. 433). To understand Cociovich, it is also useful to consult the Archive of Noé Cociovich at the IWO.

In Chapter 7, the massacre of the Lefebre family is reconstructed on the basis of the dossier (available at the General Archive of Santa Fe Province: Expedientes Criminales, no. 30, 1871); books by Juan Jorge Gschwind (*Historia de San Carlos*), Darío Barriera (director of *Deudas impostergables*, published in the *Archivo del Crimen* series), and Roberto E. Lance and Juan Carlos Pedroni (*Raíces de San Jerónimo del Sauce*); and short works including José Larker's very helpful "Manifestaciones del bandolerismo rural y de la acción estatal en la Provincia de Santa Fe. Un caso particular: la trayectoria delictiva de los hermanos Alarcón (1865–1871)," Aldo Gastón Green's "El escuadrón de lanceros del Sauce: Una aproximación a las transformaciones operadas en una sociedad india durante la 19° centuria," and Javier Leandro Maffucci Moore's "Indios, inmigrantes y criollos en el nordeste santafesino (1860–1890): Un caso de violencia en una sociedad de frontera." I also drew on the newspaper *La Patria*, from Rosario, in its issue from October 26, 1869.

In Chapter 8, the rescue of books after the AMIA attack was related to me by Ester Szwarc and is also recorded in the documentary *Los jóvenes que rescataron la memoria*, by Rodolfo Compte, which also has a name-sake version in book form (*Atentado a la AMIA: Crónica de los jóvenes que rescataron la memoria*).

In Chapter 9, I was able to gather the details for the trip through time around February and March 1898 by reading copies of the newspapers *La Nación* and *La Prensa*, as well as several editions of the magazine *Caras y Caretas* to complete the portrait of the epoch. The Gallery of Suspects from 1898 (held at the Juan Vucetich Police Academy, in Buenos Aires Province) was shared with me by the historian Diego Galeano.

Throughout the chapter, Mijl Hacohen Sinay's autobiographical series published in the magazine *Der Shpigl* (The mirror) was an indispensable source: the dialogue between Sinay and Joel Rosenblit was reproduced from there.

To learn more about Liachovitzky, I was able to consult the Archive of Jacob Sh. Liachovitzky at the IWO.

In Chapter 10, I have based the contents of *Der Viderkol* and the references to Jewish journalism in Argentina on the reports of Pinie Katz (in "Apuntes para la historia del periodismo israelita en Argentina"), Shmuel Rollansky (in "MHS, el pionero de la palabra escrita en Argentina. En su 70° aniversario" and "El periodismo, las letras y el teatro judíos en la Argentina"), Lázaro Schallman (in "Historia del periodismo judío en la Argentina"), and Mijl Hacohen Sinay himself, in his autobiographical series.

The words of Carlos Ulanovsky were taken from the book *Judíos & Argentinos: Judíos argentinos*.

In Chapter 11, the portrait of Vermont has been constructed thanks to the aforementioned books by Pinie Katz and Mijl Hacohen Sinay's autobiographical series, in issues 345, 346, and 347 of the magazine *Der Shpigl* (The mirror).

Everything relating to Jaim Reitich arose through interviews with his descendants.

In Chapter 12, to reconstruct the murder of María Alexenicer, I based my work on interviews with her descendants, the article by Mijl Hacohen Sinay, and on the series of news pieces that were published in the newspapers *La Prensa*, *La Nación*, and *Nueva Época*. Information on the political chief of San Cristóbal, Ramón Vázquez, can be found at the General Archive of Santa Fe Province: Sumario instruido a Ramón Vázquez, jefe político de San Cristóbal. Ministerio de Gobierno/Sección Gobierno, Expd. 19, Sec. 1, 1906.

In Chapter 14, I was able to write about the night in honor of Mijl Hacohen Sinay thanks to newspaper articles that are held in his archive at the IWO. In addition to the texts cited in this chronicle, I have been told about his life by my father, Horacio, my uncle Sergio, my grandmother Mañe, and my father's cousins, Moisés, Cora, and Ana Luz. And a great deal was provided to me by Don Gil Sinay, Mijl's nephew and my grandfather's cousin, who, when I visited him at his home in Santiago, Chile, was 102 years old. Don Gil and his family (Rebeca, Jorge, Jaime, Felipe, Daniela, and Catalina) welcomed me with generosity and shared everything they knew about Mordejai Reuben Hacohen Sinay and Mijl.

A complete history of the JCA has been written by Theodore Norman in his book *An Outstretched Arm: A History of the Jewish Colonization Association*. And the Archive of the Jewish Colonization Association at the IWO serves to enrich it.

Acknowledgments

I would like to express my gratitude to everyone who assisted in the enthralling and arduous task of writing this book.

To Natalí Schejtman, for her illuminating vision. To Paula Salischiker, for her interpretation and search for genuine images.

To Jana Powazek de Breitman; to Ezequiel Semo; to Silvia Hansman, Abraham Lichtenbaum, Ester Szwarc, Débora Kacowicz, Cynthia Fidel, and other contributors from the IWO Institute; to Perla Sneh; to Eliahu Toker; to Ana Weinstein; to Sabrina and Julia from the Centro Marc Turkow at the AMIA; to the staff of the Buenos Aires Jewish Museum; to Alejandro Dujovne; to Iván Cherjovsky; to Andrés Kilstein; to Batia Pelz; to Rabbi Mendel Gorowitz; to Mónica Szurmuk. To Héctor Camilleri. To Moisés Kijak; to Alan Astro; to Adam Gruzman; to Yaacov Rubel. To Máximo Eseverri and Ana Lía Rey. To Alicia Novizki and the Alpersohn family. To Isaac Waxemberg. To the consul of Belarus, Sergei Lukashevich. To historians Diego Galeano, Gisela Galassi, Lila Caimari, María Gabriela Micheletti, Guillermo Stämpfli, José Larker, Carolina Piazzi, and Laura Naput. To Ricardo Levisman. To Osvaldo Aguirre. To the journalists Rodolfo Palacios, Sergio Olguín, Daniel Capalbo, Rafael Saralegui, Santiago Casanello, Daniela Pasik, Julián Gorodischer, and Juan Ortelli.

To Ignacio Román, for generosity and engagement.

In Moisés Ville: to Abraham "Ingue" Kanzepolsky, Eva Guelbert de Rosenthal, Sofía Gun, Judith Blumenthal, Golde Gerson, Emilio Hoffman, Osvaldo Angeletti, Lucas Bussi, and the other community members. In Rosario: to Ester Davidov, from the Julio Marc Museum; to Carina Frid, from CEHIPE. In Esperanza: to Franca Biondi, from the Museum of Colonization. In the city of Santa Fe: to Pascualina di Biaso and Mercedes Valdez, from the General Archive of Santa Fe Province; to Dr. Noemí Calvo, from the General Courts Archive (of the Santa Fe Judiciary); to Néstor Flores.

To everyone who contributed their testimony. Each one was essential.

To Leila Guerriero, for her edifying editing and constant support. To Mariano Roca and Paola Lucantis, from Tusquets Editores. To Lucila Schonfeld.

To the Sinay family: Horacio and Mery, Sergio and Marilén, Iván & co., Ana Luz, Paula, Moisés (in the United States), Cora, Gil, Rebecca, Jorge, Jaime and company (in Chile), Silvia (in Rosario).

To Patricia Catterberg.

And to Malena Higashi, who caught the heart of this story at first glance.

About the Author

JAVIER SINAY is a writer and journalist based in Buenos Aires. His books include *Camino al este*, *Cuba Stone* (coauthored), and *Sangre joven*, which won the Premio Rodolfo Walsh of the Semana Negra de Gijón, Spain. In 2015 he won the Premio de la Fundación Gabo/former FNPI for his story "Rápido. Furioso. Muerto" (Fast. Furious. Dead) published in *Rolling Stone*. *The Murders of Moisés Ville* is his first book in English. Visit loscrimenesdemoisesville.com and javiersinay.com to learn more about *The Murders of Moisés Ville* and Sinay's other works.

About the Translator

ROBERT CROLL is a writer, translator, musician, and artist originally from Asheville, North Carolina. He first came to translation during his undergraduate studies at Amherst College, where he focused on the short fiction of Julio Cortázar. He has worked on texts by such authors as Ricardo Piglia, Hebe Uhart, Gustavo Roldán, Javier Sinay, and Juan Carlos Onetti.

RESTLESS BOOKS is an independent, nonprofit publisher devoted to championing essential voices from around the world whose stories speak to us across linguistic and cultural borders. We seek extraordinary international literature for adults and young readers that feeds our restlessness: our hunger for new perspectives, passion for other cultures and languages, and eagerness to explore beyond the confines of the familiar.

Through cultural programming, we aim to celebrate immigrant writing and bring literature to underserved communities. We believe that immigrant stories are a vital component of our cultural consciousness; they help to ensure awareness of our communities, build empathy for our neighbors, and strengthen our democracy.

Visit us at restlessbooks.org